D0831200

STONEHENGE
TO
STAR WARS

DISCOVERING THE PRESENT BY
EXPLORING THE PAST

Mark R. Horowitz

Dow Jones-Irwin
Homewood, Illinois 60430

This publication is designed to provide accurate and
authoritative information in regard to the subject matter
covered. It is sold with the understanding that the
publisher is not engaged in rendering legal, accounting, or
other professional service. If legal advice or other expert
assistance is required, the services of a competent
professional person should be sought.

From a Declaration of Principles jointly adopted by a Committee
of the American Bar Association and a Committee of Publishers.

Sponsoring editor: *Jeffrey A. Krames*
Project editor: *Jane Lightell*
Production manager: *Diane Palmer*   **47400**
Jacket design: *Image House*
Compositor: *TCSystems, Inc.*
Typeface: *11/13 Century Schoolbook*
Printer: *The Book Press*

Library of Congress Cataloging-in-Publication Data

Horowitz, Mark R.
   Stonehenge to Star Wars : discovering the present by exploring the
past/Mark R. Horowitz.
      p.   cm.
   ISBN 1-55623-245-4
   1. History, Modern—1945-   2. History—Philosophy.   3. Perspective
(Philosophy)   4. Continuity.   I. Title.
D842.H58   1990
909.82—dc20   89-71409
                                                              CIP

Printed in the United States of America
1 2 3 4 5 6 7 8 9 0 BP 7 6 5 4 3 2 1 0

To

Nels M. Bailkey and Francis G. James
for showing me the landscape

Mark A. Kishlansky and Jerald C. Brauer
for giving me the road maps

and

Barbi, Whitney, and Tristan
for allowing me to take the journey

INTRODUCTION

Everything has been thought of before,
but the problem is to think of it again.

—Johann Wolfgang von Goethe (1749–1832)

Those who believe that we are somehow apart from history miss a fundamental truth about human beings: we *are* history. That's because nothing is truly new, and we continue to act and react in the same way since we stood up on our hind legs and walked. Furthermore, we are not doing such a great job of understanding the present, or planning for the future, because we have lost much of the past through ignorance and oversight. Given the complex, interconnected, nuclear-armed world we occupy at the end of the 20th century, such neglect could prove ominous.

This book is an attempt to alter the perceptions of the past. It is not a history book; it is about the present: a journey through time to discover our present world by exploring what has gone on before our time. Often, when we have a problem or a dilemma requiring a solution or explanation, we immediately demand *new ideas,* which don't always succeed. Well, until our own century, such talk would have been anathema to the most knowledgeable of men and women during the last 5,000 years of recorded history. When a problem arose or an explanation was needed, people turned to old ideas—those that were used before their time. Even the most productively creative period of the last thousand years, the Renaissance, was but new wine in old bottles. Renaissance, we must remind ourselves, simply means *rebirth*—of old ideas, old forms, old concepts. It clearly wasn't a new birth, as any Renaissance man or woman would have freely admitted.

The late 20th century represents the most ahistorical group of people inhabiting the planet to date. We think technology can solve all our problems—never mind the problems and outright dangers technology creates. We believe that much of what we confront is unique, different, unknown . . . new. We believe wrongly. Long before our era, there was war, famine, inflation, unemployment, disease, greed, ambition, trade, treaties, work, marriage, taxes, illiteracy, crime, revolution, invention, poverty—look around you—and these have been around a long time. Unfortunately, we are not as enlightened as our ancestors when it comes to understanding the present and planning for the future. They would look to the past for guidance, instruction, familiarity, comfort, continuity, answers. We are unable to do this because we don't know what happened.

Some great thinkers have pondered the purpose of knowing the past, and we might pause to hear them out. One of England's more thoughtful prime ministers, Benjamin Disraeli, observed: "The more extensive a man's knowledge of what has been done, the greater will be his power of knowing what to do." Oliver Wendell Holmes, Jr., an associate justice of the U.S. Supreme Court, said, "When I want to understand what is happening today or try to decide what will happen tomorrow, I look back." Patrick Henry, that firebrand orator of the American Revolution, wrote, "I know of no way of judging the future but by the past." Andrei Sakharov, the Soviet dissident and father of their hydrogen bomb, wrote, "A people without historical memory is doomed to degradation"—a clear condemnation of his country's policy of rewriting or ignoring history.

Each of these thinkers knew something we seem to have missed. But it was the philosopher George Santayana who informed us how dangerous a lack of knowledge about the past can be: "He who refuses to acknowledge the past is condemned to repeat it." Just read the newspapers of the last 50 years and Santayana appears visionary. In truth, he was only observant.

I hope you will find this journey as fascinating as it continues to be for me, one that will bring out some unexpected emotions: anger, laughter, sadness, pity, and perhaps some optimism. We will be reacquainted with familiar people: Napoleon Bonaparte, Julius Caesar, Charlemagne, Pope Urban II, Michelangelo,

Henry VIII, Hannibal. We will also encounter some not-so-familiar characters: Charles the Rash, the Duke of Norfolk, Theresa of Portugal, Hezekiah, Ptah-hotep, Abbot Irminon. We will visit different empires and civilizations, with many stops in Great Britain and the Roman Empire because of their longevity over time and the events taking place within their borders. We will hear from different thinkers, some more than once because they had a lot on their minds.

And we will explore the problems, daily situations, and pressing questions in our own lives from the perspective of others facing similar circumstances long ago. The past is present—we just need to find it for ourselves to understand why we do what we do, and that we have done it before.

Mark R. Horowitz

ACKNOWLEDGMENTS

It would take too many pages to mention the people who have influenced or helped me in my never-ending quest for understanding the present from the vantage point of the past. My first opportunities to *go public* with my thoughts were with articles written for newspapers using an historical perspective. They first came about through the patience and advice of two respected journalists who are no longer with us: Hoke Norris of the *Chicago Sun-Times* and Charlotte Curtis of the *New York Times*. When I began writing editorial pieces in earnest such a perspective was risky for editors, who were fearful of going against the conventional editorial format and content. Yet a few took the chance and several need to be mentioned. Peter Prichard, and later Sid Hurlburt, both of *USA Today,* have given me opportunities to express my perspective on their editorial page. Dotty Brooks, for many years the financial editor at United Press International, asked me if I could sustain a weekly column using an historical perspective that focused on economics, business, and finance. I suggested we give it a try, and at this writing there have been more than 150 columns, in no small way because of her enthusiasm and support. After Dotty's departure from UPI, I received wonderful help and advice from Mitch Martin, Roz Liston, Bob Webster, Heather Clancey, and Nena Baker. Much of this book is based on research and writing for the UPI column. I must also express gratitude to a very enlightened executive editor at WMAQ-AM All-News Radio in Chicago, Scott Herman. He took a gamble on allowing me to give a weekly radio commentary, called "Taking a Step Back," to offer his listeners a 60-second journey each week showing how the past and present are but dots on a common line.

Family and friends have put up with a lot of argument and storytelling from me over the years, and it would be impossible to thank them all. My parents, Edie and Larry, and brother and sister-in-law, Ken and Crystal, have been supportive and understanding throughout my studies and writings. My wife Barbi has endured several trips abroad and long days and months of watching her husband hermetically seal himself in his study to contemplate a commentary from the past. Her thoughts on a draft of this book proved invaluable to me, especially in keeping me on the road to where I was going—it's easy to stray off a 5,000 year path. My children, Whitney and Tristan, have been more understanding than children have a right to be, and I thank them for "letting Daddy write" on those holiest of days, the weekends. Sir Geoffrey R. Elton of Clare College, Cambridge, has graciously kept up a lively correspondence with me for over a decade, and his insights as our foremost Tudor historian and as a personal friend have given me much food for thought. Finally, a quick but long-felt thank you to Dean Stellas, Scott Schirmer, and Greg Schamber, friends who have always cheered and waved as I marched through time, sometimes wondering the wisdom of it all, but never doubting the necessity, or the goal.

M. R. H.

CONTENTS

1

ON WAR, REVOLUTION, AND OTHER TEAM SPORTS

Since any era of history usually finds itself immersed in conflagrations of various sorts, it is with such activities that we begin our quest to discover the present—and future—by exploring the past. Ever since the first cave man bonked the head of his neighbor to acquire a cave, turf, or a woman by force, warfare has remained a human expression we seem unable to live without. Not surprisingly, humans are among the few animals that fight to the death; other animals fight to submission. We therefore need to investigate what war is, how it has been fought, its inevitability, and if, indeed, it can be avoided. And considering what the *ultimate* war will look like, our journey begins with a rather significant first step.

THE HITTIES, HITLER, AND WHY WE WAR

A professor of ancient history once noted two reasons for why we war: *economic rivalry* and *fear*. These reasons make sense, especially in ancient times when city-states vied for commercial superiority, and when the growth of ancient empires—from the Egyptians to the Israelites, Hittites, Assyrians, Persians, Greeks, and Romans—often led peaceful nations into war through the fear of being gobbled up or enslaved.

A third reason, however, seems to run through the last 5,000 years of recorded history and gives further clues about the meaning of wars, their causes, and their prevention: desire for *political advantage*. This quest may be for internal or external gain. Internally, a country uses war as a means to quell unrest, dissatisfaction, or just to vent anger at the ruling government or the outside world. This worked well for Adolph Hitler and Benito Mussolini; indeed, war was a safety valve for Germany and Italy in the late 1930s during a time of economic collapse, with the by-product of giving those dictators complete control of their countries. Today, Eastern Europe is experiencing the throes of internal upheaval due to economic and political failure. Whether war will be a result of these changes remains to be seen.

Absolute rulers continue to use war as a national *distraction* from discontent at home to avoid political turmoil and possible overthrow of the government. The Iraqi-Iranian war allowed two absolute rulers a chance to let their repressed populations run at each other's swords and momentarily forget both the misery at hand within each of their borders and those who might be at fault for such misery, namely the leaders themselves. In ancient times, rulers of overpopulated states in the Mediterranean world encouraged their people to colonize other lands—leading, of course, to warfare between the colonizers and the home team. Nevertheless, getting rid of some of your people offered a means of relieving internal dissension caused by frequent famine, political unrest, or loss of control by the ruling monarch or family.

In seeking political advantage externally war is used as a means to get a leg up on the competition. Historians will argue for many years to come why the United States ventured into Vietnam, despite warnings from France in the mid-1950s that it would be a lose–lose situation. And the U.S.S.R. is just beginning to discover from their machinations in Afghanistan whether they bought anything politically useful by invading that country.

Late medieval Europe used warfare as a political bargaining chip, one we don't seem to be very good at today because we don't know when to stop. In the latter part of the 15th century, England frequently went to war with France, not to recover land it once claimed, but to gain a political advantage for future bargaining situations. King Edward IV (died 1483) invaded France for a short time, then stood still and allowed himself to be bought off with a yearly bribe from the French king. Edward's future son-in-law, King Henry VII (d. 1509), did the same thing. It brought money into the English coffers and bought for France a neutral country, thus allowing the French kings the opportunity to grab pieces of Italy without England butting in.

NAZIS, NORTH KOREANS, AND OBJECTIVES

Economic rivalry, fear, political advantage—disparate but interconnected reasons for going to war. Yet once this option becomes the means to solving a problem, an objective is required. After all, why bother slugging it out if you have no idea what you want if you win? A few objectives have been put forth recurrently over the centuries, ranging from reacquisition of land or destruction of territory to world domination. Some objectives have been defensive in nature, such as stopping the Nazi onslaught (World War II) or crushing a change in the political winds (Czechoslovakia). Toppling Hitler was a clear-cut objective that most democratic societies could buy into without difficulty. The sending of American troops to North Korea (a country of 46,540 square miles) to somehow stop the rampage of communism from the U.S.S.R. (241,748,000 sq. mi.) and China (740,000,000 sq. mi.) never gained a following; nor was there an understanding of what the desired outcome should be, or if it was really feasible. Wars are not only destructive, they can be worthless in the long run.

If the reasons for war lead to certain *objectives,* then it might be useful to look at a war that failed, despite initially having both a reason and an objective. No, not a recent war, although it could be argued that Korea, Vietnam, and Afghanistan are good examples because they seemed to have reasons and objectives that somehow got lost in the actual activity of war. Rather, it is an ancient war—between Rome and Carthage—that allows us an interesting observation: It is almost impossible to rally support at home for a war if no one understands the objective or agrees with it.

THE ELEPHANT MAN: HANNIBAL MISSES HIS CHANCE

At some time in their lives, those who made it a point to *read* during their years of formal education came across the name *Hannibal* and vaguely put together a picture of a daring man leading lots of men and big elephants over the Alps to invade Italy. The picture then fades in memory loss (what happened anyway?) or survives only in humor (who cleaned up the mess from all those elephants?)—without any real thought about why some egomaniac would cajole elephants to walk to Italy and go against the power of Rome.

While it is always fun to retell the story—and it will be related dutifully, and with brevity here in a moment—there is a larger theme involved: the notion of going to war for a reason, and losing the opportunity to fulfill the objective once the decision is made to fight in the first place. As just mentioned, Korea, Vietnam, and Afghanistan might become examples of either failing to define the objective for warfare clearly or failing to meet the objective for reasons unrelated to the war. Hannibal is an example of missing both free throws.

By the mid-third century B.C., Rome was already a great power in the Western world, that is, the countries and lands surrounding the Mediterranean Sea. With rising nationalism and a desire to protect her trade lanes, Rome began conquering foreign lands. In 230 B.C., Greece was invaded; soon after, the Gauls of northwestern Europe became a target, with the Roman objective of driving them out of northern Italy. Through alliances, treaties, and a huge victory against the Gallic armies in 225, Rome was positioned as a growing empire—and a menace to those cities and countries intent on maintaining their independence.

One of those cities was Carthage on the northern coast of Africa, a rising trade center that frequently raided the Italian coastline and engaged in outright warfare against the might of Rome. The most famous of these altercations was known as the Punic Wars. Here is the background: After 241 B.C. internal rebellion by unpaid mercenaries all but destroyed Carthage; when the mercenaries were finally crushed, the Carthaginians discovered that during the rebellion, Rome had been busy grabbing nearby territory. The times were growing ripe for another Carthaginian-Roman confrontation, and thus began the Punic Wars.

Enter a 26-year-old named Hannibal, who in 221 was named leader of the Carthaginian army. Bent on revenge against the might of Rome—and let's not forget *economic rivalry* and outright *fear* —Hannibal had developed into a brash, egotistical upstart with a single objective in mind, or so he thought: to crush Rome. The Roman writer Livy noted that Hannibal was "the first to enter the battle and the last to abandon the field"—your basic Oliver North–type personality. Before long, Hannibal took his armies into battle against allies of Rome, the beginnings of a war that seemed impossible for the Carthaginians to win.

In 218 B.C., Hannibal made the fateful decision to march his 50,000 infantry and several thousand cavalry across the Alps. It was not a pleasant journey. The army fought off frequent attacks by marauding tribes, to say nothing of the occupational hazards that went with convincing elephants to walk through mountain passes. By the time Hannibal penetrated into Italy, he had lost half his soldiers and many of the perplexed pachiderms.

When the Roman Senate heard of Hannibal's progress and entrance into their country, they quickly raised the hue and cry for an army. While numbers are always unreliable in ancient texts—although in our own era the "official" numbers reported from the Vietnam war also instilled little belief in their veracity—one estimate boasted that Rome mustered more than 300,000 infantry, 14,000 cavalry, and 500,000 reserves. In 217 B.C., one of the Roman armies encountered Hannibal's forces, but through a clever decoy tactic, Hannibal was able to encircle the Romans and kill most of them.

Although now in control of northern Italy, Hannibal was greatly outnumbered and required the aid of local cities willing to revolt against Rome. This never happened, so Hannibal decided to let his troops loll in the sun along the Adriatic shore. Had he taken time to discover what Rome was up to, he might have continued plundering Italian towns and seeking encounters with Roman armies, which could have led to the defeat of Rome. Why? Because the Roman Senate suddenly went into a daze, believing that Hannibal would just *go away* after succumbing to internal strife and disease. But fortunately for Rome, Hannibal's seaside sabbatical gave her time to come to her senses—with the Roman Assembly taking the lead—and soon a superior Roman army met the refreshed Carthaginian contingent, which was now bolstered by 16,000 Gauls.

Hannibal, ever the master at reading people if not political situations, knew that the Gauls would head for the hills once they saw the Romans advance—who wouldn't? He therefore put them in the center of his battle alignment, and when the Gauls indeed started a mass retreat, the Romans followed them, only to be enclosed by the Carthaginian regulars on all sides. Of some 80,000 Roman infantry, more than half fell at the battle of Cannae. Most of Hannibal's losses were Gallic fighters.

Rome was completely vulnerable—but Hannibal did not advance. Why not? Apparently, the Carthaginian leader believed the prevailing press clips: that Rome was mighty and could not be taken. Whatever the reasons, he decided to make camp north of Naples and wait for reinforcements from Carthage and her allies . . . and wait and wait—long enough for Rome to build up her military force again. When further help from Carthage was on the way, crossing the Alps as Hannibal had done, it was met by a Roman army and defeated. Rome now took the offensive, sending troops to Africa to invade Carthage while keeping Hannibal at bay through intermittent skirmishes.

In 202 B.C., Hannibal returned home to face a Roman army on his native soil. The 45-year-old Carthaginian tasted defeat for the first time, and Carthage was forced to surrender most of her war fleet and pay a large tribute to Rome. The Roman Empire was now a fact—one that lasted more than half a millennium. Hannibal went into hiding after trying to bring law and order to his beloved Carthage, and in 184 at the age of 67 the once-daring general took poison rather than submit to capture by the Romans. By 146, the Punic wars were over and Rome annexed Carthage and her territories.

So what was this war all about? It was about rival nations—although not nations as we use the word today. It was about revenge, economic fear, and political superiority. And it was an example of missing an opportunity by not considering the whole picture. As a strategic thinker, Hannibal was the best our planet has produced; as a tactician, he could win battles against armies of far superior numbers. But as a leader concerned with meeting the objective, Hannibal didn't cut it.

Another problem: Hannibal did not articulate his objective to his country very well. That's why he failed to receive the support needed, when he needed it. The same was true in the United States with the Vietnam war: Those asked to fight and die in that war never really had a handle on what the objective was, or the very necessity for fighting the war. That lack of understanding was very clear at the time: The student protests of the 1960s were but an outpouring of fear and disgust at a war the government couldn't define in terms that were acceptable and reasonable. Ironically, it took a 1989 report published by the U.S. Army Center of Military History, "The Military and the Media," to *discover* that, lo and behold, it wasn't the kids or the media that lost the war. Rather, it was lost because the government couldn't show the enemy that the people of the United States were 100 percent behind the war effort. "To do that," the report said, "the administration had to first convince the American people that South Vietnam was either worth a prolonged war of attrition or that U.S. forces could win in the end without a major sacrifice of lives and treasure." The conclusion, evident 20 years earlier by those against the war, is telling: "Neither alternative was possible . . . [the enemy] could lose every battle and still win. He had only to endure until the cost of the war for the United States increased to levels intolerable over the long term."

Hannibal also had too narrow a view of what he thought he wanted to accomplish, or what his country would buy as a rational reason for a prolonged war. For him it was attack for the sake of attacking, not fight for an expressed purpose in mind that would have long-term consequences and a final resolution. This makes one wonder why go to war at all if the objective has a chance of getting lost in the thick of battle or through the passage of time. That is a question all governments must ask themselves before they commit to this ultimate exercise in mass violence. Nations will always war, history shows us, because humans are at war with themselves. Perhaps wars can be kept to a minimum once the reasons are identified and the judgment is made that, indeed, the objective can and will get lost, and therefore hardly merits the fight, or the destruction.

Hannibal never understood this subtlety. Perhaps it didn't matter over the course of time, since Rome was in an expansion mode that apparently no one could stop. But Hannibal had a chance and muffed it. That he could muster such enormous support was a testimony to his leadership abilities. Indeed, the great early-modern consultant of princes, Niccolo Machiavelli, in discussing Hannibal, noted that "men are moved by two principal things—by love and by fear." Soldiers always will have at least these two personal reasons to follow a leader into battle. This, of course, bears little on the overall objective, or the opportunities lost or gained once war becomes a reality.

So go empires; so go the leaders who would make or break them. But war as a last resort has found success or failure linked to objectives and the ability of a country to accept and support those objectives. It is an old game, hardly worth playing except to win. That is why the United States was at first reluctant to invade Panama in 1989 to rid the country of a drug-dealing dictator: The objective had to be articulated clearly and *sold* outright to the American people before a commitment to military force could be made. But once the government believed that Americans would rally around an invasion, it was launched with impunity in late 1989. When goals are set and acceptance is reached, governments can rush out full force and endure whatever consequences arise from that action. World War II was such a "good war" that the price of 50 million lives was tolerable to countries who saw the objectives clearly. The loss of 20 or 30 lives in Panama were just as acceptable since the objective was clear and agreeable to the majority.

GETTING NASTY: PLAGUES, TREACHERY, AND BIOLOGICAL WARFARE

Nuclear weapons are not the only deadly landmines added to the playing field of war. Because conventional wars have a better chance of getting started than nuclear ones, there is a potentially deadlier menace than the glow in the dark from plutonium: death from the spreading of disease.

Biological warfare may be debated on ethical and moral grounds today, but it should be understood that there is an historical element to the argument. For one, dying in war from disease has always been a common occurrence, from the plague-hit Athenian soldiers during the Peloponnesian War (5th century B.C.) to the disease-ridden Union soldiers at the Andersonville, Georgia, prison in the American Civil War. But it was also true that disease was deliberately spread to kill enemies, often with results more grim than expected.

Plagues hit Europe and the Middle East in several waves during the 14th century, sometimes decimating whole towns. But such death was also made use of in war. It was not uncommon for corpses of plague victims to be dropped down the wells of enemies to contaminate the water supply. This activity was especially effective in desert warfare, where water was scarce yet essential for survival. And when we think of the British soldier, visions of red uniforms, proper etiquette, and sportsmanship may come to mind, but that was not always the case in war. When Great Britain fought on the North American continent against the French and the Indians in 1756, they battled an alliance of fighters conditioned to a harsh environment unfamiliar to the British. So the soldiers in red resorted to germ warfare. They acquired blankets used by smallpox victims and had them distributed to the Indians. The results were disastrous, one estimate being that 95 percent of those Indians exposed to the disease died from it.

We can, of course, remind ourselves that such cases were "in the past," and that the 1925 Geneva Convention forbade use of disease-producing microorganisms as weapons. But they were nonetheless used in both world wars. During World War I, German secret agents infected U.S. cavalry horses with the bacterium glanders, which caused ulcers in the respiratory system. In 1940, the Japanese air force reputedly dropped grain containing plague-infested fleas into populated Chinese towns, hoping to start an epidemic.

Today, biological agents dwarf the medieval Black Plague in effectiveness. One well-distributed ounce of the strain Q fever (*coxiella burnetti*) can infect 28 billion people. This horror suggests that we might spend a little more time thinking about what to do with our stockpiles of biological weapons—instead of putting all our energy into diminishing the nuclear threat. The fundamental question remains: Will countries continue to develop biological—and for that matter, chemical—weapons? From an historical perspective, the answer is quite clear: of course! Such weapons find their way into war, especially when the objective is to win the war, at all costs. Is it inhumane? If it is, then inhumans have been using them for centuries.

Which brings us back to the notion of warfare. For mankind has recognized the destructiveness of war through its weapons for millennia, and the two—weapons and warfare—go, well, hand-in-hand: If you are going to strike a blow, it is usually more effective to use something on the downswing to make it stick. So if being human is being warlike, maybe wars can be prevented by outlawing the deadly weapons of war—a step in the right direction, correct? Well, we've been there before with some disconcerting results. And as we shall see, banning deadly weapons looks nice on paper and plays well in the village square, but it just doesn't work.

PREVENTING WAR—PART I: THE TREATY

If war is a breakdown of the desire to find peaceful solutions to international (or intranational) problems, human beings are blessed, for better or worse, with a box of bandages that often bind peaceful coexistence beyond what reasonably might be expected for the species: treaties. Such attempts at getting on with thine enemy go back to the earliest civilizations and are admirable for their approach to peaceful solutions. Yet treaties, for all their good intentions, are after all mere pieces of paper, ready to be ripped up or revoked once one of the parties decides that the agreement no longer satisfies the reality of the day.

Americans carry much historical baggage involving the abandonment of treaties with their own indigenous population, the Indians. And World War II was brought to us, in part, by the repudiation of the punitive World War I Treaty of Versailles (1919) which, in fact, proved that to the victor go the spoils . . . until the losers become the spoilers by starting up the war again. Today, of course, the stakes are much higher than tanks rolling out of the Rhineland; we now have the power to destroy the earth many times over. But while we search for SALT treaties and START negotiations, we must inquire into the usefulness of deal-making when to break such agreements could spell the end of mankind as we currently define it.

In another era there was, if you will, an attempt to put together a Strategic Arms Limitation Talks (SALT) treaty of sorts because of the fear of a deadly weapon and its consequences in war. The results from that effort, however, do not portend well for our present treaties, negotiations, and arms limitations talks. The weapon which many feared would destroy mankind, or at least the "man" part of mankind, was the crossbow. Although its origins are obscure—the Chinese may have invented it—it appeared in Italy during the 10th and 11th centuries as an improved engine of war. The bow and arrow had existed before 10,000 B.C., as did other missiles and "bombs." But, like the atomic bomb, the crossbow presented a deadlier outcome than its predecessors because of its construction and the materials used to build it, as well as its ability to kill lots of people efficiently and effectively.

Its destructive nature was quickly recognized by Christendom, the *national* force behind a divided Europe in the late 11th century. Pope Urban II, the promoter of the First Crusade and no peacemonger by anyone's papal score sheet, actually banned its use officially at the Lateran Synod of 1097. Unfortunately, the ban was broken before the ink dried.

In the year 1139, at the Second Lateran Council, Pope Innocent II forbade "under penalty of anathema the deadly and God-detested art of slingers and archers." The decree, of course, covered only *Christians,* allowing open season on non-Christians. About the same time, Conrad III of Germany banned the use of the crossbow in his army and kingdom. Wonder of wonders, it seemed that the "disarmament" of a deadly weapon for war was at hand through the combined efforts of major world leaders.

But again, the ink had little time to dry. Wars were waged, crossbows were used, and lives continued to be lost in battle. In England, where the Welsh longbow remained the foremost weapon, crossbows were nonetheless used by the mercenary armies of Henry I (1100–35), Stephen (1135–54), and Henry II (1154–89). King Richard the Lion Heart (1189–99) was reputed to be a good shot with one; ironically, he died from a crossbow wound sustained while laying seige to a castle.

Decrees, bans, treaties—none could defeat the fact that a weapon of destruction existed in the world, to be used whenever the need arose to war and to conquer. This rather bleak illustration of mankind's effort and failure to limit or ban the use of a deadly weapon is not reassuring for the modern age. Yet it appears that the medieval epoch—and the powers running the show—went further in striving to avoid death and war with a dangerous weapon than we are presently willing to endeavor. One thing is certain: It is folly to think that dangerous weapons—nuclear weapons, biological weapons, or chemical weapons—can be legislated or written out of existence. We must keep close vigilance and continue the dialogue on reducing armaments, but we must never deceive ourselves into thinking that dangerous weapons will just go away. They won't. Ever.

PREVENTING WAR—PART II: THE SUMMIT

This brings us to another technique for reducing the chances of war. It may appear a recent game but, as with everything we do, is quite old: the "meeting of the minds," or at least the meeting of leaders with like minds who are interested in agreeing on something. These we call *summits,* and modern American presidents feel it important to have such meetings with the designated world enemy of free society, Russia. And as most news-watching people now know, world powers—whether friends or foes—are supposed to meet to solve problems or begin a new dawn of cooperation.

Or are they? There have been thousands of such meetings between "world powers" over the last few millennia, and some no doubt resulted in better relations between countries. But taking the *long view* —something Americans are especially loathe to do in this age of instant news and next-quarter results—one wonders about the efficacy of such summits and what they actually mean down the road. Let's look at three meetings we might call summits to see if our presidents have their expectations misplaced, beyond the appearance of leadership that such exercises are supposed to suggest.

Pope Leo the Great met with Attila the Hun in 452 A.D. to prevent the belligerent warrior from invading Italy and destroying Rome. From this meeting, "the scourge of God" (Attila's nickname) was persuaded to turn back his armies and leave Rome intact. (Note: If people in the 5th century knew that the Huns were suffering from plague and hunger brought on by their own pillaging, Leo might not have appeared so "great" after all.) The long-term results from this meeting, however, lessen the renown of this admittedly incredible tête-à-tête between Attila and the Pope. In 476 A.D., the western Roman Empire collapsed to hordes of barbarians, bringing about what older historians have called the Dark Ages. Thus, one meeting between antagonists became little more than a blotch on the blotter of history.

In 61 B.C., Julius Caesar, by then a powerful general, met with his two equally powerful counterparts—Pompey and Crassus—to work out a way to rule the expanding empire peacefully. From this meeting they formed a *triumvirate,* with each man governing Rome equally. And given the willingness of three avowed opportunists to suppress their individual ambitions, the future looked bright—the near future. Crassus continued to seek military glory and upstage his partners by vanquishing Rome's enemies until, in 53 B.C., an enemy Parthian general vanquished Crassus. Meanwhile, Pompey, who had married Caesar's daughter, Julia, to seal the coalition, became more and more jealous of Caesar's military victories. Julia died, and after a falling out between the other two generals, Caesar took a legion across the Rubicon in January 49 B.C. to dismantle the government and form one around himself. Pompey tried in vain to defeat his former father-in-law, and ended up fleeing to Egypt where he was unceremoniously murdered. So much for triumvirates.

Perhaps closer to the present call for summitry is the meeting between those two Renaissance kings, Henry VIII of England and Francis I of France. Meeting in 1520 outside Calais on what was to be called the Field of Cloth of Gold, the two archenemies and cousins got along splendidly—although Francis purportedly threw Henry to the ground in a wrestling match. That two such protruding egos could actually meet was no mean feat. Francis would, and did, break any oath for a parcel of land in Italy, and Henry's moods could run from saintly to psychotic, as several of his wives witnessed.

Yet soon after this meeting to patch up differences, Henry VIII allied with the enemies of Francis I, and within three years Francis managed to get himself captured and imprisoned after starting some mischief. Henry went to war against France late in life, and the two countries have remained on uncomfortable speaking terms ever since, with occasional warfare or ill will between them for old time's sake.

These examples do not mean that summits are useless coffee klatches that provide little world comfort beyond photo opportunities and fashion statements by the leaders' wives. Nor is it being suggested that perhaps world leaders should wrestle instead of talk, although a good show is better than no show at all, and we must never forget the entertainment value of summits. But it is very clear that we must be wary of putting too much good faith into a meeting of world powers, or too many expectations on how such a meeting will secure a peaceful future.

If history is the bookmaker, the odds at long-term success are very long indeed.

KING CHARLES I, THE SHAH, AND REVOLUTION

So far we have looked at external warfare and have observed that we today are merely playing out a repetition of activities involving war and peace that go back centuries and millennia. Another aspect of going to war is, of course, warring with oneself: civil war, or revolution. We use the word *revolution* today as if it means something new: a revolutionary detergent, a revolutionary breakthrough in painkillers, etc., *ad nauseam*. Not true, and the creative directors at advertising agencies had better take note in case "truth in advertising" laws suddenly begin to take correct word usage into account.

Revolution means what it says: Making a full circle and coming back to where you began—a complete revolution. But, how can that be, especially with a "brand new, revolutionary cheese spread?" Look at the American Revolutionary War—didn't we throw out a king and start something completely new? Not really, and many would argue that we simply replaced Georges at the top (George Washington for King George III) and rearranged the English parliamentary system. But there *were* changes, and that leads to a better definition of revolution: a revolution, whether peaceful or violent, does constitute change, but usually change that includes returning to an arrangement similar to the one that existed at the onset of the revolution.

If we can understand this concept and what it means when future revolutions occur—and they will—we will have more options available for what to do and how to react. And there is no better example than the revolution in Iran, one that caught the American government off guard through a lack of understanding history. (Obviously, we need a Department of History in the government, with Cabinet status, so that Administration decisions can be relevant and informed!) From a historical perspective, there were few surprises coming out of the Iranian revolution. Moreover, we have precedents that provide us with a scenario on just what might happen to Iran down the road—and the world ought to be prepared.

One example is the English Revolution or civil war, and although 17th-century Englishmen and present-day Iranian Shiite Moslems have little in common, their revolutions do have parallels that should be considered. Here's how the English revolution played out:

Tensions existed in England long before the revolt, but from 1639 to 1649 a governmental crisis between King Charles I and his Parliament developed into civil strife. Religion played a part in this rift. The Puritan aristocrats, the middling sort, and commoners demanded a more austere, "English" religion than the pompous, often "Roman" (*read* "Catholic") practices of the king and his churchmen. Toward the end of the decade, one pious leader, Oliver Cromwell, sought remedies for the social, political, and economic injustices brought about by the king. The lack of any panaceas led to civil war, the execution of Charles I in 1649, and the establishment of a commonwealth.

That sequence seems repeated by certain events in Iran, beginning in 1979. Although there were key economic concerns,

religion became the rallying point for Iranians, with the Ayatullah Ruhollah Khomeini leading the way for the establishment
of an Islamic, "Iranian" republic in place of the Shah's immoral,
"Western" orientation. But the Shah, like Charles I, refused to
share power or redress the grievances of the country. Had the
Shah not taken a "vacation," he would have lost more than his
throne, as did Charles I some 330 years earlier.

So what happened in England once the revolution deposed
the regime? One might say that a revolution occurred literally:
a complete circle returning to the original point of departure.
Oliver Cromwell spent the next nine years trying to find a legitimate basis for his government. Beginning with a conservative
ruling body, the government went to a radical, religious group of
"saints," and finally to governance by major generals in charge of
an England divided into a dozen districts. Cromwell became the
Lord Protector. Government did remain viable in the 1650s, but
Cromwell died in 1658, failing to establish a better power structure than the one he destroyed under King Charles I. His son,
Richard Cromwell, took the reins of power ineffectively for two
years, and in 1660 the late king's son, long in exile, was invited
back to England as King Charles II.

Iran for the last decade has been seeking to establish a viable
government to replace the Shah's. The summary executions of
"royal" supporters have no parallel in the English experience, but
religious fervor pervaded both revolutions: the Puritans abolished Christmas, the Iranians outlawed alcohol. And, of course,
many of the Iranians take their religion to great extremes, toler-
ating no criticism of their beliefs or their nation, Salmon Rushdie
and *The Satanic Verses* particularly. Under Cromwell, there was
actually some freedom of speech and religion not known under
the king.

Yet it must be emphasized that when Charles II was "restored" to the throne of England, it only appeared to be a complete revolution returning to where the insurrection began two
decades earlier. There were changes—irrevocable ones. Charles
II, unlike his father, was to be a constitutional monarch, dependent and beholden to Parliament. Although Charles did not keep
all of the promises he made upon his return, he did have to
answer for his actions to a powerful group of influentials.

So what will happen in Iran? Well, as it happens, the Shah of Iran, like Charles I, has a son and heir, Reza Pahlavi. And Pahlavi has been waiting in the wings all these years for the possibility of returning to his homeland as the head honcho. When that might happen, if at all, cannot be scripted out with certainty. Oliver Cromwell died leaving a son, but the son was a shadow of his charismatic father, and it took two years for the English to realize that maybe the bad old days under a king really weren't that bad after all. The late Ayatullah Khomeini also left a son, Ahmed Khomeini, but if he ever reaches the position of supreme authority in Iran he will confront the same problems that plagued Cromwell's son: The son of a revolutionary rarely commands the respect or power attained by the father. Furthermore, the Ayatullah Khomeini reached almost demigod status in Iran; the son could never aspire to such a pedestal. Much depends on how long the Iranian people can live with their continued repression. How strong is their yearning for a pre-Khomeini era of greater, if guarded, freedom and stability, however oppressive were the days of the Shah?

If the Shah's son returns (or someone else representative of the "old days") he will not be like the Shah of Iran—that's where the *definitive* revolution stops. Pahlavi would have to share power with the ruling factions and find a way to balance the desire for stability with the need to incorporate the Iranian culture into a form of government. Constitutional monarchies can work; they have in England for three centuries, and the Spaniards restored one after the Franco revolution ran its course. There is something about human nature that allows us to repress past evils in our memories and bring to the forefront the old sparks of light that make the present look dreary. Whether Iranians will allow the Shah's son to hold the candle is an interesting option worth watching and planning for with care—especially when you consider that Moslems may account for a quarter of the world's population in the next 30 years and presently make up between 50 and 100 percent of the population in 40 of the world's countries. No small numbers. We need to get smart quickly, and to understand the history of these fascinating people, and what it means.

DEMOCRACY: A REVOLTING IDEA

There have been a spate of revolutions lately, peaceful or otherwise, that seem to have a common ideology about them that bears a little comment. The first major revolt was in the Philippines, where a lady in a simple yellow dress rallied her people against a perennial dictator and his wife of many dresses. The reason: a desire for more freedom, justice, and opportunity, or what we in the West might call "a little democracy." Then we've seen evidence of democratic yearning from recent events in the U.S.S.R. and demonstrations in its satellites; and from the student uprisings and massacres in China. One wonders if a little democracy is a dangerous thing, and worth the risk of revolution. Indeed, the Romanians, who may have suffered thousands of casualties in overthrowing the government in late December 1989, will learn the worth of democracy in the next months and years.

The notion of democracy goes back to the dawn of civilization, and we get the modern derivative from the Greek *demos,* or "rule of the people." The Greeks flirted with the idea, even came up with some interesting possibilities in the 6th and 5th centuries B.C. America, of course, took a shot at it and seems to have pulled it off: At this writing, the United States has the oldest working democratic constitution in the world. The French assiduously watched the Americans in the late 18th century and emulated them with their own bloody revolution for "liberty, equality, and brotherhood." England, as has been seen, beat the Americans and the French to the punch, toppling a king to establish an evolving democratic society that nonetheless maintains the fiction of a monarchy because, to the British, change is a painful thing.

Those ancient Greeks, who relentlessly debated all forms of government, would have been the first to applaud the virtues of the democratic ideal, and perhaps even the recent attempts to achieve it. Pericles, the Athenian "father figure" and hero of the Peloponnesian War (431–404 B.C.), noted the *superiority* of democracy over other forms of government: "Our constitution is called a democracy because power is in the hands not of a minority but of the whole people. When it is a question of settling private disputes, everyone is equal before the law."

This belief, of course, was in stark contrast to that of the militaristic Spartans, the enemies of Athens at that time, and we might easily see a modern parallel in the difference between the United States on the one hand and the hardliners in the U.S.S.R. and China on the other. Missing from Pericles' summation, however, was the "price" of democracy—but another Greek astutely noted the cost. Plato, (427–347 B.C.), as observant as he could be cynical, said that civil war was prelude to the establishment of democracy:

> And when the poor win, the result is a democracy. They kill some of the opposite party, banish others, and grant the rest an equal share in civil rights and government. . . . Yes, that is how a democracy comes to be established, whether by force of arms or because the other party is terrorized into giving way.

Plato would hardly be surprised at the events of the 1980s, which are sure to continue to the end of the century. Revolution may be nature's way of telling humans it's time to rearrange the political furniture, but democracy seems to have become the interior decorator in vogue. This is not new, just new to most people occupying the current time frame who have no reference points about revolution. The only shock should be in suddenly gaining such knowledge, and not in what is happening.

COMING TO TERMS WITH DOOM

The philosopher Georg Wilhelm Hegel once fatalistically declared, "man learns from history that man doesn't learn anything from history." Add to that Sir Walter Raleigh's observation that "the ordinary theme and argument of history is war," and one begins to feel a cloud of hopelessness setting in. But the true prophecy of doom, unintentionally stated, can be traced to a prediction in a letter written to Franklin D. Roosevelt on August 2, 1939: "it may become possible to set up a nuclear chain reaction in a large mass of uranium." The letter was signed by Albert Einstein.

Yes, war is inevitable—our journey in this book began with the belief that mankind will always be at war, and that such wars arise from curious reasons: economic rivalry, fear, and the need for political advantage. Ideals often enter into the picture, and here revolution usually gets its day in court, most recently from a romanticized notion of democracy and all it has to promise.

The difficulty in living with war lies in what military force means at this particular juncture of what we call history: Unlike the possible outcomes of all other wars, we now possess the power to obliterate ourselves, and undoubtedly take the earth off the "habitable planet" chart as well. Are we helpless? Hopeless? Doomed? If treaties and summits didn't work in the past, will they not fail in the future, with the outcome being death and destruction?

Nasty questions, uneasy answers. Perhaps there are two approaches we can take—approaches stemming from ideas coming from the past. The first, quite simply, is to be aware of what will always be and what will never work. Yes, there will be wars. Yes, men and women will seek treaties and meetings and guarantees against future wars and the use of deadly weapons. Yes, such activities will fail when the losing side decides it doesn't want to lose. Yes, we can destroy ourselves.

This is not a rhetorical exercise. It is an understanding of where we are and where we have been: the lessons of history. Remember, until the present century, mankind used the past to understand the present and future, and sought answers and options—and criticism—from all that went on before. The world can become less complex and less frightening if we are willing to unpack the historical baggage we carry with us and hang it up for all to see. So awareness will keep our expectations in perspective and allow us to act and react realistically.

MEDIEVAL KNIGHTS AND MX MISSILES: AN IMMODEST PROPOSAL

The second approach may sound like a heroic war movie, where the leader of each side decides to fight it out to the death in order to spare the slaughter of thousands: Let's make leaders culpable and directly responsible for the weapons they vote to make, the troops they deploy, the agreements they sign, the words they speak to other leaders. Make them so responsible that if something goes wrong, it goes wrong with them first!

How do we do that? Well, there are enough creative political minds in the world to fill in the details, most of which could be cribbed from history. But we can have a little fun in illustration by using what we might call "The Weapon That Would Not Die," aka the MX missile. For it seems that every few months or years this indestructible idea surfaces, plaguing congressmen and senators and giving editors new copy for their bewildered readers. It also gives us an example of the larger question: How can people in power be held accountable for all aspects of war?

In the early years of the Reagan administration, fear ran rampant in Congress that the United States was behind the Soviets in nuclear strength and the ability to respond to a nuclear first strike. Indeed, the notion of a strategic defense system of laser-packed satellites circling the earth—aka *Star Wars*—came out of this hysteria. Moreover, in the race to build weapons—any weapons, at any cost—there was no sense of responsibility on the part of those voting for the weapons. Indeed, the prophets and politicians engaged in arming the United States to the teeth had perhaps overstepped their moral—and historical—bounds. How so?

In medieval times, the knight was responsible for supplying his own armor and fighting for his country. He gathered about him loyal men to fight by his side, at first through feudal obligation, later by cash payment. If the knights lost in battle, the people lost the war. Irony of ironies, when Parliament began as a quasi-representative institution in England, the members of Parliament "elected" from the counties were called the Knights of the Shire, and they usually were. Thus, those responsible for defending the realm, and dying for it, also represented the people in Parliament.

Since today we elect our senators and congressmen to protect our country as well as our liberties, it is only fair that they take on the role of their chivalrous ancestors and bear the arms they ask *us* to pay for. (The medieval knight paid his own way—times have changed!) In this way, those people elected to defend us militarily will have direct responsibility for doing so.

When soldiers are needed to fight a war, each congressman

and senator should return to his district or state and take charge of the muster. After all, who wouldn't fight for their country if they could see Senator Smith or Congressman Jones in the lead, charging up the hill . . . or, more likely, trudging through the desert? And when new bombers or submarines are requested by Congress, wouldn't it be equitable to have our representatives in the cockpits or behind the periscopes, protecting both our nation and the results of military spending? The medieval precedent speaks loud and clear: Put your sword where your mouth is. This ensures that our wars will be essential and our weapons in perfect working order.

But can we apply historical accountability in the nuclear age where buttons, not spears, become the means of destruction? No better example exists than the MX missile machinations. Before President Reagan made a decision to put the missiles in hardened silos, this silliness—part of our urgency to rearm and overarm—involved "hiding" missiles in Utah and Nevada, using underground railroad tracks so that the weapons could be frequently moved from spot to spot. The theory was that the Soviets would be unable to hit a moving target. The theory forgot that a little Soviet ingenuity might simply favor nuking Utah and Nevada altogether.

But there is a better way of protecting these missiles so that the Kremlin—to say nothing of the Pentagon—would be confounded: Let those responsible for promoting MX missiles each be in charge of one, wherever he or she may go. Not only would this satisfy our desire to allow our elected officials their historical right to protect their country personally, it would be far more reasonable than painting bull's-eyes on silos. After all, do you know where all of our congressmen and senators are right now? Do you know where they'll be 10 minutes from now?

The Army would assign teams of technicians and engineers to follow each congressman and senator, 24 hours a day, with an MX missile. When Congressman Jones goes home to visit his constituency, a missile is close behind. When Senator Smith hops a plane to visit six European countries on a "fact-finding" mission, so goes a missile. The Soviets will be baffled beyond belief. If the General Accounting Office can't keep up with our officials, how could the KGB?

There are other benefits that go with this MX missile plan. With the frequent travels of these elected citizens, our NATO allies will be pleased to know that at any given time a few missiles are close at hand, ready to protect them. And when a senator or two travels to meet with an unfriendly head of state, that leader may be encouraged to act more friendly when he realizes what is resting in the 20-car garage next to the visitor's quarters.

Besides, congressmen and senators are much harder targets to hit than Utah and Nevada.

"War is hell" a professional soldier purportedly said. It is also the sport of kings, the exercise of governments, and the entertainment or horror of the masses, depending on which channel you're watching. But if nothing else, war is old—an almost institutionalized icon of human aggression, whether it be called Ares, Mars, Xerxes, Alexander, Hannibal, Caesar, Attila, Tamerlane, Napoleon, Patton, or Hitler. Our future depends on understanding war, why it happens, and how to anticipate it. This is not moralizing; it is simply seeking knowledge from a recently untapped source: the past.

2

ON WEALTH, POWER, LEADERSHIP, AND TOWERING EGOS

It is time to move on to another aspect of our lives that we need to understand and ponder from the perspective of the past: the desire for wealth and power. Like the reasons for war, this attribute of human beings is manifested each day. Moreover, the wealthy and the powerful have been around a long time, and they pretty much have their act together and know their role in society. To understand the Trumps and the Rockefellers and the Kennedys, the Rothschilds and the Goldsmiths and the Toyodas and the Krupps, we must discover where they are coming from. Then perhaps we will have a better notion of where they are going, and what it means to us all.

THE ARISTOCRACY: WHEN CLASS AND CASH COLLIDE

The wedding of Prince Charles and Lady Diana in July 1981, followed by the births of their offspring, have given us occasions to focus our attention on the aristocracy. Who they are and what they do is a curiosity for Americans and other peoples who, for whatever reasons, choose not to support the ideal of an aristocracy. Furthermore, we are not sure what the upper class thinks of the rest of us *common folk,* let alone those of us who would be "aristocratic."

The answer, perhaps, is: Not a whole lot.

The aristocracy of a society—in any era of history—has never enjoyed sharing its pedestal. Indeed, the noble life represented something one was born into, and not something that could be acquired in this life. America, a country that once threw out the rule of a king, claims no such hereditary class privileges. Yet such a group does exist in the world's most powerful democracy—an elite based on cash and confidence. But this threat to the elite is not new; it has plagued "true" blue-blooded aristocrats for millennia. Over 2,500 years ago, the Greek aristocrat Theognis lamented the rise of the common people in his city near Athens. When the lower strata of society began seeking political power, Theognis wrote, "We the rest, their betters nominally, once the best; degenerate, debased, timid, mean! Who can endure to witness such a scene?" Theognis was not a very pleased patrician: He resented people beneath him striving to be like him.

But how could that happen if birth represented the only criteria for nobility? Things change. The inception of a cash society complicated the once-pure upper echelon of noble birth and power. This was expressed in the ancient observation: "Wealth throws lineage into confusion." For now people with *accumulated* wealth—not inherited wealth—could put pressure on the airy aristocrats to allow them to enter the cloudy domain of the privileged few.

The growth of modern society in England, a country with a long aristocratic tradition, included this disdain for the *nouveaux riches* and their craving for power and respectability. Perkin Warbeck, a pretender to the throne of King Henry VII (1485–1509), sought support for his cause by proclaiming that the king not only married off royal princesses "unto certain kinsmen and friends of simple and low degree," but also chose his chief ministers and advisers from "caitiffs and villains of simple birth" — horror of horrors to the snuff and pinky-in-the-air set. Perkin was right but he neglected to draw the logical conclusion: that many of those men of "lower degree" would—and did—become wealthy landed nobles in the ensuing years, much to the consternation of the old families. And in time, the new rich became the old rich.

In the 16th and 17th centuries, England witnessed a role reversal of sorts in the fortunes of nobles and the middle-class gentry. While some nobles lost financial ground, the gentry became a rising class of landowners and businessmen. It must have been upsetting to the aristocrats when a newsletter, circulated in 1628, proclaimed that the House of Commons could buy out the House of Lords "thrice over." To protect economic as well as ancestral interests, the old "lords" of the land now had to roll up their sleeves and take care of business: a most disagreeable circumstance for the well-washed.

By the end of the 19th century, both England and America had an aristocracy based on great wealth: the "green blood" of finance overshadowed the "blue blood" of history. Gilbert and Sullivan could spoof the mentality of the entrenched older nobility in their musical *Iolanthe* ("dating from the Flood, Blue Blood"), but reality portrayed a class of wealth foreign to inherent gentility and grandeur. In America, dynasties were forged from the sweat and brains of men of "simple birth." All that remained necessary to build a foundation for this new definition of nobility was the passing of time while the wealthy families grew wealthier . . . and respectable. Thus a clerk and bookkeeper named John D. Rockefeller founded a powerful dynasty of philanthropists, entrepreneurs, and politicians by shrewdness and determination. A tenant farmer from Ireland, Patrick Joseph Kennedy, migrated to Boston and became a cooper (caskmaker), and planted the roots for several generations of wealthy entrepreneurs and U.S. senators and congressmen, one becoming president of the United States. Similar stories are found throughout the world where cash could be had and accumulated through one's own hard work, or the work of others on their behalf.

Where wealth abounds so does a new sense of respectability, honor, and achievement. Wealth has thrown lineage into a new realm of validity. Today, the American dynasties prevail, stretching from the early history of the country across generations of investments and opportunities. The present-day winners of million-dollar lotteries and the get-rich-quick inventors of schemes and machines must wait until time has established their credentials for entry into the nobility of America. The

American watchword for "blue blood" defies the old European ideal that legitimacy breeds "good breeding." In the United States, a country that rejected belief in an *ancienne noblesse*, such a development was inevitable, given the ideal of wealth as the goal for the good life.

The genie is out of the bottle—or perhaps we should say the dollar is out of the cookie jar. Wealth is a major factor not only for success but for respectability, and it can be acquired in this lifetime. It sounds almost religious, substituting for the confessional booth the bank stall (to clip coupons). This, of course, is irrespective of how the rest of the world is faring, whether at war, in poverty, or at environmental risk. We can expect the rich to continue doing what they do best: acquiring and protecting money. It's not their fault; they are just on the stage of a play we all have written for ourselves. We just didn't get the parts.

THE RICH, "FILTHY LUCRE," AND ALL OUR PROBLEMS

Of course being rich means shouldering the burden of guilt until proven innocent when things go badly and it looks like the well-to-do simply *must* have had a gloved hand in it. And that goes for our economic ills as well. In the mid-1970s with an oil shortage, rising interest rates and prices, and underemployment, the oil companies—and those who controlled them—were accused of making "windfall profits" at the expense of the rest of us. Well, in the ill-informed, little-understood world of Tudor England (1485–1603), the malaise of the day—poverty, high prices, or underemployment—was attributed to the rich as well. The drive for reform in America of 1976 differed little from that in England of 1576, with darts aimed at wealth and the wealthy.

Yet are we of the well-informed 20th century more knowledgeable than 16th-century Englishmen about the perpetrators of our plights? The problems Tudor writers complained about are familiar to the late 20th century. Prices were rising after 1510, and had increased more than fourfold by 1600: a moderate rise by our standards but devastating to a world familiar with stable prices for centuries. Add to this a "Christian ethic" frowning on profit (lucre) and excessive wealth, and it is little wonder that tempers flared up. Many also believed the population of England was decreasing; whole towns stood deserted, and starvation and disease were ubiquitous. People felt there were wanton *enclosures:* arable land converted to pasture for the more profitable raising of sheep, leaving the peasant farmer less and less plowland. Someone had to be blamed for these "evil times."

But 16th-century Englishman assessed their economic woes incorrectly. The population was actually increasing, and at a rapid rate, contributing to high prices, starvation, bulging cities—and great profits to those who had the wisdom and luck to manage their farms and fields effectively. Most of the large-scale enclosures and desertions condemned throughout the 16th century actually occurred *before* the Tudor period; what critics observed was the result of a long-term development. Furthermore, peasants as well as patricians enclosed land for sheep-raising and profit in a time of great demand for wool and cloth. So those who could take advantage of events—rich or poor—did extremely well.

But the Tudor writers could not comprehend the causes of their maladies. Hence, they pointed the finger at the obvious villain to their minds: the rich, be he nobleman, gentleman, or bishop. High prices were caused by "high rents," wrote Henry Brinklow (d. 1546), a London social reformer who blamed the landlords for "rackrenting." An ardent enemy of the Pope during the Reformation, Brinklow recommended confiscating the properties of bishops, deans, and landowners and giving one-tenth to the crown (for the good will and support of Henry VIII, no doubt), and the rest for social reforms. No wonder this brazen son of a Berkshire farmer was banished by the bishops—those "forked caps," as he called them.

Hugh Latimer (d. 1555), as well, believed that "covetous landlords" caused the problems facing young King Edward VI. Even the king should "refrain from having too much," he wrote. Latimer apparently didn't know very much about monarchs. Thomas Becon (d. 1567) added his invective against the "covetous, ostentatious" gentlemen, and Robert Crowley (d. 1588) believed the poor rebelled because of the greedy "lawyers, merchants, knights, and lords." Crowley's solution, of course, followed contemporary beliefs: The oppressed should "refer their cause to God"; the oppressors should "lament their sins, defend and help the innocent poor," and allow the people to have "Godly ministers."

The 20th-century citizen might have been hesitant to ask God to mediate between the oil companies and John Q. Public. The latter could complain about the "windfall profits" of the former, but it was "filthy lucre and covetousness" of the 16th century all the same. Only a future history book can postulate what caused the problems of the 20th century, and why the writers and reformers of our era picked their particular villains. For the present, blame will undoubtedly fall where it has always fallen: on those who need not fear the malaise of the day. Another generation will determine if our assessment was correct.

THE DEVIL AND HIS WEALTHY WIFE

There are no hard numbers on this, but it is a reasonable supposition that wealth and happiness do not necessarily go hand in hand, especially during a stroll down the matrimonial aisle. We have seen how the nobility have tried for thousands of years to protect themselves from the madding crowd, unsuccessfully, and that they often bear the brunt of blame for the problems of the world. But although historically the upper crust have believed that somehow noble genes were different, clearly their personal situations in life were very similar to their nondesigner genes' counterparts.

This was known throughout history—those of wealth and aristocratic heritage still suffered the burdens of human beings, and in one special area in particular: marriage. We read today about wealthy movie stars happily married for days or weeks on end before the separation, divorce, and ritualistic feeding of the lawyers for The Settlement. The same is true with multimillionaires who have the uncanny ability to whittle down their fortunes with each ensuing marriage. One story comes down to us from the 13th century that reminds us of the shortcomings of wealth, or at least its inability to bring happiness. It was told by Jacque de Vitry, the Cardinal Bishop of Tusculum who died in the year 1240. He wrote several books of sermons that were woven from stories illustrating some moral, including one about the Devil and his wife.

It seems the Devil decided to take human form (once again), this time as a servant to a very wealthy patrician. Because he worked hard and was loyal, the rich man gave the servant his daughter in marriage, along with a great fortune. While on the surface this medieval marry-the-boss's-daughter scene might appear desirable, it was anything but for the Devil. As de Vitry related it, "Every day and night . . . she quarreled with her husband, and gave him no rest." After a year of this, the harassed husband called it quits. He confronted his father-in-law and said, "I want to leave and return to my country." The father-in-law was puzzled. "Haven't I given you many things so that you want for nothing?" he asked. "Why do you want to go away?"

At first the Devil refused to give a reason—when you're Satan you can afford to be coy. But when his father-in-law pressed him about where exactly home was, the Devil decided to spill the beans. "I shall tell you without concealing the truth," he said. "My country is Hell, where I have never endured such discord and annoyance as I experienced this year from my quarrelsome wife. I prefer to be in Hell rather than stay with her any longer." And with that, the Devil disappeared from sight forever—although some would argue he simply changed residence.

While it is true that the female of the species is here being blamed for the conjugal breakup, the moral revolves around wealth and its inability to ensure happiness. Perhaps it is the expectation of what wealth can bring: so much security in the area of material things, and therefore surely security in all areas of human experience. Not so. The rich find it out the hard way, by being there. Jacque de Vitry knew all along, and he had a hell of a way to demonstrate it.

PASTA PATRONAGE: DISHING IT OUT, RAKING IT IN

Wealth continues to be a mountaintop people aspire to climb, for better or worse. And while their expectations may or may not be realized, if they acquire wealth they will soon discover that "the rabble" suddenly have expectations of the rich: the belief that those who have it ought to share it with everyone else.

Donating money is a very old exercise, one that brought benefits not only to the beneficiaries but to the donors as well. Today, businesses give money to good causes and it is called "social marketing": finding ways to look good and reap some kind of financial reward from the largess. This may be through increased product or company awareness among consumers, or by shortening the sales cycle with promotional "good works" tie-ins with retailers or distributors. Wealthy people also give of their fortune—with the benefit of establishing positive perceptions among peer and plebeian alike that this is a "good person." "We need him or her on our board, or in our organization, or at the next dedication or ball or presidential fundraiser." And let's not forget the power the wealthy obtain over those who benefit from their gifts. It's real . . . and it's real useful.

The Italian merchant-princes gave freely during the Renaissance, bringing them popular support and a strong power base. Kings gave freely for the same reason; those that didn't usually had briefer tenures in office. Perhaps the greatest benefactors were the Roman emperors, who could add to their prestige and power by spending sums of money on good works. And the credit they received pales compared to what our current corporate heads and philanthropists might expect from their own activities.

The emperor Claudius (41–54 A.D.) did nice things for a town in Caria, and a monument was erected there in his honor that began "[Dedicated] to Tiberius Claudius Caesar Germanicus Imperator the divine Augustus, pontifex maximus, in his twelfth tribunician power, five times consul, acclaimed imperator twenty-one times, father of this country, the protector and benefactor of mankind"—that sure beats getting a plaque for the wall in the study! The inscription further noted that Claudius gave funds to "wash out the public bath, and in the same year, while serving as markets commissioner, he arranged for the products sold in the market to be sold below cost price in his term of office"—a discount that probably was a public success but did not amuse the retailers in Caria.

In Lycia during the 1st century A.D., the priest of Artemis and chief magistrate was cited on a monument as the author of "the greatest benefits of the city" when, during a famine, he "gave advances of money for the purchase of wheat." And in a town in Macedonia about the same time, Gaius Popillius Python "paid the head tax for the whole province [and] repaired roads at his own expense." It was no coincidence that he was named lifetime chief priest.

Sometimes benefactors had to make a little noise in order to receive public recognition, which after all is the real name of the game when it comes to handouts from the rich and powerful. In 145 A.D., the emperor Antoninus (138–161 A.D.) notified the chief magistrates, council, and people of Ephesus that "the generosity which Vedius Antonius has vouchsafed to you I have learned about not from your letters but from his." Vedius let the emperor know in no uncertain terms about the buildings he donated and other public works, and that the city did not "appreciate him properly." The townspeople, who were no dummies, simply reprinted the emperor's letter and posted it in a public place.

There was little doubt that being a benefactor, and letting those in charge hear about it, could help one's career. In 129 A.D., the emperor Hadrian (117–138 A.D.) caught wind of the good public deeds of Lucius Erastos, also of Ephesus. The emperor told the city leaders that Lucius "wishes to be elected councilman, and I put his candidacy up to you. If there is no obstacle and he qualifies for the office, I will pay upon his election the fee that councilmen pay. Farewell." Needless to say, any obstacles would have instantly disappeared: A letter from the emperor usually made it to the top of the in-box.

It's not that easy today, as can be seen from the nominees who get turned down for jobs by legislative bodies or committees despite their dedication and "good works," and their connections to government leaders. But the wealthy learned long ago that, at the very least, in order to keep their hands on their money they had to give some of it away. Once other benefits were discovered—public offices, greater power, and influence in the community—it became clear that donations and gifts were the way to go. This will continue, self-interest being a strong force in the lives of the elite. Fortunately, some of those fortunes will benefit the less fortunate: What better way to spread fortune around?

THE POWERS THAT BE: SOME OBSERVATIONS

When we think of Lee Iacocca of Chrysler Corporation or John Akers of International Business Machines Corp., we think of leaders wielding enormous power over their companies and their employees, as well as over their industries. For better or worse, those who enter the corporate world with personal ambitions often set their sights on positions of power, almost as an end unto itself. So from power breakfasts and power lunches, they move to power cocktails and power aerobics. A power ticket to the boardroom, it is argued, will not be too far ahead. The same is true of the powerful rich—the wealthy families who wield power through the influence they enjoy from their fortunes.

The notion of power has preoccupied great minds over the centuries, and we might pay heed to their words. For one, power is not necessarily evil. The late-19th-century American lawyer John Foster believed that "power, to its last particle, is duty." After all, someone has to steer the ship and take on the heavy responsibilities associated with leading. How to exercise that power is as important as holding it. Honoré de Balzac, the 19th-century French novelist, wrote that "all human power is a compound of time and patience." The 19th-century English novelist, Edward Bulwer-Lytton, noted, "power is so characteristically calm, that calmness in itself has the aspect of power, and forebearance implies strength." This quiet approach to power was also recommended by the 1st-century A.D. Roman philosopher Seneca, who wrote: "He who has great power should use it lightly."

Developing a focus is also a key to successfully managing power. Johann Goethe (1749–1832), the German dramatist and philosopher, gave this warning: "Beware of dissipating your powers: Strive constantly to concentrate them. Genius thinks it can do whatever it sees others doing, but it is sure to repent of every ill-judged outlay." Using power for good works rather than for personal aggrandisement must also be a cornerstone for those who possess it. The early-20th-century American banker, Frank A. Vanderlip, said that "since nothing is settled until it is settled right, no matter how unlimited power a man may have, unless he exercises it fairly and justly his actions will return to plague him."

Still, most people realize that power can corrupt, and although the New Testament declares that "the powers that be are ordained of God" (Romans 13:1), those wielding power often go astray of their duty. The Latin historian Tacitus (1st century A.D.) declared that the "lust of power is the most flagrant of all the passions"—a lust that can no doubt blind the possessor to rational behavior once power is attained. Caleb Colton, the early-19th-century English clergyman, wrote that "power will intoxicate the best hearts, as wine the strongest heads. No man is wise enough, nor good enough, to be trusted with unlimited power." Those who hold power must therefore walk a tightrope over immense temptation.

The 1st-century A.D. Greek biographer Plutarch saw the exercise of power as the ultimate trial for one's virtues: "It is an observation no less just than common, that there is no stronger test of a man's real character than power and authority, exciting as they do every passion, and discovering every latent vice." Knowing that more power exists than should be used makes the true leader. The 3rd-century B.C. Greek geometrician Archimedes saw power as limited only by what was in one's grasp: "Give me a lever long enough and a prop strong enough, I can single-handed move the world." Using power effectively and fairly means leaving a few levers untouched.

STONEHENGE AND THE SEARS TOWER

Isn't the money, the power, the fame, the prestige enough? Isn't that a leading question? Why? Because if it were enough, the rich and powerful would simply spend all their time trying to become richer and more powerful. But since most people, including the rich and powerful, are aware of the life cycles of human beings and are settled in the fact that "we can't take it with us," how can the elite gain advantage over that great equalizer, Death?

Well, unlike other animals roving the planet, human beings have long memories that can be shared with succeeding generations. And that means if you want to be remembered, you have to create something memorable and leave it lying around for others to notice once you've checked out. Since it is difficult for anyone, wealthy or poor, to plan out their own mythology to guarantee at least immortality in verse, there is the next best thing if you possess the shekels to do it: Leave something monumental behind. We saw how the Romans did it, with stone monuments erected to their names and deeds, hoping to beat the clock of mortality by telling future generations of their greatness.

Or of their terrible power. The 14th-century conqueror of Central Asia and parts of Europe, Tamerlane (or Timur Lenk, Tamburlaine, Timour or Timur, depending on who was cursing him), had written on his tomb "Were I alive today, Mankind would tremble." He couldn't take it with him either, but he made sure people got queasy just thinking about him.

When we look around at the skylines of major cities in the world, we see that they are dotted with what are often called monuments to our technology: huge skyscrapers made of steel and concrete and glass towering above the streets. Interestingly, they continue to be built even when vacancies are high in nearby buildings, and one wonders if the same motive is in operation as was with those ancient wealthy wishing to be remembered. The Sears Tower in Chicago, currently the world's tallest building, may indeed be no more than the muscle-flexing of a giant corporation. So, too, with Chicago's John Hancock and Amoco buildings, and others around the world. Moreover, there is continuous talk of such structures being built to top the Sears Tower, even when the need for more office space is nonexistent. Prodigious building projects satisfy the ego, corporate or otherwise. But this is hardly new to civilization, as we have seen. Most people are aware of the great pyramids of Egypt which, beyond being monuments to VIPs, did no more for their earthly remains than a six-foot plot of dirt could have accomplished. But it was not so much for a person's remains as for a constant image for mankind's collective memory that such structures were built. They continue to be built today for the same reason.

King Mausolus of Caria (d. 353 B.C.) wanted to ensure that mankind remembered him by building an enormous tomb, a tomb that became one of the Seven Wonders of the World. Today we remember his name—he gave us the word *mausoleum*—but we don't remember what he did or why he wanted us to remember him. Mausolus blew it. The builders of Stonehenge in England started out small—a ditch and holes—some 5,000 years ago, until the descendants of the original builders decided to erect an enormous monument of megalithic markers. We are still trying to decipher what the thing means (see Chapter 8), and we are not sure who was buried there, although several human remains have been found. A legend putting King Arthur's father beneath Stonehenge—which Merlin the Magician then erected—at least makes sense when we see what the pharaohs were doing. But if the structure was built by the priestly upper class to instill fear and awe in the people for all eternity, it didn't go much beyond the evening performances and occasional matinees. We don't have the names of the builders or the leaders, their deeds, or their thinking.

There are many famous ancient monuments that went far beyond your garden variety graves and buildings to become prodigious wonders in stone. Their construction required millions of man-hours and thousands of tons of materials over many decades, even centuries. The stone monuments and rows around Carnac in France attest to the incredible lengths a ruling class would go to in order to build giant memorials that could withstand the weathering of time. Closer to our own experiences, the Italian city-republics of the 13th and 14th centuries were made up of rival families and "consorzerie" *(consortia)* who spent enormous sums of money constructing towers from which to defend themselves against enemies. The towers were the pride of the families—no doubt Shakespeare's Romeo and his Juliet came from rival towers in Verona. Yet to see them today in Padua or San Gimignano makes the visitor question the wisdom of erecting these hollow edifices whose function was purely egotistical and defensive in nature—there was no benefit beyond showing off power and wealth.

In centuries to come, today's office towers will surely draw visitors to such "ancient" sites as Midtown Manhattan, downtown Chicago, and other metropolitan centers of commerce. The visitors will question what purpose, beyond providing working space and glorifying their creators, these towering, enormously expensive structures served—to their citizens. The answer may become all too apparent: None. Egos are costly and take time to satisfy; smaller, more utilitarian edifices just won't do. Pyramids or Stonehenge or the Empire State Building—they all become monuments of the desire to create respect for the powerful through powerful reminders. In the short run they work; further on, the memory dims as the monument decays.

"ALADDIN'S LAMP": SOME OBSERVATIONS

Money has become the medium of measurement for wealth, whether in liquid form (cash) or another form with comparable worth (land, buildings, art, gold). Since the first coins were minted long ago, the notion of money, its importance, and the problems it creates have not gone unnoticed by those inclined to put quill in hand to write about it. Their thoughts on money are varied and poignant, and a few bear repeating in light of our discussion about those who would acquire lots of it.

Aristodemus (c. 750 B.C.), the legendary ruler of Messenia, purportedly said that "money makes the man," and many in the world today would agree. The 18th-century French satirist Chamfort noted that "to despise money is to dethrone a king," and even the romantic Lord Byron felt that "ready money is Aladdin's lamp." But while famous writers such as Jonathan Swift could point out that "money is the lifeblood of the nation," others were less sanguine about its accumulation. The 17th-century English philosopher and statesman Francis Bacon observed "money is a good servant but a bad master," and the 19th-century British novelist Dinah Mulock rejected Aristodemus' money-makes-the-man view, stating, "there is a vast difference in one's respect for the man who has made himself, and the man who has only made his money."

The New Testament did not look kindly on the coveting of wealth, as in I Timothy 6:10: "The love of money is the root of all evil." And in John 2:15: Jesus "made a scourge of small cords" and drove the money changers from the Temple in Jerusalem. Whether money is good or bad—and Bacon felt that "money is like manure, of very little use except it be spread"—the usual way of acquiring it today is through business. Here the sages of other eras also had some thoughts, not all of which were favorable. The German social leader August Bebel (d. 1913) flatly said "the nature of business is swindling," and of late, this would be difficult to dispute on Wall Street. Howard Scott, the American economist, was even less kind: "A criminal is a person with predatory instincts who has not sufficient capital to form a corporation."

Once money is acquired, whether in vast amounts or on a more modest level, there is the whole issue of what to do with it, and how to manage it wisely or lose it foolishly. Robert Frost, in his poem "The Hardship of Accounting," might have been speaking to a wealthy person, or perhaps the U.S. General Accounting Office:

> Never ask of money spent
> Where the spender thinks it went.
> Nobody was ever meant
> To remember or invent
> What he did with every cent.

Or, if you have to ask how much a Mercedes Benz is, you can't afford it anyway.

Money may not be all things to all people, but it clearly brings out the best and the worst in us. The 17th-century English journalist Sir Roger L'Estrange understood this when he wrote, "Money does all things; for it gives and it takes away, it makes honest men and knaves, fools and philosophers; and so on to the end of the chapter." Those with vast amounts of money no doubt find themselves somewhere in L'Estrange's observation. Those who would be rich or suddenly become so might pay attention to both the fortunes and the follies that money brings, often with a vengeance.

BLIND AMBITION AND CHARLES THE RASH

We have looked at wealth and the wealthy, discovering that this group of people has been around a long time and continues to flourish in much the same way as did their distant cousins. Moreover, the distinction of "old rich" and "new rich" is blurring, thanks to the infusion of money as a means to wealth and, ultimately, nobility. Money may not be the cure-all; indeed, it can't buy happiness and it often leads men and women astray. But it can afford a life of leisure and the satisfying of the ego.

Wealth can also afford power, but that is only one side of the coin. For there is another road to power besides the one that is paved with money: ambition. Indeed, wealth sometimes induces the need for the rich to prove themselves, something that money can't buy. John F. Kennedy could have lived the life of a wealthy, European playboy (and, indeed, he apparently did, but on a freelance basis); instead he went after and won the presidency of the United States. But he had to overcome prejudices against not only his Catholic religion but also against the vast wealth of the Kennedy clan. Actor James Stewart could have rested on his motion-picture laurels and wealth; instead he commanded a bomber wing in World War II, was awarded the Distinguished Flying Cross, and through dedicated service earned the rank of brigadier general.

Others of the elite strove for nonpurchaseable power and glory to no avail, without knowing when to quit. Nelson Rockefeller wanted to be president, but despite prodigious spending and numerous attempts, it just was not to be. The same has been the case for another Kennedy: Edward M. The ambition is there but the cards are stacked against him, whatever the reasons may be. And money doesn't make any difference.

Trying to reach a goal at all costs is a human trait of the few, not the many, regardless of wealth or station in life. One such person, Charles the Rash, followed his obsession for winning to the grave. In the mid-15th century, the duchy of Burgundy was divided into two parcels of territory completely subservient to the French king, Louis XI. The Count of Burgundy, Philip the Good, had little desire to change this situation. But his son, Charles, was cut from a different cloth. He took charge of his father's armies and waged bloody battles to gain control of his duchy's destiny. Charles was a young man in a hurry, eager for his father to pass the reins of power to him so he could unite Burgundy and throw off the yoke of French rule.

In 1465, unable to contain his son's ambition, Philip gave the government over to Charles. The young count dreamed of carv-

ing out both a country and a name for himself in history, and he
established perhaps the best army in Europe for the purpose.
Charles was singular in his determination, taxing the people
beyond their means to establish a steady flow of capital for his
enterprise. His ambition soon bore fruit: towns were taken, often
with unprecedented slaughter, and when his father died in 1466,
the son became known as Charles the Rash, though he is commonly, and erroneously, referred to as Charles the Bold.

Charles made one miscalculation: Louis XI of France was as
egocentric and single-minded as himself, and in no way would he
allow Charles to impinge upon French overlordship. Charles'
ruthless treatment of those he vanquished didn't help his cause
either, and soon France enlisted the aid of the Swiss, the most
experienced soldiers of the day. In 1476, Charles' armies were
routed, and the beleaguered count was on the verge of insanity
from his defeat. People in the lands he had conquered saw an
opportunity to take advantage of this setback and revolted
against Burgundian rule.

But Charles was nothing if not fiercely determined to reach
his goal of establishing a sovereign state. In 1477, marching with
a newly formed army, he encountered France and her allies in a
field near Nancy. It may not have been his finest hour, but it was
his last. The Burgundians were defeated and, at age 44, Charles
the Rash was killed in battle. Within a short time, all of Burgundy was absorbed into France.

Keeping your eye on the prize is important when deciding
what course of action to take to reach that goal, and most parents
tell their children to try again if they do not succeed on the first
attempt. But understanding your limitations while judging the
strengths of the competition are just as important. Otherwise the
ego will disallow any realization that the goal cannot be obtained
and must be changed or abandoned. For once reality is denied,
defeat is not far off.

THE PRINCES IN THE TOWER

Thanks to William Shakespeare, an image has come down to us
of a man so obsessed with a driving desire to be king that he has
come to represent everything that is evil with ambition: King

Richard III of England. For here was a man respected by commoner and peer alike as a generous, fair noble and a princely, brave soldier who supported his brother and king, Edward IV. What he did to bring upon his head the wrath of centuries tells us as much about perceptions as it does about truth. It is the fate for leaders such as Richard Nixon, Margaret Thatcher, Mikhail Gorbachev, and Francois Mitterand, who wonder what the world will think of them decades or centuries from now.

Although the chronology of events is not completely clear, certain facts are known about this "murder mystery" that the late actor Laurence Olivier played to perfection on the stage. King Edward IV died on April 9, 1483, leaving two sons and five daughters. The two boys were named Edward and Richard. Both boys were minors, and while the eldest was declared King Edward V, a Protector was named to watch over the realm until the young king came of age. The protector was Richard, Duke of Gloucester, the dead king's brother and therefore the uncle of the two boys.

Some time in the spring or early summer of 1483, the two princes disappeared from public view. At the same time, it was announced that the late Edward IV's children were illegitimate due to prior marital "commitments"—not entirely unbelievable because Edward fooled around before and after his marriage. The Protector was proclaimed King Richard III on June 26, and nothing more was heard of the young Edward V and his brother. In 1674 bones discovered behind a staircase in the Tower of London were thought to be theirs.

The new king ruled for a little more than two years during a time of threats, rebellions, and evil rumors at home and abroad that he did away with his two nephews. In August 1485, a 28-year-old adventurer named Henry Tudor, who had rather anemic claims to the throne and a modest following, marched an army against the troops of the king. The two forces met near Market Bosworth on August 22, Richard III was slain, and Henry Tudor was proclaimed King Henry VII on the battlefield, with the dead king's crown upon his head—or so the story goes.

So what really happened to the two princes? The only widely accepted evidence is a statement by Dominic Mancini, a writer who left England in July 1483. He wrote that the princes resided in the Tower of London, "and day by day began to be seen more rarely behind the bars and windows, till at length they ceased to appear altogether." Both Richard III and his successor, Henry VII, required the deaths of young Edward V and his brother to secure their claims to the crown: You cannot be a king if there already is one. Henry Tudor was abroad during Richard's accession and 26-month rule, giving Richard III ample time and opportunity to help the boys depart this world for the next. But if Richard had allowed his nephews a secluded life in the Tower, then it would have been left for Henry VII to decide their fates—no easy matter since Henry was planning to strengthen his claim by marrying the boys' sister, Elizabeth of York, which he did.

Richard III got blamed for the murders, mainly because he lost the throne and the Tudors kept it for the next 118 years. The Tudor writers committed themselves to a smear campaign that culminated in Shakespeare's masterpiece, *Richard III*. The physical deformities attributed to Richard—a hunchback with a withered arm—were clearly added by the playwright to further demean the king and portray his cruel ambition. What we can never know is how much of Shakespeare's evil Richard is real and how much is fiction.

There is nothing wrong with being ambitious—that's how we left the cave and ended up in condominiums over the last few thousand years. But it is perception—what people think you want and how you plan to get it—that in the final analysis becomes the "true story," regardless of the truth. Richard had other options to play, including the *arrangement* of his nephews' demise as an accident if indeed he were the vicious monster of lore. We know that King William II of England died from an arrow in his back during a hunting expedition in 1100—and that his younger brother, Henry, quickly became King Henry I. No one knows for sure if Henry had a hand—or a bow—in the whole affair, but Henry I's older brothers had been a king and a duke, and Henry didn't want to be the odd man out. Richard III knew the story and could have followed suit.

In our age of mass communication and instant news, we must realize that most bold, visible actions will find immediate analysis by the media and their audiences, and that such analyses depend on how those actions are perceived. It means that ambition must be tempered, and that "what people will think" must be considered in advance and taken into account *prior* to any action. Richard III might be a hero today if he had handled his nephews differently or found a way to satisfy his ambition without violence or without incurring a public outcry against his actions. Instead, he is vilified for all time. Whether a murderer or not, his image is set for the ages.

So before someone enters the next foray into fame, fortune, and power, the possible perceptions of such actions should be considered and taken into account. Even the best of intentions can look dreadful in the public forum. With Richard, we will never know exactly what those intentions were, or if he even accomplished them.

RUNNING FOR OFFICE ON THE WALLS OF POMPEII

Seizing the moment is one thing; trying to get elected to an office without violence is quite another. Countries with electoral apparatus spend millions to help satisfy the ambitions and egos of those who would govern their fellow beings. Sometimes elections are bought or owned: England has had a history of "rotten boroughs," where the regional patron simply put in his man and that was that. And, of course, many an elected official has been bought by those interest groups which got him the office. The American humorist Will Rogers put it rather poignantly: "We have the best congressmen and senators that money can buy."

Because we are witnesses to present elections and have limited knowledge of past exercises in choosing the "right man," it is easy to think that television advertising blitzes and mass mailings are very modern—an invention with no precedent. Wrong. We have seen that the Romans had no problem "advertising" the good deeds they accomplished for their fellow men and women; they also used advertising as a means to get elected to office. In fact, we are rather backward in our slick, and often dirty, attempts to get messages across to the public through advertising. The Romans were pointed, frank, and refreshingly honest. They made it very clear why candidates should win and what each would do for the empire. There were no television sets or print ads. The Roman ad men used *walls,* creating graffiti as well as paintings and formal signs. The remains of the town of Pompeii, buried by the eruption of Mount Vesuvius in 79 A.D., provide us with examples of Roman political advertising copy.

We may think that political action committees (PACs) and special-interest groups are modern inventions. Not so. Look at the fruit dealers who supported Marcus Priscus for the office of douvir (magistrate): "The fruit dealers . . . unanimously urge the election of Marcus Holconius Priscus as duovir with judicial power." It should be noted that for similar offices, the goldsmiths wanted Gaius Cuspius Pansa, and the muleteers "urge[d] the election of Gaius Julius Polybius."

Often, the advertising was done by individuals and was of a personal nature. One person, who agreed with the muleteers, wrote: "I ask you to elect Gaius Julius Polybius . . . he gets good bread." Another wrote: "If upright living is considered any recommendation, Lucretius Fronto is well worthy of the office." Today, media buyers worry about their ads appearing at the right time in front of the right target audience. In Pompeii, some worried about their ads lasting out the day. One supporter wrote: "His neighbors urge you to elect Lucius Statius Receptus [to the office of] duovir with judicial power; he is worthy. Aemilius Celer, a neighbor, wrote this. May you take sick if you maliciously erase this!"

In modern day elections, any dark past of a candidate is carefully guarded by managers and advisers, although as presidential candidate Gary Hart proved in 1988, it is often impossible to protect the candidate from himself. The ancient Romans had no problem advertising what a candidate was really about. Two happy-spirited writers thought they could help their candidate out by writing: "[We] ask you to elect Marcus Cerrinius Vatia to the aedileship. All the late drinkers support him." And one unsavory group let their feelings be known with the line: "The petty thieves support Vatia for the aedileship." Or perhaps Vatia's opponent had that written—we'll never know.

As unpleasant as an electoral contest might be, those wishing to obtain power over their fellow citizens must recognize the dual nature of this process: appearing truthful, while holding back any truths that could be harmful to getting elected. Advertising has become the medium for this dual track approach, to the point where the unsuspecting public becomes bombarded with contradictory messages that would boggle the minds of the most well-meaning 12-member jury seeking the truth. And since we are in an age where perception by far is the "bottom line" for making decisions, countries and local governments will need to take longer looks at political advertising, and how it affects both the electoral system and the quality of the candidates winning office.

We will continue to be inundated with advertisements flaunting the best qualities of the ambitious and the egocentric; whether the qualities are accurate is academic. Perhaps one day the public will cry out to end all political advertising, and replace it with forums more conducive to learning both the character of the individual and the truth behind the message. And instead of news reporters asking the questions, maybe a group consisting of a cross section of the country might make for a more meaningful dialogue.

One anonymous writer on the walls of Pompeii probably reached the point of "ad exhaustion"—maybe *ad nauseam* is more appropriate here—when he wrote: "I wonder, O wall, that you have not fallen in ruins from supporting the stupidities of so many scribblers." Let's hope today's hapless voting public reaches the same degree of understanding come the next major election.

DRESSING FOR SUCCESS, MEDIEVAL STYLE

In today's impressionable business world, which has its share of the ambitious and the powerful, how you appear often means more than what you are. This has led to an entire field of thinking centered on the notion that appearance can be as valuable for success as accomplishment—or taking the political electoral process to the office place. So we hear about guides on how to cajole a raise out of a boss—merit or achievement notwithstanding. And we listen to consultants on everything from how to position yourself in a résumé to how to be impressive in an interview . . . even if your résumé isn't.

One interesting aspect of this stress on appearance is the

concept known as "dressing for success." This runs the gamut from what colors to wear—blue for dominating chief executive types—to what shirts or blouses to buy. Proper attire has become a major concern for those entering the business world and those hoping to sit on top of it. But while the innocent of heart ponder the primary need to "dress the part," we might take pause to consider another perspective on dressing for success. Only from this view, success meant staying alive.

The business suit in question was one of armor, a covering worn not to protect a weak personality or an anemic job application but to shield the body from an assault by weapons. Yet the goal was the same as in the business world today, or in any social arena: winning. Indeed, today's corporate heads and their lieutenants talk of setting objectives, planning strategies, and implementing tactics to win a campaign—all military terms coined by those same people who dressed for those campaigns. But it was armor, not the business suit, that got the job done.

Some of the earliest armor, made of bronze, was worn by the ancient Sumerians (c. 2500 B.C.), consisting of small conical helmets and leather or fabric cloaks with metal scales attached to them. For the business of war, this was an important business suit that afforded protection from flying projectiles or blows from handheld weapons. Even a thousand years later, the ancient Egyptians manufactured similar suits, as did the ancient Greeks for their Hoplite foot-soldiers. But unlike our lightweight two-piece suits, ancient armor accompanied by a spear could weigh more than 70 pounds: a burden no one today would welcome during a sweat-generating interview.

By the 11th century A.D., mail of linked rings of iron or steel replaced the ancient armor. Manufactured mainly in central and western Europe, this armor soon was reinforced with strips of leather or steel plate for added protection. In Japan, samurai armor was also made of steel plates topped with a helmet. But not only did the helmet protect the head in battle, it was given frightening features to instill terror in a samurai warrior's opponent, something our hat designers should consider for those on their way to the executive suite.

In the mid-14th century, metal plate had all but replaced chain mail, with the most artistry accomplished in the next two centuries. Although it is easy to imagine modern business stars falling down the ladder of success in spite of their terse tailoring, the popular belief that knights in armor once fallen stayed felled is false. Despite the weight, a knight in armor could lay down and get up, climb a ladder, and even run a little. Whether he wanted to is another story. (See Chapter 4 on Frederick Barbarossa.) Armor went out of style because of the development of the gun, since stopping a bullet would have required enormously thick armor. Battles were still fought at close quarters, but without the bulky armor that for 4,000 years meant the best chance for success for the soldier in arms.

Dressing for success is a good first line of defense in today's cutthroat business world where impressions are as important as one's performance. But rarely has a battle been won by hiding behind the armor. A suit never wins a battle; people do. The ambitious knight understood the difference between shining magnificently in his armor and using skill and brains to win the battle. It is obvious that as more ascending stars tumble from the upper echelons of success due to incompetency or bad judgment despite their immaculate attire, those who would be leaders will have to rethink "looking the part" versus "being the part." There are just too many choosing the former, not enough the latter. Those "being the part" eventually will climb the ladder and stay at the top, should competency and judgment ever come into style as being essential tools for leadership.

"IF THOU ART A LEADER"

Just because people strive to win the game and become *the boss* doesn't mean they have any specific qualifications for that lofty position. Would-be presidents or popes don't really have all the requisite experience to fill those positions from day one. They have to *learn* to be president or pope through doing it, despite their knowledge and accomplishments. Having said that, it is also clear that certain skills and experience can help make this transition a smooth one. And it can be aided by obtaining advice from those who have been there—easier to do for presidents, harder for popes since the new pope often has no inkling he will be the new pope, and when he does the old pope is already dead.

Although there are numerous books, articles, and manuals on how to be the top dog, nothing can replace the advice from those who have been there, or *near* there. And, yes, past ages have worried and wondered about the training of their leaders, often resulting in the writing of books about the subject. Perhaps the most famous is *The Prince* by Niccolo Machiavelli, and we will seek his advice when we talk about the business world at length (Chapter 4). Yet almost 4,000 years before Machiavelli printed his thoughts on leadership, another adviser was penning his ideas about what it took to be a good ruler.

In about 2450 B.C., Ptah-hotep, the chief adviser to a Fifth Dynasty pharaoh in Egypt, set down instructions for his son so that the young man could achieve the worldly success of his father as an adviser. The instructions began with Ptah-hotep telling the pharaoh of his old age and the desire to have his son succeed him as the king's visier. The pharaoh replied, "Speak unto him. No child is born wise." One lesson Ptah-hotep imparted to his son was to avoid being an intellectual snob, a good piece of advice for our Harvard and Stanford MBA graduates seeking the fast elevator to the top floor: "Be not arrogant because of thy knowledge," Ptah-hotep wrote, "and be not puffed up for that thou art a learned man. Take counsel with the ignorant as with the learned, for the limits of art cannot be reached, and no artist is perfect in his excellence."

When it came to leadership and conduct, Ptah-hotep made it perfectly clear that honesty was the best policy: "If thou art a leader, commanding the conduct of many, seek for thyself every good aim, so that thy policy may be without error. . . . He who departs from its laws is punished. . . . Wrong-doing hath never brought its venture safe to port." Looking at the trouble that current leaders around the world get into, this advice is perhaps more relevant today than it was almost 4,500 years ago.

Ptah-hotep also spoke of how to lead people, something every leader today needs to consider before declaring a policy or ignoring what people have to say. And his observation gives us a simple yet powerful tool to be effective rulers: listening. "If thou art a leader be kind in hearing the speech of the suppliant," he said. "Treat him not roughly until he has unburdened himself of what he was minded to tell thee. The complainant [sets] greater store by the easing of his mind than by the accomplishment of that for which he came."

Ptah-hotep knew how to work with the leader, as a confessor and as an adviser, and his accomplishment would be envied today. He wrote, "It is no small thing that I have done on earth; I have spent one hundred and ten years of life, which the king gave me, and with rewards greater than among the ancestors, through doing right for the king even unto the grave." Every ruler needs a Ptah-hotep as counsel. But more important, the wise Egyptian has left us with some thoughts to consider when we elect leaders or become them: honesty, humility, listening. Analyze the fall of any world leader or person of power—from Marcos and Khashoggi to Uno and Papandreas—and it's a good bet they missed one of Ptah-hotep's precepts for effective leadership or the handling of power.

THE FORCES OF ORMUZD AND AHRIMAN

Leaders are wealthy or powerful or good or evil—they lead none-theless. But how about their conduct, their *ethics*? A tricky subject that—and we will explore it further in Chapter 9—since one person's ethical behavior is another person's immoral perversion, or some such perception. Yet even leaders themselves believe they have a grasp of what is ethical and right and appropriate, as if their position affords them an opportunity to unravel this philosophical puzzle that so often claims victims of "high moral fiber."

So Albert Einstein, who helped father the atomic age and spent the remainder of his life loathing it, preached about a world government and the need for justice for all. So Lee Iaccoca, who helped father the Ford Mustang and the 'New' Chrysler Motor Company, expounded on how to govern and, in the process, take care of those less fortunate and in need. So Albert Szent-Gyorgyi, who helped father Vitamin C, ranted about the need for world peace, or else. And who would argue with those powerful enough to gain a platform? They feel fortunate—although some feel justifiably rewarded—and they want to share their acquired wisdom about mankind now that they have a clear, loftier view of things.

Having strong opinions on ethical behavior, and finding a stratospheric perch to preach from, was the preoccupation of an ancient philosopher and religious leader known to us today as Zoroaster, or Zarathustra (meaning "owner of old camels"). This Persian reformer, whose unknown dates vary from 1000 B.C. to 530 B.C., saw the world in a perpetual conflict between good and evil. And like a present-day leader—or any person of importance with a platform for pronouncements—Zoroaster had ideas to make things better. As with most dynamic leaders he had visions, although of the heavenly variety. He also felt that his solutions were the only ones to be followed: "I am thy chosen one from the beginning; all others I consider my opponents." (Zoroaster was not one for taking negative reviews kindly.) He identified two main forces in the battle of good and evil: Ormuzd, "the wise lord," and Ahriman, "the spiritual foe." Each had armies at their command and their final conflict depended upon which side mankind would support.

What appears refreshing to the modern reader in looking at Zoroaster's thoughts is his code of ethics, not a few of which would help purify the often tainted world of the affluent, in or out of business. Those following his teachings swore to abstain from robbing or stealing the property of others, and to lead a good life. They also promised to speak the truth and act honestly. Even the environment was of concern to the prophet—an environmentalist in ancient Persia! He enjoined his followers to keep the earth, air, and water free from defilement. He even went so far as to prohibit burial or burning of the dead for fear of polluting the elements. Burial was done high above the ground.

Zoroaster's motto, repeated many times in the sacred *Avesta* scriptures, was "I profess good thoughts, good words, good deeds." Not a bad motto, for the people at the top and for us all.

A GOTHIC TALE OF PUBLIC TRUST

Power wielded is power unbridled if it works in a vacuum, unaware of those affected by it. Those in power for power's sake often fall from grace—if not from this mortal life—because they forget that power involves responsibility to those who allow themselves to be ruled. The 1980s will be remembered as an era in the United States when Ronald Reagan wielded power. And he must wonder how exactly he will fare in future history books about what he accomplished and for whom: himself or those who looked to him for help. In one area, economics (or Reaganomics), he will be judged very thoroughly since it represented a blend of avoiding federal government financing of public and social works and encouraging such funding at the local level of government and through private enterprise . . . often leading to no funding at all. This economic philosophy was in part a reflection of his personality—a hands-off leader remote from everyday affairs, and perhaps the country at large. Economists and historians are just now assessing what the effects of his policy mean for future generations.

Long ago, another leader with similar managerial experience to Mr. Reagan set out to make his mark on the world. But in doing so, he also realized the importance of taking charge personally, whether or not his moves were popular. And he understood the need to listen, as our friend Ptah-hotep wrote about many years earlier.

The story begins in the late 5th century A.D. when the Western Roman Empire was in its death throes, though the Eastern Empire, centered at its capital city of Constantinople, continued to thrive. Numerous tribes from Europe wreaked havoc throughout the old Western Roman domains, and the invasion by Attila the Hun (Chapter 1) added to the chaos that permeated Italy and Northern Europe. One of those tribes, the Ostrogoths (literally *East Gothics*), began threatening Rome in the wake of Attila's victories. Theodoric, the seven-year-old son of the Ostrogoths' king, was sent as a hostage to Constantinople, ostensibly to check the Ostrogoths from destroying Rome. Ironically, this little maneuver became the instrument of further Roman invasion. The young Theodoric, while not formally educated, learned the arts of government and war by observing and participating; he apparently never learned to read. In 488, at about the age of 34, he led the Ostrogoths across the Alps into Italy against the Roman emperor, Odoacer, beginning a five-year war of attrition.

Theodoric, probably tired of waiting for victory and with a clear objective in mind (unlike Hannibal, who seems to have enjoyed sunbathing), invited Emperor Odoacer and his son to Ravenna, where he wined and dined them . . . and then killed them by his own hand. Now in charge of the Western Empire, Theodoric protected the forms of government he found. His greatest achievement, however, was in restoring economic prosperity. He increased military pay—a sore point among soldiers—and gave two thirds of the Italian soil to the Roman population, leaving one third for the Goths. He ordered the draining of the Pontine marshes for cultivation and, believing in a regulated economy, issued an "edict concerning prices to be maintained at Ravenna." No price list survives, but it was later reported that food prices dropped by one third during his reign.

In moves that we recognized in the Reagan agenda, Theodoric also reduced government personnel and salaries, and he kept taxes low. Despite all these budget-cutting measures, he still had the revenue to repair much of the damage caused by previous invaders; he even built a few churches and palaces.

Theodoric's kingdom collapsed soon after his death. But his accomplishments, especially in the realm of government and the economy, point to a leader in touch with the problems of the time. Moreover, at the age of 70, when his days were numbered and others wanted to take his place, Theodoric wrote a letter to his counterpart, the Eastern emperor, that showed his understanding of good leadership. He wrote: "The most dangerous heresy is that of a sovereign who separates himself from part of his subjects because they believe not according to his belief." Future generations will judge Mr. Reagan on Theodoric's warning. Present leaders must take it into account before they proceed to exercise the power they possess.

MOSES, THE DOGE, AND THE DUKE OF NORFOLK

Much has been written about the graying of America and what it means to both the marketplace and the leadership of our country. This has been underscored by having experienced a septuagenarian president in charge of arguably the world's most powerful nation. But let's face it: You can have power and wealth and fame and ambition . . . but you're still going to get old.

Nevertheless, Americans over 50—one out of every four at this writing who, by the way, control half the discretionary income in the country—should be of good cheer. Why? Because the elderly of our species have been in control throughout history: It's just been kept a secret by young people who run across this fact in college and fail to take it down in their notebooks. And that means that such octagenarians as William Paley (founder of CBS) and Armand Hammer (Occidental Petroleum Corp.) are not alone in their unwillingness to drop the baton and head for the wheelchair.

One need only delve into the Old Testament to see who was in charge of the Israelites once they fled Egypt and bondage: an 80-year-old former Egyptian taskmaster named Moses. And although Joshua was later fit for the battle of Jericho, a higher authority clearly felt he wasn't ready for taking refugees on a 40-year tour of the desert, no expenses paid. That task was left to Moses, who supposedlly died at the age of 120.

In 12th-century Venice, the office of the doge grew in importance as the city became the leading trade center of Western Europe. In 1192, the council elected Enrico Dandolo as doge—he was more than 85 years old. Dandolo hardly sat around sipping capuccino on the veranda. Rather, he built the city's trade to a point where it rivaled that great port to the East—Constantinople. In 1204, when the doge was more than 95 years old, he spurred on the Fourth Crusade and encouraged the Crusaders to take the long route to Jerusalem via Constantinople. This, of course, led to the Crusaders sacking his major economic rival, putting that city out of commission for centuries (see Chapter 6). When the doge passed on the following year, he no doubt died with a smile on his face.

Whether doing battle in the field or in the marketplace, age has never been an encumbrance to good leadership. A case in point is Thomas Howard, 2nd Duke of Norfolk and a leading English nobleman under Henry VII and Henry VIII. In 1513, the young, 23-year-old Henry VIII went sailing off to France with an army, dreaming of victory over his ancestral enemies. (Although never quite engaging the enemy, a group of French cavalry did wander into the line of fire of Henry's artillery, and their agility at retreating quickly gave the incident an embarrassing name for any would-be-conqueror such as Henry VIII: "The Battle of the Spurs," so called for the Frenchmen kicking their heels into the retreating horses.) Meanwhile, the Scottish king, James IV, decided that with Henry away it was a good time to invade England. Thomas Howard, by now 70 years of age, led an English army north, and the resulting battle at Flodden Field left 10,000 Scots and their king dead. Howard lived on to the age of 81 to serve his heroic king.

It was clear in the past, as it should be now, that elder statesmen are a real asset to any society, and that we shouldn't simply put them out to pasture or on some innocuous commission for their "advice and counsel." Right or wrong, Ronald Reagan was an effective leader in getting many of his programs pushed through. And with a shift in age brackets in the United States, it is important to realize that the nation, and not just the youth, can be served by those who possess vast experience, and experiences.

Leaders and those who were once powerful never fade away—they just find a smaller group of followers to lead. We would be wise to use their wisdom on a grander scheme, to everyone's benefit.

MAGNA CARTA, CHARLEMAGNE, AND GREATNESS

When you tie all of this together—wealth, power, leadership, ambition, ego—you easily arrive at the word *legacy:* what that person actually leaves behind besides a record of actions, deeds, and a large estate. One goal that no doubt comes to the minds of those in this elite group is greatness, the assessment by future generations that something or someone was truly great in the historical track of time allotted them.

Whether someone can seek greatness is chimerical at best, since to be called *great* is relative to time and circumstance and definition. One example of something viewed as great was the Magna Carta, or Great Charter, reluctantly signed by England's

King John in 1215 at Runnymede outside London and reissued at various times. Historians have argued as to why it was great in the first place. Some saw it as the birth of rights for the common man; others felt it was a reactionary declaration to restore the once-powerful rule of the barons. Either way, neither baron nor king thought it to be a "great" event for future generations to hold in awe—they just wanted to get on with their lives.

The charter was definitely referred to as great not long after its creation, but apparently the name simply referred to its length, which was considerable as medieval charters go. Worse for those who seek icons to worship, it was really the 1225 issuance of the charter that was the important one for generations of Englishmen, and it came in the reign of John's son, Henry III. So much for 1215 and the lengthy document at Runnymede.

Although other examples exist of things called great (the Great Wall of China, for instance), the word usually has been applied to a handful of historic personages who for one reason or another were deemed great by later generations. Alexander, son of Philip of Macedon, conquered much of the civilized world in the middle of the 4th century B.C. and is known to posterity as Alexander the Great. Fortunately for him, the word great only acknowledges his tenacious accumulation of real estate and not its retention, since it was divided by royal generals soon after his death.

Charlemagne, or Charles the Great, followed much the same career path in the West as did Alexander in the East, but on a smaller scale, suffering similar territorial losses among his successors (see Chapter 7). Alfred the Great, the only British monarch to earn that epithet, united much of England against the Danes. But that accomplishment only made the country a more unified place to be conquered by the Normans 150 years later. Julius Caesar, on the other hand, subjugated quite a bit of territory but was never called great. This probably would not have concerned him, for he ended up being deified, and his name became a title for future emperors and dictators: Caesar (and its later variants, *czar* and *kaiser*).

So what of greatness? Surely it was a fleeting moment in time to those called great. Furthermore, many of the realms that achieved greatness in size, power, or wealth—such as the Assyrian, Persian, and Hittite empires—were great for but a short span of time measured against the history of civilization. So even if one aspires to greatness, it will rarely be acknowledged in that person's lifetime, and should it come to pass, it may merely represent a short-lived accomplishment or feat. Only time can decide how significant was the journey, how prodigious were the achievements of those who dared to be great.

Our elite will always be with us, forged from inheritance, acquired wealth, power, leadership, ambition, conquest. The door is open for anyone to enter—that is a certainty. But it is a rather long, arduous climb to that pedestal, where few wish to move over and make room for one more. Most people nonetheless dream of reaching it, though few are willing to attempt the trek, or to make the sacrifices along the way. Regardless, the journey is ancient and ever present, and there will always be those who rise above their fellow human beings because they are perceived as having risen.

Most important, the vehicles for getting there remain the same; so do the challenges, the rewards, the pain, and the satisfaction. Envied or hated, they are part of our experience on earth. And they do provide a good show. Di (Princess of Wales), Fergie (Duchess of York), George (Bush), Donald (Trump), Lee (Iacocca)—the stage is full and we all have front row seats.

3
C H A P T E R

ON WOMEN, WINE, WIZARDS, AND SOCIETY AT LARGE

We have explored certain elements of the present from the perspective of the past, and it should be coming clear that we have "been there before." Yet the reasons, and consequences, of war, wealth, and power do not touch most of our lives on a day-to-day basis. Few of us will start a war or rule an empire, let alone amass a fortune or run a government. We therefore need to look at aspects of society that reach us on a more personal level. While an all-inclusive list would take volumes of space to explore, a few are here proffered to show that our current societal problems and situations and "changes" are not *current* at all. They may or may not provide comfort to the present, but a different view will surely emerge of what we will encounter, and presently witness, as the 20th century comes to a close.

WOMEN AND MEN—PART I: THE ROMAN APPROACH

Biblically speaking, marriage as an institution has been around ever since Adam and Eve decided that, despite the lack of competition, a formal arrangement requiring loyalty and fidelity was a good idea, the Serpent in the Garden notwithstanding. This bond had a profound effect on society: There would always be failed crops, disease, wars, death—but humans could depend upon the stability of the marriage pact. That's why the ancient Greeks could accept the decision of their forebears to embark on a 10-year war with the Trojans because the wife (Helen) of a Greek (Menelaus) was abducted by a Trojan (Paris, or Alexander)—never mind that the lady failed to object with any vigor. Religion also recognized the efficacy of marriage, declaring that the union of woman and man was ordained by God and supervised here on earth through the ministrations of God's employees (priests, rabbis, ministers, shaman). The Christian church went so far as to make marriage one of its seven holy sacraments that ran the course of a person's life from birth until death.

But things change. Today, there are as many divorces as marriages, and women recognize—once again—that the marriage bond can position them as second-class citizens and several paces behind the male of the species. So we now witness that when people marry, if at all, it is later in life after some self-exploration and career fulfillment; babies are arriving when couples are in their thirties—a far cry from the Old Testament when a 13-year-old boy was a man ready for procreation, or from medieval times when teenagers such as Romeo and Juliet could consummate a marriage.

One example of this change that, as will be seen, isn't a change at all, can be seen in the work force. A new statistic from the 1960s, which we might call the *Triple W,* or "Women Who Work" number, relates to a current trend in what is taking place in the United States and other countries. More than half the women in America—some put it at 70 percent—are gainfully employed, in part because of some interesting cultural gymnastics as the family gets redefined and the workplace struggles to accommodate the fairer sex as they demand exactly that—fairness.

Throughout history, there have always been exponents of female freedom of choice in a male-dominated society. But those were usually exceptions to the rule of the male, who ran the roost as well as the realm. Women such as Aspasia (5th century B.C.), the Greek courtesan and mistress to the charismatic Athenian leader Pericles; or Queen Eleanor of Aquitaine (12th century A.D.), married to a French king and later an English king, providing offspring for both, bestrode the male-oriented world to the tune of their own minstrels, and their own agendas. But it takes a ripping of the cultural fabric—some say the 1960s did just that—to allow thousands and millions of Eleanors their chance at achievement. And more often than not, the unraveling first begins with the marriage bond, literally.

During the 1st century B.C., the wealthy members of the Roman Empire grew wealthier while politics became more corrupt and morals hit the skids—developments not all that foreign to our own world! The proverbial oldest profession, prostitution, increased its cultural value as brothels competed for business among the wealthy. Indeed, some gratified politicians actually organized a guild of brothelkeepers (*collegium lupanariorum*) to consolidate a loyal source of votes. As the marriage pact became a farce, so, too, went any sense of morality traditionally linked to that union. Most wealthy women had at least one divorce under their togas, and men found wives solely for their money or political connections. Two leading politicians and generals, Pompey and Sulla, were each married five times for political and monetary advantage. Cato the Younger (95–46 B.C.) angrily observed that the Roman Empire had become a matrimonial agency.

When a husband decided the marriage was no longer useful, he simply sent his wife a letter announcing their divorce. No reason was necessary, and the newly liberated husband was free to seek another investment. Many men chose to play the concubine game; and many well-to-do women avoided having children so they could do the same. One Roman official, Metullus Macedonicus, implored men to marry and have children, but the trend toward rich, childless couples continued. As one historian noted, children were now luxuries which only the poor could afford.

This situation encouraged women to look beyond marriage for fulfillment, and freedom of movement became a way of life. Women divorced their husbands as easily as did the men, and many women took up cultural activities, from dance and singing to studying philosophy and giving public lectures. Not a few entered into business. The marriage bond took on a new meaning; so did the position of a woman's place in society.

Today's working woman is a product in part of the redefinition of the female role in marriage—a situation similar to the Roman era. But so far we have not had a total collapse of moral stability. The free moral posture, especially toward sexual activity, that accompanied the loosening up of female stereotypes since the 1960s seems to have been checked. There is also another factor we cannot as yet assess regarding this halt on the road to moral decay—acquired immune deficiency syndrome, or AIDS, which requires playing sexual hot potato to see who gets caught when the music stops . . . permanently.

Time will tell if women take the lead in moral laxity traditionally pioneered by their male counterparts. For as with men, they now have the freedom to do so. But it is important to understand that the institution of marriage is always in flux; it is not cast in concrete and its shifting precepts have periodically changed the roles of men and women in society, and toward each other. Women have sought power and independence throughout history. Maybe a search into the past will give the present generation of women the next plan of action, or a peek at what they need to consider, or avoid. For women have been there before—it just takes an acknowledgment that the late 20th century is yet another replay of some very old stories.

WOMEN AND MEN—PART II: THE EARL AND THE PROTESTING LADY

If love and marriage, as in the song, "go together like a horse and carriage," then we have seen in recent years the horse being put out to pasture while the partners fight over who owns the carriage. Such prattle over property partly stems from a rash of famous palimony and divorce cases, with Hollywood leading the way with such names as Joan Collins, Clint Eastwood, and *E. T.* creator Steven Spielberg, whose bill for divorce may pale the one his extraterrestrial received for "phoning home." Added to this mauling of matrimony is the prenuptial agreement, which explores the current discovery that love is nice but does not ward off a lawyer's pursuit of gross assets in a divorce settlement.

Marriage as an institution is ancient and still viewed as a binding force for family and society despite the changing attitudes of men and women toward such partnership. But the dual aspects of its nature—socio-religious and economic—have always come into conflict. For while religious leaders, as we have seen, defined the marriage act as something sacred and inviolable, civil leaders sought to protect the inheritances and landed wealth associated with the union. A marriage may be "made in heaven" but its value was often found not in poetry but in the bank. And as the Devil learned (Chapter 2), even the sound of coins cannot always buy that elusive yet essential ingredient in the human makeup: happiness, and its pursuit.

By the 12th century, the canon law of the church in Europe—which ostensibly concerned religious matters but in fact spilled into temporal life—was being challenged and supplemented by the rediscovery of a body of Roman law, passed on from the latter period of the great empire. The results were a convoluted assortment of laws that often depended more on the political situation than a legal solution. And no better example of this state of affairs—and how it affected women—comes down to the present than the law on marriage.

At this time, marriage was a rickety institution. (We just explored the same set of wheels more than a thousand years earlier in Rome!) Divorce was now forbidden, spouses often died at young ages, and property was commonly the motivating force behind a matrimonial union. Both church and state wanted to get into the act, trapping couples in legal conundrums. This, in fact, is what happened to the earl of Oxford in England.

The earl, an important figure in the court of King Henry II (1154–89), was betrothed to the daughter of a royal offical. Before the marriage could be consummated—then defined as the time a couple required to perform successfully in the marriage bed—the official fell from royal favor and lost his lands. Since the young lady was no longer an heiress, the earl quickly "fell out of love" and lost interest, deciding that she was not quite marriageable, a conclusion easily supported by his king. (Henry had married Eleanor of Aquitaine primarily to bring her vast lands in Western France into his Norman empire—he knew what marriage was all about!) But the earl's lady, in an unlikely move for that century, protested too much and ended up imprisoned by her former fiance, who vainly tried to have her drop the claim that he had broken a sacred vow.

The Pope and several bishops heard of the lady's plight, but they were in a political bind. This was the time when Henry II was feuding with his recalcitrant archbishop of Canterbury, Thomas Becket. Rather than alienate Henry—a good son of the church, that is, a large contributor—the Pope and his prelates did nothing about the matter for several years. But Becket's murder in 1170, brought about willingly or not by Henry II himself, gave the Pope the leverage he needed, and a formal ecclesiastical investigation was held into the earl of Oxford's case. Wonder of wonders, the earl lost on canonical counts, and spent the next 20 years with a landless but fruitful wife who produced several heirs for her faithless spouse.

So while we continue to watch live-in pals get million-dollar settlements and hapless mates seek the fortunes to which they have recently become accustomed, we might take a pause for reflection. Perhaps those who marry for the wrong reasons may get their payment down the road, when changing political winds and new laws catch them. In this, women have become the equals of men.

WOMEN AND MEN—PART III: VIKING "DINKS"

Another apparent stride for women in partnership is the DINK. DINK? Well, nowadays it's important to speak in acronyms (which often make the parables of the New Testament positively understandable). These include acronyms for everything from prolonging the planet by reducing strategic nuclear weapons (START) to aging gracefully in spite of nuclear weapons (AARP). But the DINK is an economic affair of the heart: Double Income No Kids. Such couples often are envied by both the unmarried and the very married. After all, there's all that discretionary income that never departs for the never-ending landscape of disposable diapers (nappies if you're across the Atlantic), pediatricians, and new shoes every three months.

Yet DINKS are people, too, despite their two cars, two jobs, and probably two different views of marriage since there is so little time for discussion and a meeting of the minds. DINKS no doubt quarrel, divorce, cheat on each other, and commit the other unpardonables that all married couples are susceptible to—kids or no kids. But let us pause a moment—this marital arrangement is hardly new, as we have already seen in ancient Rome. Nor is it as harsh or downright dangerous today as it could be.

A DINK relationship during the time of the Vikings of Northern Europe a thousand years ago would have been open to many perils since customs were very different from our own. For one, marriages were usually arranged by the parents, often for money. Although a free woman could veto any arrangement, there was a catch: If she married without the consent of her parents, her husband was declared outside the law (outlaw) and thus became open season for any of the bride's relatives who decided it was time for her to become a widow and start over. Divorce was rather tricky, too. A man could divorce his wife, but if the reason wasn't good, he stood the risk of being killed by his wife's family. Divorce was justifiable, however, if a spouse was caught wearing the clothing of the opposite sex—it is best not to touch *that one* when considering today's various permutations! Dealing with adultery was easier than with divorce. If a man caught his wife with another man, he could kill the intruder without bringing down the wrath of the lover's family: a rather enlightened view of breaking that particular Judaeo-Christian commandment and one we might want to send to committee.

The female member of a modern DINK household no doubt strives for stability in her marriage despite double workloads and little time for intimacy. A Viking wife also worked, but she had no qualms about setting her husband and other men to fighting each other for her affections. Viking women were also valuable advisers to their husbands, especially in business affairs. And they obtained financial benefits over time: one third of the husband's wealth immediately, increasing to one half after 20 years of marriage, a sort of 401K pension program for spouses.

The Viking DINK couple did have certain things in common. They were great lovers of singing, and both male and female enjoyed playing musical instruments, especially the harp. (A King Gunnar purportedly could play the harp with his toes. It is not known how adept his wife was on the same instrument.) Although virtual pussycats at home, Viking men talked big once they left their houses and congregated among themselves—a custom carried on today in pubs, bars, and other watering holes.

One Viking poem about Odin, king of the gods, gives an idea of what men thought of their women: "At evening the day is to be praised, a sword after it is tested, a woman after she is cremated." Viking men did not mince words.

Today's men caught up in a DINK relationship probably look more kindly upon their counterparts than did the Viking men of old. For while divorces rarely end in murder, those costly lawsuits with potentially diminished lifestyles encourage the male to make the marriage work. Otherwise, winding up a *"single income no kids"* divorced male means winding up a SINK.

THERESA AND THE FOUNDING OF PORTUGAL

The American public, and those abroad who follow politics in this country, are aware of strong-willed First Ladies who have influenced their presidential husbands in the decision-making process. In recent years, Nancy Reagan has been both praised and criticized for her involvement in policymaking, and in another era Eleanor Roosevelt often officiated over the Oval Office during Franklin Roosevelt's heyday in the White House.

The same is also true in everyday life, where the male of a relationship wears the appearance of being the decision-maker, while his "better half" actually *suggests* the courses of action to be taken. This is in part the result of more historical baggage carried into the 20th century: the male hunter protecting his personal interests and making the tribal decisions for the benefit of all. What males hate to confront is the observation that they prolong their adolescence well into their twenties and thirties, therefore often having to rely on the advice of the fairer sex for grownup help, while absentmindedly forgetting to give them credit for the *ultimate decision.*

Women, of course, carry their own baggage, including the rather self-serving male argument that females are too "emotional" to make rational decisions: Leave it to the male to cut through the hormones and reach the "right" decision . . . with, perhaps, some occasional help from a lady or two to "bounce ideas around." Well, none of this will wash as we approach the end of another millennium: 2000 A.D. Women are not only behind male power but often out in front of it all. Yet it's an old story, one that both sexes should review before they condemn the other for stepping out of character.

More than 800 years ago, a strong-willed woman helped her husband not only implement his business at hand—becoming king—but carve out a new country: Portugal. In 1095, King Alfonso VI of Castile and Leon gave his daughter, Theresa, in marriage to a famous Crusader, Henry of Burgundy. As part of the package, Henry received a parcel of land from the domain of Leon called Portugal, after the Roman seaport of Portus Cale. Henry, however, wanted to be a king, not a count beholden to his father-in-law. So he and his wife schemed to make their lands a separate, independent kingdom.

Unfortunately, Theresa's husband died in 1112, but that failed to stop her from continuing their quest. Through her efforts, the upper classes became indoctrinated with the notion of an independent Portugal, and she helped fortify Portuguese cities for war. Theresa also led her armies into battle—when she wasn't busy receiving visits from poets, musicians, and lovers. The going was not easy. At various times she was defeated, captured, deposed, and reinstated. When she finally died in 1130, it was in exile with her lover.

But Theresa had been a good teacher to her son, Affonso I Henriques (1128–85), who now took it upon himself to achieve what his mother set out to do. When the king of Castile promised Affonso any land he could capture from the occupying armies of the Moors, the son of Theresa plunged headlong into battle to carve out a large country he could call his own. In 1139 at Ourique, Affonso defeated the Moors, thus creating the possibility of establishing a large kingdom under his rule. The king of Castile was hardly thrilled at the news, even though he had promised Affonso any land he could wrest from the enemies.

The matter of who owned the land went before the Pope, who favored the claim of Castile. But Affonso, like his mother, was not one to give up. He offered to hold the lands of Portugal as a domain under the auspices of the Papacy, and even agreed to pay an annual tribute to the Pope. It was an offer too good to turn down. In 1143, the Pope recognized Affonso as king of Portugal, thus fulfilling the dream of his father and mother.

It cannot be proven that behind every successful man there

is a woman pushing him on, especially today when women are doing just fine on their own. But it sure doesn't hurt the male of the species to have the support, courage, and expertise of his mate, if not his mom. It is a situation males will have to accept; if they are wise, they will seek it out. It is not a new idea, and kingdoms have been forged because a woman carried a vision beyond dreaming and taught the males around her how to make it happen. It's time to throw open the windows of history and throw out all that prejudicial, stereotypic baggage.

FONTEVRAULT AND THE WOMEN'S CLUB

The gathering of males, as with eagles, is a lofty sight to behold. For thousands of years, males have sought to establish groups of influence through clubs, societies, schools, and other artificial aggregates that stood as bastions of power and a mystery to the uninitiated and the unwelcomed. Women, of course, were summarily excluded from such organizations and it has only been in this century that the men's clubs are being threatened either with female members or extinction, some preferring to fall on the sword rather than sheath it.

Groups meant power; in England during the 17th and 18th centuries, the Whigs and the Tories had their own clubs for meetings and planning political strategy. Today, women are just starting to establish such nuclei of influence, whether it be the National Organization of Women or the council of 200 (women in business) in Chicago. But there have been such gatherings before the current "discovery" of inequities between male and female power bases; moreover, they wielded enormous influence both on commoners and the highest born.

The ancient Greeks had their Amazons, the Romans their Vestal Virgins—women in groups who controlled their own destinies or who held influence over males. In the case of the Romans, it was religion that served as the source of power, and it was religion—Christendom—that held Western Europe together after the fall of the Roman Empire.

One powerful group of women held sway over the affairs of men during the height of Christendom in the 11th and 12th centuries. (Moreover, men were allowed to enter "the group"—women were way ahead of the unenlightened male clubs to follow.) That group of women was at Fontevrault Abbey in France, founded in 1099 by a hermit seeking to create a Christian community for meditation. Since it was imperative to house men and women separately, convents for women were built within the abbey grounds under the name of St. Benedict. The monks built for themselves the convent of St. John. Because the founder dedicated the abbey to the Virgin Mary, it became necessary to appoint an abbess to rule over the entire community. Both nuns and monks owed complete obedience to her, and her power extended to help the poor, lepers, and prostitutes.

The abbess took orders from no one but the Pope in spiritual matters and the king of France in earthly affairs. The prestige and authority given the abbess made her and Fontevrault a power base at a time when religion was bigger business than trade. At its height, nearly 5,000 men and women—including 300 nuns—inhabited the abbey, and it was the *in place* for women of repute. All 36 of the successive abbesses from the 12th century on were descended from nobility, and many of the nuns came from the blue blood of Europe. Fourteen princesses actually became abbesses; five were from royal families. Some names—mostly forgotten to us—give an idea of this exclusive institution: Matilda of Anjou, daughter of Fulke V (fourth king of Jerusalem), widow of a grandson of William the Conqueror and aunt to King Henry II of England; Mary of Champagne, widow of Eudes II, duke of Burgundy; Alix of Champagne, granddaughter of King Louis VII; Eleanor of Brittany, granddaughter of King Henry III of England; Isabella of Valois, great-granddaughter of St. Louis (Louis IX).

The power maintained by the abbess made her a formidable ally, and kings and queens traveled to stay at Fontevrault, seeking both comfort and political support. Eleanor of Aquitaine, mentioned earlier as the wife of the stormy King Henry II of England, was a benefactor of the abbey and visited the place frequently, as did her husband, who died in 1189, some 15 years before his wife. Although constantly at odds in life, both Eleanor and Henry are buried together in the abbey, along with their heroic son, King Richard the Lion Heart. In his dying days in

1199, Richard recognized the importance of the women and works of Fontevrault: "I know that when the time comes for me to expiate my sins, I shall be hard put to it to escape the pains of hell, be it not for the mercy of God and the prayers of the hand-maid slaves of Christ at Fontevrault, whom in my lifetime I held in great affection." (To see why Richard may have feared the "pains of hell," see Chapter 9.)

Fontevrault, like other religious houses, succumbed to the ravages of the French Revolution in the late 18th century, with only the magnificent buildings surviving. But it stands as a memorial not only to the services rendered to God by dedicated people, but as a reminder that women have taken charge of affairs that have influenced the judgment—even the course of events—of the males who would be kings or counts or other stations of import. The same is true today, only women do not need a cloistered life to establish spheres of power and influence. They can now work on equal ground with their male counter-parts, with the goal of accumulating authority and influence once held on a grand scale many centuries ago.

"THE APPLE OF WISDOM": SOME OBSERVATIONS

What all this boils down to involves the recognition that equality among the sexes remains an old game—it seems new to us be-cause we don't have much of a reference point for comparison. Moreover, women continue to change their focus on what is important to them, in part because of male reaction; in part because the female in society constantly requires redefinition, as does society itself. Indeed, some experts contend that the "new woman" of today is really the "old woman" of bygone eras: de-sirous of a home, hearth, husband, and offspring. Desiring a career, it is now said, comes in second place. This flies in the face of the *corporate woman* who wants to have it all: career, success, self-earned rewards, babies, and—ah, yes—a husband to have and to mold, if educating the male becomes necessary.

No matter how you cut it, the ultimate challenge here is women and men trying to relate to each other while struggling to understand themselves. The *Triple W* (women who work) situation only exacerbates the difficulty, with men unsure of fast-track women and corporate females suspicious of inflexible male managers. Yet women and men have always gone at each other, and women have, on occasion, taken shots at their "lesser half." Some famous ones have left us with their thoughts.

The 18th-century French writer Madame de Stael wryly observed that "the more I see of men, the more I like dogs." The American commentator Helen Rowland also had a few jabs: "The only original thing about some men is original sin." And to counter the male's belief that aged women fare worse than their male counterparts, she said, "Nowadays most women grow old gracefully; most men, disgracefully." The 19th-century novelist George Eliot admitted that women were less than perfect but gave the reason why through one of her characters: "I'm not denyin' the women are foolish: God Almighty made 'em to match the men."

Of course, women have been the historic victim of verbal abuse by men. The late-19th-century writer and wit Max Beerbohm went after female appearance when he wrote, "Most women are not so young as they are painted"; and an anonymous commentator said that "women's styles may change, but their designs remain the same." In fact, their being fashion conscious was noted by none other than the 19th-century German poet and critic Heinrich Heine: "As soon as Eve ate the apple of wisdom, she reached for the figleaf; when a woman begins to think, her first thought is of a new dress." Dr. Johnson, the 18th-century English critic and writer, was surprised that women could think at all. He wrote "Sir, a woman's preaching is like a dog's walking on his hind legs. It is not done well; but you are surprised to find it done at all."

Clearly these views have become entrenched down to the present, and it will take time to alter attitudes and recognize that it is in everyone's best interest to treat women equally with men. We marvel that recent history has revealed women leaders such as Indira Gandhi (India), Golda Meir (Israel), Margaret Thatcher (England), Benazir Bhutto (Pakistan), and Gro Harlem Brundtland (Norway). We marvel falsely, since women have been at the forefront, or the driving force behind the leader, throughout recorded history. Men and women alike must understand that the struggle is old, the aim the same, the need more pressing as goals and values change while advances in science, technology, and childcare allow women greater freedom from the biological burden of childbirth and child-rearing than ever before. Once we get over the hump of this age-old battleground, attention can be spent on working out society's problems together.

DRINK, DRANK, DRUNK, AND ROWENA THE SAXON

The current drug crisis in the world—illegal drugs doing awful things to young and old alike—puts alcohol and its abuses into the background, but only momentarily. Drug usage has been around a long time, further back than that 19th-century pioneer drug user Samuel Taylor Coleridge who rhymed about ancient mariners and the like; further back than the ancient Chinese, Greeks, and Romans, who used mushrooms, poppies, and other curious flora to stimulate their brains in ways that greatly magnified the joy we get from eating a chocolate sundae. But the consumption of distilled or fermented liquids of the alcoholic sort have been a constant in human life and living. And we need not wait for a comeback—it never really left us.

Americans have traditionally enjoyed occasions—or excuses—for imbibing wine and spirits. Some recent statistics show that American adults consume almost 3.5 gallons of wine per person and 2.5 gallons of distilled spirits on the average annually. Upon first reading that may not sound too debauched if spread over a year's time. But, according to the dings of liquor store cash registers, annual liquor sales total about $18 billion—nothing to blink at but a lot to stagger around about.

Drink has been with us since the dawn of civilization, or at least the wee hours of the civilized morning. Moreover, it has always been an acceptable practice to take drink with food. A 6th-century A.D. Roman chaplain and writer named Venantius Honorius Clementianus Fortunatus exhorted members of the legal profession to take it easy and put their work in perspective . . . through a glass of wine:

Drop business, lawsuits on the Palatine.
This festive table bids you dine and wine.
Let din of law and wrangling cases rest.
The day is joyous. To relax is best.

Good advice, but not when the legal fee meter is running at $250 an hour.

Wine and spirits have always been linked to ceremonial and relgous observances, from the libations offered the gods by the ancient Greeks to the wine served at the Passover meal and at the Last Supper. One semi-myth about a toast gives us the origins of the Christmas drink *wassail,* as well as the uses of spirits in solidifying alliances. While not quite the three-martini lunch between businessmen cutting a deal, the precedent is rather clear, and rather old.

According to the 12th-century writer and mythweaver Geoffrey of Monmouth, a 5th-century Celtic leader named King Vortigern fell in love with the Saxon king's daughter, Rowena. Vortigern—whose overthrow eventually led to the rule of King Arthur—had made an alliance with the enemy Saxons, to the dismay of his fellow Celts. But a deal is a deal and Vortigern became infatuated with Rowena, who encouraged his desire by offering the king a gold goblet filled with wine.

"Lord King, wacht heil!" she said.

Although delighted with this little ceremony, Vortigern needed an interpreter to figure out exactly what the young lady had uttered.

"She called you 'Lord King' and honored you with an expression of greeting," the interpreter explained. "What you ought to reply now is: 'Drinc heil!' "

Vortigern, seeking to fan the flames of his newfound love, went along with the game. According to Geoffrey of Monmouth, "From that day to this the custom prevailed in Britain for a person who drinks at a banquet to say to another: 'Wacht heil.' " It was only a small etymological leap to turn this phrase—and the drink that accompanied it—into wassail.

Social drinking is acceptable today despite the movement to curb the intake of drinkers who drive and to keep alcohol away from minors. This differs from drugs markedly. "Social drugging" is widely practiced but has yet to gain expressed respectability, either in conventional conversation or in the law courts. So we will continue to imbibe the brew and lavish the liquor at parties and celebrations. It is an old custom, aptly described in a poem from the medieval songbook *Carmina Burana* that shows just how pervasive drinking was long before our time:

> Mistress drinks and master drinks.
> Knights get plastered, clerics clink.
> This one drinks and that one, too.
> Servants can and maids oft do.
> The swift, the slack,
> The white, the black,
> Of booze they never have a lack.

HOW PERSIANS MADE DECISIONS THROUGH DRINKING

Before we move on to more edifying aspects of our lives as seen through the eyes of the past, we might stop off in ancient Persia to view a rather unusual, almost contradictory use for alcoholic beverages. Today, executives or politicians caught drunk on the job would have little recourse but to resign. While we all drink in the privacy of our homes or at local chuggeries with friends, we simply will not tolerate our well-paid leaders tying one on during working hours or before public view. Most people have some cloudy notion of ancient Greeks and Romans lying around sloshing wine down the esophagus, often in the company of leading politicians, but that was then and this is now.

Well, alcohol did in fact have its day in court, an imperial court. A story comes to us from Herodotus, the 5th-century B.C. Greek historian and gossipmonger, who wrote a long book on the growth of the Persian empire and its invasion of Greece. His observations give us a peek at the Persian way of life, although even the basically objective Herodotus had trouble understanding all he wrote about.

In one passage, he related how Persians went about making decisions. Because the Persians were "very fond of wine," much activity centered around the banquet table, where "the main dishes at their meals are few, but they have many sorts of dessert, the various courses being served separately." Although wine flowed freely, Herodotus noted that the Persians had a code of etiquette of sorts, for "no one is allowed to vomit or relieve himself in the presence of another person"—a notion we today probably would not need to consider. Herodotus then discussed the decision-making process:

> If an important decision is to be made, they discuss the question when they are drunk, and the following day the master of the house where the discussion was held submits their decision for reconsideration when they are sober.

It is here that the final disposition of a decision is determined: "If they still approve it, it is adopted; if not, it is abandoned. Conversely, any decision they make when they are sober, is reconsidered afterwards when they are drunk." Given the outcome of many corporate decisions made today, this process may have some merit.

Where the Persians were fond of imbibing spirits, they could be rather cold sober when it came to lying: They detested it. Almost as bad were those who went into debt. According to Herodotus, "they consider telling lies more disgraceful than anything else, and, next to that, owing money."

It is difficult to loathe the Persians for their practice of decisions by the dram, especially when we today spend millions and billions studying how best to act, and often end up doing the wrong thing anyway. Moreover, wine was a way of life with them; they recognized its benefits and dangers, and they were willing to give sobriety a chance after a banquet's-worth of thinking and drinking. And when you consider that they despised two practices embedded in our own lives—lying and owing money—maybe we should reconsider our priorities and what causes the most damage. This is not to say that "Advocates for Alcoholic Decisions" should be duly formed and followed; it simply means that in different eras, society has recognized the pros and cons of drinking spirits, and that the Persians found an interesting use for them that actually produced positive results. And most of us would drink to that, in moderation one would hope.

SOCIAL REFORM FROM "DOWN UNDER"

Marriage, sexism, drunk driving, inequality at work and at law: these fall under the general umbrella of social reform, and they span decades and centuries of concern, action, or indifference. When we think of reformers, our minds usually travel to England or America, those two bastions of democracy and social justice, for examples of the poor being fed, the sick treated, the disenfranchised reinstated. Well, we missed a place where social reform was very much on the minds of those in power, and they did something about it: Australia. Furthermore, the boys and girls down under often had a jump on their giant Western cousins.

For some time now, Australia has been the flavor-of-the-month in America. It may have begun with the Mad Max movies and continued on with Australia's version of the good-natured cowboy: Crocodile Dundee. Regardless, everything from beer to koala bears are selling briskly as the laid-back, "no problem" attitude of the Australians firmly roots itself in the minds of impressionable consumers. It is interesting, however, that the image of the outback adventurer is about all that Americans and many Europeans have to go on, partly because shrewd manufacturers see advantage in merchandising this image. But beyond a dusty memory of Australians descending from criminals, it would be shocking to learn that Crocodile Dundee's ancestors were social reformers before it became fashionable in the rest of the Western world.

It is true that, soon after the English explorer Captain Cook made a pass at Australia in 1769, a contingency of English convicts were transported to the continent, and that other such settlements were founded. But these newly spawned adventurers were not hardened criminals. They were debtors and political outcasts who could gain freedom after seven years of forced labor on this virtually unexplored land mass. These freemen did a good job of exploration and settling, and soon other immigrants came to this new land of opportunity. Raising sheep became the main industry, and agriculture developed as a bulwark for the economy.

Gold was discovered in Australia soon after the 1849 rush in California, and as the economy began to grow so did the railroads and the areas of land under development. From 1850 to the outbreak of World War I, the population increased more than tenfold from about 400,000 to almost 5 million. New Zealand, consisting of islands 1,000 miles off the Australian mainland, began its modern history in much the same way as its gigantic neighbor. Wool also became a chief staple, and as methods of refrigeration advanced, New Zealand exported meat, fruits, and dairy products.

But something else developed within this new nation peopled by foreigners. Free from the constraints of governmental traditions and much of their cultural traditions, the colonists of Australia and New Zealand took a different view of society and what it meant to the individual. Maybe it was the land, or the distance from Western Europe, but the pioneers of the southern continent took their pioneering spirit into their way of life.

In 1855, the state of Victoria in Australia instituted holding elections using secret ballots—an innovation later copied by the United States, Great Britain, and other parts of the world. The right for women to vote was introduced in New Zealand in 1893 and in Australia in 1902, well ahead of similar efforts in the United States and Britain. New Zealand also adopted a program of noncontributory old-age pensions in 1878, an enlightened approach to aid their fellow men and women. And in 1907, a national infant welfare system was established. Australia followed suit with both programs soon after.

So as we sip our Australian wine coolers, balance our Australian throwing knives, and mimic a crude "G'day," we should remember that much of what we have come to know as social reform got a boost in a remote part of the world by some rugged, free-spirited people. Those down under were downright out front when it came to helping their fellow citizens.

POVERTY: SOME OBSERVATIONS

While it may be quaint to take note of the anonymous observation that "God loves the poor, and that is why he made so many of them," poverty and all the tragedies surrounding it (homelessness, disease, child mortality) remain an important political and social issue around the world. And in any democratic society, poverty and the poor are difficult to sweep under the carpet.

The early-19th-century English clergyman Caleb Colton wrote that "If rich, it is easy enough to conceal our wealth but, if poor, it is not quite so easy to conceal our poverty. We shall find it is less difficult to hide a thousand guineas, than one hole in our coat." Hand in hand with the guilt a democratic society harbors over its poor is the recognition that it is the poor who cannot benefit from the freedoms inherent in a democracy. William Cobbett, the late-18th-century Anglo-American journalist and political writer, noted that "to be poor and independent is very nearly an impossibility."

But moralistic virtues aside, it costs money to help the poor—a realization that enters the realms of politics and economics, especially in an election year. There are, however, arguments that suggest reasons for helping the poor, and they are not new. The most obvious one is crime, for the simple reason that the poor may have no choice when it comes to surviving. The 16th-century Elizabethan poor laws recognized the correlation between roaming criminal vagabonds and poverty. Either the poor found food or they perished—there was no economizing in poverty. The late-19th-century English dramatist and wit Oscar Wilde said that "To recommend thrift to the poor is both grotesque and insulting. It is like advising a man who is starving to eat less." The ancient Greek philosopher Aristotle wrote that "Poverty is the parent of revolution and crime." And statistics show that crime and poverty are irrevocably linked, costing billions of dollars in losses and damages each year.

The poor are also outside of society, contributing to neither the political nor economic welfare of the country. This means a loss of participation that could benefit not only a nation but the very poor who remain locked out of the process. The rich, as we have seen, are often blamed in part for the lot of the poor. Henry Ward Beecher, the 19th-century American clergyman, said, "You cannot sift out the poor from the community. The poor are indispensable to the rich." The early-20th-century English poet and novelist G. K. Chesterton felt that even when the rich helped out, it was more through acceptance of poverty than a desire to cure it: "If we wish to protect the poor we shall be in favour of fixed rules and clear dogma. The *rules* of a club are occasionally in favour of the poor member. The drift of a club is always in favour of the rich one."

Perhaps what politicians and patricians alike need to consider is the one problem of poverty that cannot be measured by loss of income, purchasing power, or crime rate: the loss of a good life. The 18th-century English author Samuel Johnson put it best when he wrote, "Poverty is a great enemy to human happiness; it certainly destroys liberty, and it makes some virtues impractible, and others extremely difficult." We must consider the total picture when we develop the next "poverty program" for debate and consideration. For it is not just food and clothing, or even a job—it is the dignity of the person and the loss of freedom that is at stake. And dollars cannot buy such things, only understanding and a willingness to restore and nurture. We have known this a long, long time.

AMERICA AND ITS SOUTH AFRICAN "COUSIN"

Racism and dealing with it have occupied a great deal of activity and media coverage in the last half of the 20th century. During that period, South Africa has been the focus of attention for those countries who believe that equality and human rights extend to all people of all colors. Moreover, many sanctions and obstacles have been put in the way of the white-controlled South African government, both to inveigh against the laws of apartheid and to instigate change. These have included everything from trade embargoes to exclusion of South African athletes from the Olympic Games.

The United States, of course, is behind this assault on apartheid, since legal slavery is anathema to the moral dictums of the American culture. But it wasn't always that way. In fact, just a century ago America looked a lot like, well, South Africa. Slavery was an acceptable institution in the United States ever since the first black slaves landed in the Colonies in 1619. By the early 19th century, groups arose to abolish slavery, but most of their preachings and writings fell on deaf ears, especially in the South where slavery was part of an economic system of labor.

Although Britain abolished slavery in 1833, it persisted in

their former colonies, to the dismay of the British foreign secretary, Lord Palmerston. There was no love lost between Palmerston and the rebels across the sea, and the foreign secretary decided to use slavery as the issue to isolate America. He reached treaties with several countries that allowed the British navy to stop and search ships suspected of carrying slaves, and he said his policies enjoyed the support of "every state in Christendom which has a flag that sails on the ocean, with the single exception of the United States of North America."

He was wrong. France was not in favor of such seizures, and many ships, fearing searches, simply ran up the stars-and-stripes when a British ship approached. The *Creole* affair in 1841—when slaves successfully mutinied an American vessel, killed a white passenger, and were allowed to live as free men in the British port of Nassau—only made Anglo-American relations worse. It took the political fall of Palmerston before better relations were restored, but a Civil War before the United States gave up its hold on slavery.

This was an interesting role reversal from today, with Britain playing the United States . . . and the United States playing South Africa. But today as with yesterday, it remains difficult to effect change through international treaties and pleadings with the offending country. Putting pressure on countries to adhere to human rights is important, but ultimately change must come from within. In America, a Civil War initiated a change that, more than 120 years later, is still slowly chugging along. South Africa may need its own internal, and perhaps bloody, upheaval to overturn the long-held customs and dogma of the white minority. It is not a pleasant thought—just a realistic one.

EQUALITY: SOME OBSERVATIONS

Economic equality, racial equality, equality for the sexes, equality for religious worship: many meanings for this relative word that has been used over the centuries as an idea and as a weapon. The 4th-century B.C. Greek philosopher and teacher Aristotle had several thoughts on the subject. Noting that the concept of equality was as important as the benefits it could bring, he wrote, "It is not the possessions but the desires of mankind which require to be equalized." Aristotle also cited inequality as a key reason for discontent: "When quarrels and complaints arise, it is when people who are equal have not got equal share, or vice versa."

The German-born American psychoanalyst and author Erich Fromm (d. 1980) saw the need for equality as part of a process. "Just as the modern mass production requires standardization of commodities, so the social process requires standardization of man, and this standardization is called 'equality.'" The late President John F. Kennedy echoed this belief while recognizing that ability and equality can remain mutually exclusive: "All of us do not have equal talent, but all of us should have an equal opportunity to develop our talents."

Equality—whether in the workplace or in day-to-day living—has a utopian ring to it, partly because of mankind's inability to achieve it fully. Thomas Hobbes, the 17th-century English philosopher, wrote in his book *Leviathan* that "there is not ordinarily a greater sign of equal distribution of any thing, than that every man is contented with his share." One would be hard-pressed to find a time when such mass content existed. But how content would the man or woman of greater talent or ability be to share equal status with those less endowed—a criticism often bestowed upon equal opportunity legislation? John Stuart Mill, the 19th-century English economist and philosopher, said that "it is an abuse of the principle of equality to demand that no individual be permitted to be better off than the rest if his being so makes none of the others worse off than they otherwise would be."

Or as the futurist writer George Orwell put it in his novel *Animal Farm,* "All animals are equal, but some animals are more equal than others."

The debate over equality in a variety of contexts will continue through the century, with some redress of certain grievances and the exposure of others. But it is clear that the late 20th century has made great strides toward fixing age-old prejudices that have stifled many a career, many a life. Aristotle might provide us with a pithy plaque for our desks or walls to remind us of the vigilance required to keep equality a constant goal: "Equality consists in the same treatment of similar persons." The trick will be to define "similar" to everyone's satisfaction.

ART AND THE ART OF MAKING MONEY

While it is true that art may appeal to the emotions and the senses, there is also another side to the fruits of talent and aestheticism: Money. Artists, like any other people pursuing a livelihood and the sources of next month's rent, want to get paid for their work. Vincent van Gogh (1853–90), who died poor and depressed before reaching the age of 40, would have had a hard time understanding why a Japanese company paid $39 million for one of his paintings less than a century after his death. He might also wonder the wisdom of people investing in art as a hedge against inflation and economic uncertainty. Van Gogh invested much of his time creating art, but it did little for his pocketbook.

Vincent clearly was not a businessman, as are many of today's artists and sculptors. Nor did he follow in the footsteps of some of his more material-minded predecessors. The Italian Renaissance artist and sculptor Michelangelo, for example, often contracted to do a work of art to ensure payment for his efforts. No doubt he would have been pleased to see the Academia, housing his *David* in Florence today, with its overflow of tourists staring in awe at this beautiful work of art. But to be possessed with the need to create did not preclude getting paid for it.

One art form that started generating profits for those who created them was the tomb effigy. Since ancient times, people who could afford to be remembered after death spent money to commission elaborate effigies of themselves made out of wood or stone. These were placed over their graves to show the pictorial likenesses of the departed, or soon-to-be departed. By the year 1200 in Northern Europe and Britain, a new form of tomb effigy caught on in popularity, giving both work and profits to the artisans capable of making them: monumental brasses. These were flat, rectangular plates of brass (copper and zinc) upon which a person's image was engraved. Brass centers in such places as Cologne and Lübeck produced sheets of brass and exported them to other countries for use by artisans adept in the art of working metal. The engraved brass plates were then countersunk in slabs of marble placed over the burial site of the deceased, usually in a cathedral or parish church.

From Sweden and Finland to Germany and Italy, brasses were all the rage for the upper classes and wealthy churchmen. In England, once the brass plates were imported and engraved, the excess metal was cut away, leaving the outline of the persons represented in the brass. Today, England boasts the best collection of brasses—about 4,000—because most were destroyed throughout Europe during successive wars, rebellions, and religious upheavals.

As with van Gogh's work, brasses today are valuable because they are limited in number and representative of a particular kind of art form and style. But where the creator of *The Starry Night* had to hope for monetary gain from what he created, the medieval artisan signed the deal before he lifted his engraving tool. That is how much of art is created today, either from commissions for particular works or the promise of an art tour that will secure a certain amount of sales. The phrase "commercial art" may dig at the purists who long for *art for art's sake,* but those who create must also eat. That's not new, and more and more artists are learning that, although it might be nice to end up in an art history book 75 years from now, it's much nicer to pay the bills and not worry about where the income is coming from while running brushstrokes across the canvas. Michelangelo knew that; royal court painter Hans Holbein knew that; the unknown makers of medieval effigies knew that. A little medieval thinking can be a profitable thing.

THE 12TH-CENTURY "BLOCKBUSTER"

Art isn't the only "big business" ticket in our world of culture. Literature has taken on a whole new meaning, with the mighty dollar sign hovering over the heads of hopeful authors as books get cranked out by the thousands each year. Publishers today are willing to spend millions of dollars publishing and promoting books they believe will become best-sellers, with big profits in the offing. It is not unusual for an author to receive a six- or seven-figure advance, if the author is deemed important enough to generate large book sales. That group includes ex-presidents, flamboyant chief executives, actors/actresses with dirty linen to hang out, and "unauthorized" biographies that promise to "tell all."

Is this a phenomenon restricted to the 1980s, or part of a trend that will reach greater heights in the 1990s? Well, best-sellers have been around a long time. People have always enjoyed a good yarn, and one need only consider that *The Iliad,* which may or may not have been created by Homer, has been delighting and mystifying audiences for almost 3,000 years. Some popular tales go back even further but lost their popularity over time—the *Epic of Gilgamesh* from ancient Sumer may have hit the Top Ten list almost 5,000 years ago, but eventually fell off the "must read" roster.

Of course, such ancient stories were usually told orally; when they were written down, they could not be duplicated in the vast quantities produced today. But certain stories did become popular, and by the 12th century A.D. in Europe stories flowed freely and were heard by greater numbers of people. As in ancient times, the epic remained the popular form of storytelling, with certain heroes becoming the focus of the plot in these *chansons de geste* (songs of great deeds). Most notable in France was the *Song of Roland,* telling the exploits of Count Roland in the company of the 9th-century warrior-king Charlemagne. Spain contributed to the best-sellers list with the *Poema del Mio Cid,* recounting the heroic deeds of the Spanish warrior El Cid against Spain's ancient enemies, the Moors.

But as with today, romantic love was also a popular topic in the 12th century, and those who put such stories together expected to get paid for it. Traveling troubadours created and recited tales of lost love, love defended, or love regained, from court to court throughout Europe, getting rewarded for their deft telling of tales. Women now had a role in these stories beyond waiting for the hubby to come back, and they were actually adored by their male heroes. An example is the description of Eleanor of Aquitaine, our previously mentioned queen and wife of kings in France and England:

When the sweet breeze
Blows hither from your dwelling
Methinks I feel
A breath of paradise.

But the true best-seller of the period was created by that great storyteller, Geoffrey of Monmouth. Born in about 1100 in Monmouth in Wales, he apparently had a father named Arturus, or Arthur, and it became Geoffrey's goal to put together a "history" of the King Arthur that lived some 600 years before his time. In about 1136, he published the *History of the Kings of Britain,* with one fifth of the book devoted to Arthur. From what we can tell, Geoffrey made up lots of his facts and borrowed freely from other myths and stories to fill in the gaps. A contemporary of Geoffrey's, one William of Newburgh, said of the book:

> Everything this man wrote about Arthur and his successors, or indeed about his predecessors . . . was made up, partly by himself, partly by others, either from an inordinate love of lying, or for the sake of pleasing the Britons.

That was a pretty harsh "book review," but it didn't stop Geoffrey's work from becoming one of the most popular books of the Middle Ages, one that remained a favorite for centuries.

The mega-novels and tell-all books of today bring in fast bucks to authors and publishers, but the key operating word here is *fast.* For most best-sellers have a short time span of success: Today's hot book is tomorrow's sale item on the Remainder Shelf. Rare is the book that lasts a year, and those that do are often quickly labeled "classics." One wonders how they would have competed with the true classics, the ones that hung around for centuries . . . and millennia. We need only try to sit down and name the classics of the 1950s or 1960s to get the answer.

ROMAN WIT AND LATIN LIT

What it all comes down to when discussing literature is taste: what people want to read at a given time in history. Whether the pop culture pieces of the 1960s or the how-to-succeed guides of the 1980s, whatever the public thinks it wants to read will become the hot topics of the day.

About 1,900 years ago, a writer named Martial used a popular form of writing that brought him great fame (but not fortune),
especially after he died; much of what he penned involved knocking other writers. Marcus Valerius Martialis was born in Spain
in about 40 A.D. and traveled to Rome while in his 20s. It was a
time in the Roman Empire when Seneca the Younger was
deemed one of the greatest playwrights and Lucan and Petronius
were established in the literary world. Martial discovered he had
an uncanny ability to weave epigrams: brief, witty poems that
usually contained enough satire and paradox to ruffle the listener's feathers, if not make them stand on end. Of Martial's 1,561
surviving poems, quite a few are pointed at his fellow writers: a
Roman critic not dissimilar to our own reviewers.

One epigram, about a poet, suggests that Martial, like van
Gogh, realized the difficulty in being acknowledged as a talent in
one's lifetime, let alone getting paid for it:

> He unto whom thou art so partial,
> Oh, reader! Is the well-known Martial,
> The epigrammatist: while living
> Give him the fame thou wouldst be giving;
> So shall he hear, and feel, and know it—
> Post-obits rarely reach a poet.

Martial was also aware of one of the dangers of writing for
the public: plagiarism. Many people today can recall author Alex
Haley's problems with a suit brought against him for plagiariz-
ing passages from a book and incorporating them into his best-
seller, *Roots*. And we need not belabor Senator Joseph Biden's
lapse in attributing numerous words that were coming out of his
mouth to others who thought of them first—this during his 1988
U.S. presidential bid. Martial had a businesslike approach to the
problem:

> A rumor says that you recite
> As yours the verses that I write
> Friend, if you'll credit them to me
> I'll send you all my poems for free;
> But if as yours you'd have them known,
> Buy them, and they'll become your own.

Yet the Roman writer realized that, even with such a financial arrangement, his words would not turn a person into a great speaker. In a quick barb, he said:

> The verse is mine; but friend, when you declaim it,
> It seems like yours, so grievously you maim it.

Today we talk of good and bad books, and critics have a great influence over the financial outcome of a new work. Martial also knew a bad book when he read it:

> Why don't I send my book to you
> Although you often urge me to?
> The reason's good, for if I did
> You'd send me yours—which God forbid!

This clever commentator of the Roman Empire also had an unkind word to say about critics, as do most writers who feel they have been unfairly panned. It is a two-line malediction of sorts that might be pondered today by those who aspire to write and those who critique them:

> Sour critic, who can here no merit find,
> May you, unenvied, envy all mankind!

PHILOSOPHIZING ABOUT PHILOSOPHERS

In today's fast-paced world, there is often little time to think: So much time is spent reacting. This situation is not simply found in the workplace. At home, on vacation, or en route to the various retail outlets of necessity, most people are hard-put to simply sit down and ponder, deliberate, question, or plan. Moreover, we often frown at those who do these things for a living—the deep thinkers who weave the world into sociological theories, evolutionary trends, psychological pathways, and other patterns that beg even more thinking.

Writers such as Martial were not the only ones valued in the world's most successful empire. Romans also recognized that thinkers had a place in society, and that these philosophers had certain rights that were recognized by law. The 6th-century A.D. Eastern Roman emperor Justinian, quoting an early constitution of the republic, stated that "a fixed number of philosophers has not been set because philosophers are scarce." He also realized that many philosophers in his day were rich men, a state not very common to today's thinkers. But Justinian felt that the very wealthy ones, if truly philosophers, would be willing to help their particular cities using their own wealth, and "if they quibble regarding their estate, they will thereby make it plain that they are no philosophers"—an interesting litmus test we might try on those who preach goodness in poverty while sitting on fat wallets.

Justinian pointed out that philosophers, along with other professionals, were exempt from serving certain offices, including market commissioners, the priesthood, jurors, or envoys. They also could not become soldiers against their will. He wrote that "only one teaching in his own city has this immunity [from offices]." If they shared their thoughts beyond the city limits, they were subject to all the public services of nonprofessionals. Justinian noted, however, that future philosophers would not even be able to take to the lecture circuit in order to enrich themselves: congressmen and senators, take note!

Inscriptions from the 2nd century A.D. at Delphi in Greece show that philosophers were given privileges. One such thinker, Gaius, son of Xenon, received the following benefits for himself and his descendants:

> Priority in consulting the oracles, public-guest status, front seating at public spectacles, priority in the law courts, personal inviolability, total immunity from taxation, the right to own land and a house, and the other honors that are granted to men of distinction.

Philosophers and their deep thoughts were clearly admired and protected by an empire that lasted a thousand years and saw such thinkers housed close to the seat of power. Such advisers were deemed important to the course and scope of decisions that affected the entire empire. While it might seem a luxury today to have a Secretary of Thinking and Planning, maybe governments ought to consider how to utilize people who can have bearing on both the top priorities and the events yet-to-happen. A little thinking amid the heat of a crisis or a planning session might go a long way to ensure that the outcome comes out favorably.

"I AM TOLD YOU FORSAKE WRITING"

It was during the 1950s, the childhoods of the Baby Boomers, when parents learned that to get ahead, young adults needed a better education. Since that time, colleges have been jammed with students—notwithstanding dips in the population pool—and the Bachelor of Arts degree today is what a high school education was two generations ago: a necessity toward obtaining a decent job. But although the current crop of undergraduates probably has a better grasp of what the good life can bring if money is available in reasonable quantities, one thing has not changed since Adam and Eve taught their kids to count: Learning has its trials and tribulations.

When we think of centuries past, it is easy to conjure up visions of serious students diligently spending long hours studying and acquiring enormous amounts of information. Not so. Students will be students, regardless of the century involved. During the last millennium B.C., Egypt had declined from its previous glory as a cradle of civilization in the Near East. But a viable society and economy flourished during this time, one that allowed people to rise in stature and power through their own efforts. One major route to success was through education. The pharaohs needed educated men to serve them—our friend Ptah-hotep had been one of these centuries earlier—and a knowledgeable person could rise to importance in the government.

A scribal school existed for such training, and one ancient writer jotted down what must have been the prevailing advice of the time: "Be a scribe, who is freed from forced labor, and protected from all work. . . . He directs every work that is in this land." But going to school meant long hours for such young men, which often led to less productive extracurricular activities: "I am told you forsake writing, that you give yourself to pleasures," wrote an ancient Egyptian scolding wayward students. "You go from street to street, where it smells of beer, to destruction. Beer, it scares men from you, it sends your soul to perdition."

The colleges and monasteries of England have had a thousand-year tradition of training lawyers, scholars, and government officials. But that tradition extended to dangers lurking beyond the library or scriptorium. John of Garland was a 13th-century writer who composed a book on student conduct. His warnings to students suggest that, in his day at least, they may have gone far beyond panty raids and beer parties. John warned: "Be not a fornicator, O student, a robber, a murderer, a deceitful merchant, a champion at dice. . . . Avoid drunkards, those who indulge in secret sin, those who like to beat and strike, those who love lewdness, evil games, and quarrels."

Much closer to home than student behavior was the proverbial "letter from school," no doubt written by students to parents throughout the ages, with the same fears and needs. Thomas Sampson, a 14th-century English writer, recorded several sample letters written by students. One from a son to his father bears examination. After thanking his father for his care and support, he noted that "whatever I am, I am yours"—an indication of indebtedness that future students will come to feel as a college education hits six figures. And it is debt that he now discussed:

> The money, whereby your generosity as a father lately released me for the study of letters, is quite spent . . . I therefore crave your kindness, my respected father, devoutly, so that fatherly reverence may consider it worthy to give me some money with which I can now manage in school until the Feast of St. Michael.

A familiar request, from the Latin no less!

LEARNING, LITERACY, AND KING ALFRED

While education has been and remains integral to the growth of a person's intellectual abilities, it has become clear that even though students walk through the college door at graduation it doesn't mean they are educated. Indeed, many students cannot write complete sentences, let alone utilize minimal math skills or attempt problem-solving. And not a few are functionally illiterate, joining the ranks in the United States of some 27 million adults who cannot read a street sign, the label of a medicine bottle, or the instructions on a job application form.

We have heard American presidents past and present talk

about the need for better education, and for the eradication of illiteracy in a country that has spent more on education than any nation in history. But talking isn't enough; even funding isn't enough. Leaders—the presidents, heads of major corporations, and federal, state, and local officials—should set examples of what it means to be literate, and what it means to lack the skills necessary to function in our age of information overload.

Over 1,000 years ago, one leader of a country realized early on the need to know and to learn. In fact, his dedication to making his people and future leaders literate and knowledgeable earned him that title, previously discussed, that he alone of all English monarchs bears: Alfred *the Great*. When King Alfred ruled England (871–899), it was over a people in perpetual war with the invading Danes. After a century of plundering, the invaders decided it might be more useful to start settling in England while fighting the English, rather than simply landing and pillaging at unscheduled intervals. And it was during the century of fighting before the coming of Alfred that the major centers of English learning were destroyed, the libraries and monasteries.

Although Alfred spent much of his reign fighting the Danes, he also committed himself to promoting learning and literacy among his people. But unlike some modern leaders who put the burden of helping people learn on their subordinates, King Alfred took the lead. He began personally translating works from Latin to English so his countrymen could have easy access to them. He also prepared to have future generations schooled in the art of learning, beginning with the most basic of skills: reading. Alfred declared that "all the sons of England of free men who have means enough . . . should be set to learning . . . so that they may well know how to read written English." He hoped that by raising the level of literacy, more works could be translated and read in English, which in turn would encourage creations of new works in the native tongue of the land.

The king was determined to set an example. According to his trusted adviser and biographer, Bishop Asser, Alfred made it a habit "by day and by night, among all his preoccupations of mind and body, to read books himself or to listen while others read aloud to him." He reestablished monasteries and imported learned men to rebuild centers of learning in England. Alfred also made sure that his "senior people" were not remiss in retooling—or, in their case, simply tooling. Most of his officers began studying the liberal arts; those who could not read had their servants or sons read aloud to them.

Alfred's dedication to raising literacy to a point where works would be created in English is a watershed of sorts for the growth of ideas and all that comes from them. It became the basis for encouraging original thinking, and not just reading Latin and Greek manuscripts or translating them into English. Literacy meant access to previous information and the ability to express new information. Alfred understood that the only way a nation can avoid stagnation is to keep ideas flowing and to disseminate them to others who can build upon them, alter them, improve them. Literacy is therefore of critical importance to any society. The king of England recognized that in the 9th century; our leaders need to catch up to his enlightened view 11 centuries later.

PRAISING THE LORD, PASSING THE PLATE

While everyone has different views of society and how people should relate to each other, most humans express a trait that is commonly shared if not commonly interpreted: belief in a supreme being or beings. In fact, the oldest profession may be the priest or shaman, whose job it was to act as intermediary between those who dwelled on earth and those who dwelled above it and played some role in the affairs of men and women.

When we look at religion today, we see a mixed landscape of supposedly godless countries (the Soviet Union and some satellites); Third World and less-developed countries with devout, god-fearing people (Iran, many South American countries); and Western countries with a spectrum of religions and sects that provide a variation on a theme, usually Christianity. Most religions with large organizations require ongoing funding to carry out their missions as intermediaries, and it is apparent that those long-distance calls to the Almighty are getting mighty expensive. (Near the end of the 1980s, the Vatican was worth about $560 million, not counting its "priceless" art treasures.) And religious leaders, like any other group of competitors, are going after the same dollars to attract people to the "correct way" to heaven. Problem is, those who cough up the cash and write out the checks have no guarantees that their investments will pay off . . . in the end.

The dynamic duo of religion and money should not be viewed as something new, or even evil. Following religious leaders, and paying for the privilege, goes back to the earliest civilizations, when priest-kings ruled cities or kingdoms and held the dual roles of leader and the gods' representative on earth. The Egyptians made it even easier, positioning the pharaohs as earthly gods, an idea that the emperors of Rome found attractive enough to use in their marketing plans: Caesar as god. And just as it costs money to defend the borders of your land, so it costs money to watch out for your immortal souls. The priests made a point of that and the people paid up, regardless of the religion or the culture.

Christianity did start out as a poverty-based movement, with early Christian congregations looking more like communes than rigid hierarchies with paying members. But as noted, organization costs money and people are used to paying for organization. Unfortunately, even early on in church history, certain people with one eye on the heavens and the other on the purse strings concluded that religion was a terrific industry for realizing a good return on investment. All it took was a decent following, a bold approach to the orthodoxy of the day, and a little luck in order to avoid persecution by both the priests and the prevailing secular government.

Given America's recent spate of evangelical investment brokers (more on that later), it is almost anachronistic to read the great work on early church history by Eusebius (263–339 A.D.), who chronicled the early years of Christianity. In his book, *The History of the Church,* Eusebius outlined not only the different bishops and churches since the death of Christ but some of the heresies that prevailed over time. And in one telling discussion of the "God-denying wickedness" of a man named Paul, it is apparent that making money from religion was less acceptable in early Christianity than it is now.

Eusebius used surviving letters from learned men familiar with the cases to tell the story of Paul (not St. Paul), a religious leader who had "forsaken the canon and deviated to spurious and bastard doctrines." But of all the dogmatic deviations of Paul, the ones that seemed to have irked the early Christian leaders the most were those concerning his money matters. For example, Paul was accused of having "amassed immense wealth by committing illegalities, robbing churches, and blackmailing his fellow-Christians." And in one revealing statement, Eusebius points to a situation that late-20th-century Americans have found commonplace with the activities of their televangelists:

> He deprives the injured of their rights, promising them help if they will pay for it but breaking his word to them, and makes easy money out of the readiness of those entangled in court proceedings to buy relief from their persecutors. *In fact, he regards religion as a way of making money.* [My italics]

The church leaders, and no doubt Eusebius, were appalled at the notion of cashing in on Christ, and they probably recalled the passage in I Timothy 6:5 that railed against "godliness [as] a means of gain." But they were also scandalized at Paul's "performance" before his followers, and we can only be thankful that Eusebius missed the era of television preachers in action. In talking about Paul, Eusebius records:

> Nor need we judge the way this charlatan juggles with church assemblies, courting popularity and putting on a show to win the admiration of simple souls, as he sits on the dais and lofty throne he has had constructed for him—how unlike a disciple of Christ! . . . He slaps his thigh and stamps on the dais. Some do not applaud and wave their handkerchiefs as in a theatre, or shout and spring to their feet like his circle of partisans, male and female, who form such a badly behaved audience.

Since we are on the subject of putting on a good show for a good price in the name of the Lord, we would be remiss to pass over recent events concerning men and women of God who embraced the role of upholders of the Ten Commandments before their congregations but privately toppled a few of them. Since Eusebius used Paul as a case study, we might turn to convicted evangelist Jim Bakker, his alleged sexual and fraudulent activities and the empire he built in the name of God. Moreover, Bakker was but one in a long line of religious leaders selling a piece of heaven for cold cash.

Detractors and followers alike soon began to learn about Bakker's 2,300-acre Heritage USA Christian theme park with 1986 receipts of almost $130 million, after a former secretary in his organization publicly claimed that the mellow minister had forced her to have sex with him several years earlier. The public also learned of the humble preacher's $1.6 million salary, plush yacht, and other amenities to ease the burden of preaching humility and moderation in the name of a poor carpenter. Moreover, his fidgety wife, Tammy Faye Bakker, a chronic consumer of shopping mall goods, now appears less like a passionate gospel singer and more like a home-grown version of Imelda Marcos, with her own 50-foot walk-in closet. When Bakker was convicted and sentenced in 1989, it was for bilking $158 million from "lifetime partners" who thought they were buying into the Heritage USA complex; instead, the money was used to run Bakker's crumbling ministry, with some $3.7 million going to support his lifestyle.

Giving money to an organized church to feel more secure about one's spiritual future is one thing; what that church does with the cash is, of course, another. Yet the most rational of minds must assume that those who give feel good about what they're doing. But theme parks and television begging aside, probably the greatest sales pitch put forth by a religion occurred almost 500 years ago, and the results were no less than a revolt against that church. The vehicle for obtaining money was the *indulgence*—something one could purchase in order to be freed from the earthly penance attached to a specific sin. The Roman Catholic church long had supported the theory that Christ and the saints had a surplus of grace, and that the church could "sell" that surplus to mere mortals in the form of written documents called indulgences. Unfortunately, while an indulgence was believed to cancel the punishment due a sinner, it did not free him from the actual sin itself. He could still go to hell, indulgence or no. That didn't stop local churchmen from cashing in on this credit from heaven: many of the bridges in Devon, England, were built by workmen promised a remission of sins for 40 days of work on a bridge.

In the early 16th century, Pope Leo X, a member of the Medici family who one historian noted "would have made an excellent Pope if he had only been a little religious," wanted to finish St. Peter's basilica in Rome but ran short of cash. He therefore sent out agents to sell indulgences to raise money for the project. One agent, a man named Tetzel, got a little carried away in his sales pitch. Traveling through Germany, he told potential buyers that they would be freed not only from doing penance for a sin, but from the actual sin itself. He even went so far as to say that one could purchase an indulgence for a dead relative stuck in Purgatory; upon receipt of payment, the relative's soul would hop directly to heaven.

Humanists at the time did not take kindly to indulgences or how they were being sold. In 1501, Erasmus wrote:

> Thou believest perchance all thy sins and offenses to be washed away at once with a little paper or parchment sealed with wax, with a little money or images of wax offered. . . . Thou art utterly deceived and clean out of the way!

Martin Luther remembered Erasmus's words, and on October 31, 1517, nailed his 95 Theses on indulgences to the door of the church at Wittenberg. Luther believed that without "true inward penitence" even a pope's indulgence could not save a soul.

Or as Luther put it, "They preach no Christian doctrine, who teach that contrition is not necessary for those who buy souls out of purgatory or buy confessional licenses."

Whether raising money for Christian Disneylands or Christian cathedrals, it is those giving the money who must decide the tools required to lead a righteous, ethical life—and if they believe those can be purchased. But they must also realize that neither popes nor preachers have ever been immune to the frailties of human greed once the coffers started filling up with money. Our materialistic age feeds upon itself, demanding more money to buy more things. Buying heaven is not new; buying heaven in an age of reason, rational thinking, and sophisticated learning is an interesting curiosity that suggests we can be superstitious and medieval in spite of ourselves.

REVENGE AGAINST THE UNGODLY: AN IMMODEST PROPOSAL

When the late Ayatullah Khomeini took to reviewing books, he wanted to be sure that his version of the Moslem religion wasn't getting a bum rap. So not only did the Ayatullah demand the death of Salman Rushdie for statements the author made in his book *The Satanic Verses,* but a rumor quickly went abroad that the tomb of Dante Alighieri was to be blown up because the great writer, who died over 650 years ago, was unkind to Mohammed in his great masterpiece, *The Divine Comedy.* If the rumor were true, it would be an interesting precedent for religious revenge: a person might obtain his eternal rewards centuries ago, but the earthly remains may not go unpunished.

If going after critics of one's religion—dead or alive—is acceptable today, then there's a lot of work to be done. After all, most religions have had their detractors, and it's time to call these groups on the carpet for their indiscretions. That means the Pope needs to declare war on the Moslems for their desecration of Jerusalem and the Church of the Holy Sepulchre. True, that first happened in the 11th century, but insult was added to injury by Saladin (d. 1193), who triumphed during the Third Crusade and agreed to let Christian pilgrims enter the shrine only on a very tight visitation schedule.

Of course, while the Pope prepares for war, he had best beware. For England and the Netherlands will be planning their invasion of Italy to attack the Vatican. It was the Holy See, we may recall, that encouraged the persecution of Protestants during the 16th and 17th centuries, and successive popes called for war against England for leaving the Mother Church and pursuing a more Anglican form of Christianity. England did gain a nice victory against the Spanish in 1588 when a "Protestant" wind scattered the Spanish Armada on its way to restoring Catholicism to England. But why rest on your laurels when there's revenge to be done? And there is no time like the present to make up for the sins of the past.

Unfortunately, England will need to watch the English Channel yet again, because Spain, France, Italy, and the Catholic portions of Germany will be tooling up to invade Winston Churchill's brave little island for its apostasy. While this is a temporary setback for the European Community's plan for one state in 1992, it is nevertheless a just cause that supersedes any hopes for economic unity after 2,000 years of dissension among European nations.

Now the Russians may smile at all this, but they are hardly safe from retribution. This godless state will incur the wrath of all clear-thinking, revengeful religious nations angered by Mr. Lenin's approach to the Creation—*glasnost* just hasn't caught on fast enough. And the Hindus and the Buddhists must not be forgotten, especially since they have more ancestral bones to pick than Western minds can imagine. But while all these nations and religions prepare to avenge the criticisms of the past, the world had better be ready for a global assault by Israel. Think about it—has *any* nation missed the opportunity to persecute the Jews during the last 4,000 years? (Well, the Eskimos might be safe, but one never knows.) Even "civilized" nations such as England expelled the Jews in 1290, and if revenge is sweet, the Israelis will be busy campers as they blow up the citadels and the sites of religions and nations that have indulged in the persecution of the Chosen People.

The Ayatullah's approach to criticism of religion was, of course, not very new. Indeed, it is rather ancient and medieval, denying the indisputable fact that there is no such thing as an indisputable religion. It has taken the human race many centuries to shed its Dark Age cloak to reach a point where criticism, satire, and dissension allow us to use that frequently abused adjective when describing ourselves: civilized. If people are so insecure about their religion that they cannot tolerate criticism of it, it is time for them to head back to the altar to find a little inner strength, rather than shoot the messenger carrying that criticism, whether it be Rushdie's book or the movie *The Last Temptation of Christ*. Those who take comfort in their religion— indeed, even pay for the privilege—know that it is a personal affair, able to withstand any question, any comment, any attack. And religious leaders will be followed or rejected on the basis of that comfort.

The 18th-century French writer Voltaire said that though he could thoroughly disagree with someone's belief or position, he would also defend to the death his right to say it. We shall see how far ahead of the 18th century we are in the year 2000, or how far behind.

WIZARDS, PROGNOSTICATORS, AND RUNNING OUT OF LUCK

Since we are exploring the realm of the heavens, or at least their view from below, we might spend a little time on another aspect of belief and otherworldliness that continues to pervade our lives: predictions and those who predict. For although we are the heirs to the Enlightenment and the rational way of perceiving the world, we still wonder if magic and prognosticating are nothing more than superstitions from an age where such explanations seemed to make sense. No better example comes to us than the news in the late 1980s that President Reagan's wife, Nancy, relied on the celestial scheduling of presidential events through the stargazing stirrings of an astrologer. Granted, presidents need all the help they can get, but we raise an eyebrow slightly at the thought of returning to ancient times for guidance from the stars.

The 13th-century Cardinal Bishop of Tusculum, Jacques de Vitry, preached a sermon about the accuracy of astrology and prognostications. It bears telling the tale before our leaders and chief executives start calling in their secretaries to find out if Jupiter is aligned with Mars for tomorrow's breakfast meeting. It also shows that a bishop dead more than 700 years seemed to have knowledge about such activities that the former First Lady may have overlooked.

The Cardinal, who did not believe that "the heavenly luminaries are in the nature of signs of the future," related the story of the king's astrologer. One day a certain king noticed that his prognosticator was in a melancholy mood. When asked why, the astrologer said: "Master, I have looked at my astrolabe and I have deduced with certainty from the position of the stars that you cannot live more than six months." Understandably, the king became melancholy as well, "and every day began to be alarmed, tormented and extremely downcast, so that his knights wondered greatly and grieved."

After some heavy coaxing and cajoling, the king finally told one of his knights that his cleric, "who was an excellent astrologer," predicted the monarch's demise. Apparently the knight had a little problem with this prognostication, and for fear that "the king would be overwhelmed with grief and, incurring serious sickness, would die—for many people die through fear of dying—called the astronomer into the presence of everyone." The knight asked the reader of the stars how he was certain that the king would die within six months of his forecast. "I am sure of his death that I deduced from my art, which is infallible," he said. (Some of our present-day economists suffer this same delusion.)

The knight didn't buy it. "You must have better knowledge of yourself than anyone else," the knight said. "Do you know how long you will live?" The astrologer replied: "I know and I am certain that I shall not die for 20 years." The knight seized the opportunity, and his dagger as well. "By your life, you have lied," the knight said, plunging the dagger into the astrologer who then died, short of his prediction by about two decades. This error in the astrologer's forecasting ability seemed to have the desired effect on the king: "Then the king, [who had been] waiting for the astrologer's prediction to be proved false, [now] with renewed vigor was comforted and lived for a long time afterward."

WELSH SOOTHSAYERS AND ECONOMISTS

It is easy for reasonable minds in the late 20th century to be amazed at how important it still is for people to seek out predictions about everything from future interest rates to whether Aunt Sally is going to have a boy or a girl. Worse—if that is the right word—when it comes to economics, we take predictions very seriously and even refer to it as a *science:* economic science. (The Nobel Prize in economics is actually for economic science, which makes one run to the dictionary for reeducation.) And what with economists being human, you rarely get two of them to agree about the future; indeed, it has been said that the only consensus among economists is ignorance, and some would happily refrain from contradicting that observation.

So why does modern society, comprised of (we think) basically rational people, turn to economists for a proverbial look into their illuminated crystals—nowadays called computer terminals—knowing full well that a good portion of their predictions will be cloudy, if not dead wrong? The answer is all too simple: We have always listened to fortune tellers, and we always will. Take the example given by Giraldus Cambrensis (d. *c.* 1223), a scholar of Norman and Welsh ancestry who traveled extensively through Wales. One journey brought him to discover what we might call the ancestors of economists.

This Welsh group was the Awennithion, or *The Inspired*—a phrase also used, we might suppose, at quiet gatherings among 20th-century economists to describe themselves. The Awennithion methods for predicting the future are so similar to how our current crop of economists do it that it behooves us to consider Giraldus' observations. He noted that when The Inspired were "consulted regarding some ambiguity," perhaps something akin to the Consumer Price Index or the Gross National Product, they would be "immediately seized with a frenzied exaltation." But—and here we see an immediate parallel with our own economists—"they do not forthwith prophesy what is required of them."

How did these 13th-century soothsayers answer questions about the future? "Rather through devious obscurities and varied talk poured forth in spate; trifling and light rather than coherent, but still well-expressed." What Giraldus saw next also is familiar:

> Then you will discover two remarkable features: because after giving a response, unless they are violently aroused and recalled to themselves, they usually do not recover from such a frenzy; and, when they have recovered, they will recall none of all those things that were uttered by them in the interval.

Avoiding responsibility for what future fable might pass their lips is a trait attributable to modern economists: They rarely like to talk about last year's forecast.

But what if prognosticators are asked why previous predictions fell flat? With The Inspired, Giraldus wrote, "If they happen to be consulted on this point again or on another and have to speak, they will give utterance in altogether other and different terms." Noting the source of the Welsh soothsayer's powers, Giraldus may be closer to home for how our own prognisticators develop their predictions in the first place: "These gifts usually come to them on sleep, through visions."

But why do economists predict anyway? When one considers their book royalties, consulting fees, and enormous media exposure, it is difficult to accept academic curiosity as the sole reason. Perhaps Giraldus Cambrensis anticipated what today's soothsayers would give as the reason for their vocation when he explained why the Welsh made predictions: "Once wakened from their sleep and soothed by a melody, they declared that they offered this favor for the public benefit." One wonders if the soothing "melody" was in fact the jingle of silver in their pockets.

4

C H A P T E R

ON BUSINESS: THE VIEW
FROM ABOVE

We have looked at a variety of activities and situations that humans have engaged in since civilization became all the rage. It is now time to turn to an area that, in fact, occupies most of our conscious hours regardless of the events of the day: work. Enough has been written about early man, survival, civilization, work ethic, etc. to let us know that humans are workers. They work not simply to feed the family and survive, although that's part of the story; humans require exercising their bodies and minds through work. For many, the entire creative process centers on the ability to manifest a thought into something that can be observed by the senses: dreaming up a paperclip is nice, but the dreamer usually will not stop until the thing is actually manufactured and used. Only a very few, such as Albert Einstein, can stop at vision, although creating such visions is work unto itself.

Work—an easy concept to envision and to understand. Yet work suggests numerous areas of activity. Going to work involves a variety of financial, economic, and social components, even if we don't think about them while we are working. To approach work in a meaningful way from the experiences of the past, it might be useful to explore it from two very different perspectives: the view from above and the view from below. The first encompasses a realm of work that few of us will encounter in our day-to-day grind. This realm revolves around business practices (takeovers, mergers, banking, investment, the stock market) and business leaders (top executives). That will be our current route; the next chapter will address the perspective more people can relate to from their own experiences: the view of the worker.

MERGER MANIA AND THE
MEDIEVAL CHURCH

It is unnecessary to name recent examples of companies merging with other companies or taking them over outright. The list changes daily, and yesterday's mega-billion dollar acquisition is today's memory as corporations on both sides of the ocean vie for greater pieces of the pie, gobbling up competitors and unrelated industries alike. Mergers and acquisitions were the investment sport of the 1980s, but few can say with certainty what the results will be from the formation of these mega-companies.

Certain problems are known: Unfriendly takeovers have caused displacement of employees, dismissals of executives, and depletion of profits and resources. "White knights" (*aka* friendly suitors) taking over a company to prevent such dislocation often end up as unfriendly as those they were fighting. Yet, while this trend sometimes startles the public—especially when billions of dollars are at stake—the desire to accumulate multiple holdings is not new. Nor are the problems or perceptions that arise.

Throughout history, kings, nobles, and priests have sought to acquire power through wealth, and vice versa. Members of the medieval church in particular were in the habit—so to speak—of accumulating rich offices: bishoprics, abbacies, cardinal's caps. These offices had wealthy lands and incomes attached to them for a period of time that any present-day entrepreneur or corporate raider would envy: *all eternity*. But while acquiring companies through purchase is common enough today, obtaining lucrative church offices by cash purchase was then abhorred. Called *simony*—for Simon the magician, who tried to buy the gift of the holy spirit from the Apostles—it was common nonetheless. And often enough, the buying of an office could be as upsetting as an unfriendly takeover for those directly affected.

Viscount Berengar of Narbonne complained at the church

council of Toulouse in 1056 that when he sold a certain Wifred the archbishopric of Narbonne (which "used to belong to my uncle"), Wifred did not live up to his promised agreements. The viscount had hoped that Wifred "would be a protection to me and a shield against the spears of all my enemies"—a white knight holding the office for Viscount Berengar. But, the viscount complained, the archbishop had snatched "the castles and manors, estates and possessions of the aforesaid church, together with the revenues and possessions of the canons and what they held in common, and gave them to the devil and his servants"—perhaps a reference to Wifred's family.

Acquiring numerous church offices for wealth—the acquisition fever of the medieval period known as *pluralism*—led to charges that parish affairs suffered because the officeholder was a nonresident and rarely became involved with day-to-day affairs. This could also be argued for the architects of today's supermergers, especially when they have little understanding of the culture or needs of the acquired concern. But for the medieval church, it brought out the wrath of the public.

No greater representative of this practice of multiple holdings existed than Cardinal Thomas Wolsey of England (d. 1530). He held numerous offices, including some he had never even visited, and by 1529 he had given the English clergy such a bad name that the Holy Roman Empire's ambassador to England wrote "nearly all the people here hate the priests." Even Wolsey's illegitimate son, Thomas Wynter, went the way of these precorporate magnates: While still a schoolboy, Wynter was dean of Wells; provost of Beverley; archdeacon of York; chancellor of Salisbury; prebendary of Wells, York, Salisbury, Lincoln, and Southwell; and rector of Rudby in Yorkshire and of St. Matthew's in Ipswich.

Whether corporate mergers and acquisitions will lose their appeal as sources of profit and power is not known. Perhaps the public will decide, as it did with the medieval clergy, that contrary to corporate literature, it is not society that benefits from such activities but simply the players at the top. Should that occur, a few *Ave Maria*s might start echoing through the boardrooms.

TAKEOVERS KHAN HAPPEN WITH A HORDE OF FORCE

Irwin Jacobs, Paul Bilzerian, Asher Edelman, Carl Icahn, T. Boone Pickens, Marvin Davis—they represent a group of corporate raiders who, in the 1980s, spent billions trying to take over companies, whether those companies liked it or not. Such actions have often diminished their victims' resources and either brought about the selling off of subsidiaries for huge profits or abandoning the hapless targets altogether. When examining the motives for takeovers, greed and empire-building cannot be overlooked as root causes for such monumental endeavors. After all, why bother putting millions or billions of dollars on the line if rewards of equivalent dimensions are not in the offing?

In the financial environment of the late 20th century, it is the golden hoards of cash, stock, and junk bonds that have helped these raiders plunder and pillage. But is this behavior much different than that of raiders seeking similar rewards in other times? In the case of one organizational genius, it was indeed a golden horde that afforded a pattern of unfriendly takeovers. Only instead of leveraged buyouts and proxy fights, he used armies to make his hostile bids.

Genghis Khan (c. 1162–1227) took a population of one million nomadic Mongols and created a fighting machine that conquered most of the known world, from the Pacific Ocean to the Danube River and the Mediterranean Sea, and terrorized most of the rest. This great raider was the consummate businessman. He encouraged traditional trade between his people and the rest of the world, but he kept to his own style of commerce. He did not haggle; merchants who tried to bargain with him had their goods quickly confiscated. If, however, they simply turned their wares over to the Khan, they received more than the products' worth in gifts.

Trade with the West alerted Genghis Khan to these rich lands to be conquered. He had been unfamiliar with them because the early part of his reign was spent subduing China. But rather than show his hand, he decided to play a game familiar to today's corporate raiders: slowly infiltrate the enemy, or provoke the opponent into starting an all-out war. His target was the

Shah of Karesm, who ruled much of the Middle East in the early 13th century. The Khan sent him greetings, saying he looked upon the Shah "as a most cherished son"—a patronizing phrase that went unappreciated. So did the Khan's mention that "thou must know that I have conquered Cathay and many Turkish nations." The Shah was a Turk.

Genghis Khan's envoy carried a message offering to open trade between the two nations. The Shah acceded to this request, and commerce began between subjects of the two powerful rulers. But after about a year, one of the Shah's governors seized a caravan of several hundred merchants and reported that there were spies among them—which was entirely likely. The Shah ordered his governor to slay the entire caravan. This and other affronts forced Genghis Khan to gather his horde, starting a bloody war that brought many victories to the Mongols and expanded their empire well into Europe, where a branch known as the Golden Horde ruled Russia until 1395.

No suggestion is being made that corporate raiders are Mongols, nor that unfriendly takeovers are tantamount to bloodbaths—although not a few have been financially debilitating to suitor *and* victim. Yet raiders might very well share the opinion of the great Khan when asked what in all the world brought him the greatest happiness: "To crush your enemies, to see them fall at your feet—to take their horses and goods and hear the lamentation of their women. That is the best."

THE KING OF LEINSTER SEEKS A "WHITE KNIGHT"

One pattern for corporate takeovers is familiar to those who follow such sport: A person or group acquires a percentage of stock in a company, soon seeks a large representation on the corporate board, and eventually takes to the streets to convince stockholders to part with their shares at an inflated price to complete the conquest. As we have seen, the "white knight" has come to mean a hero of sorts who rushes to the rescue of a besieged company, offering enough money to stave off an unfriendly takeover with one of his own—a friendly one. Yet as

Viscount Berengar learned, one wonders how friendly the white knight will remain once the battle is won.

Throughout history, cities or peoples under seige have sought relief from any quarter willing to risk life and limb to effect a rescue. Sometimes the rescuer is anything but a white knight, with the operating principle simply being "the enemy of my enemy is my friend" . . . at least for now. In 13th-century Ireland, such a situation occurred that was to have a profound impact well into our present century. And the calamity took place by invitation.

Dermot MacMurrough, king of Leinster, was not a very nice man, oppressing both noble and common man with equal vengeance: an equal-opportunity tyrant. Yet he owned one fifth of Ireland and wielded enormous power. One day, according to the Norman-Welsh writer Giraldus Cambrensis (whom we met with the Welsh soothsayers), Dermot ravished the wife of O'Rourke, king of Meath, while her husband was on an expedition.[1] The author of this story, a churchman who blamed women for "almost all great disasters [that] have fallen upon the world," noted that O'Rourke sought revenge for this wicked violation. He gathered support from neighboring kingdoms and attacked Dermot.

The battle did not go well for the wicked king. Giraldus said that "after many sharp and unequal engagements with the enemy, [Dermot] finally, as though resorting to the last means of safety, took ship and fled for protection." Dermot needed a white knight rather badly—so badly that he visited his ancient enemy, England, to seek support. The English king at the time, Henry II, was off in France. But upon learning of Dermot's plight, and being a monarch well-versed at getting in trouble over women, Henry agreed to help the irate Irishman attack O'Rourke.

First, however, Henry demanded that Dermot take an oath of allegiance to him, as well as an oath of subjugation to the king of England as his overlord. Henry then granted him a document stating that "Dermot, King of Leinster, has come under the protection of our grace and kindness." Because Henry was preoc-

---

[1] It should be noted that *ravished* meant *kidnapped* and not necessarily raped. To many a medieval man, however, the difference was probably moot.

cupied with a problem concerning his archbishop of Canterbury, Thomas Becket, he sent Richard de Clare, earl of Pembroke—nicknamed "Strong Bow"—to Ireland with a contingency of Welshmen. He even got the Pope to endorse the expedition against O'Rourke.

Strong Bow was victorious, scattering the ill-equipped Irish. Dermot then learned that his foreign savior thought it a good idea to settle down and rule in Ireland—a situation Dermot failed to consider when seeking aid. In all truth, neither had Henry II, who now feared that the white knight he had sent Dermot—Strong Bow—was about to set up an empire of his own. Henry therefore went to Ireland, received homage from its people as their overlord, and established a region about 25 miles around the area of Dublin (the Pale) as an English colony. His Norman barons then proceeded to carve out a state for themselves in this region of Northern Ireland. To this day, the descendants of the ancient Irish continue to fight these "Norman" invaders who were initially invited over to help settle an internal squabble.

Finding corporate white knights can be useful in the short run when raiders are upon you. But the long-term effect can come back to haunt you well after the battle is over. Takeover targets, when considering options from "poison pills" to white knights, must also consider all the players involved and how to stop the rolling stone of rescue once it is set in motion. In Ireland, the cost is still being felt.

PLAYING "ROUGH RIDER" ON MERGERS

At the beginning of our own century, activities similar to today's mergers and acquisitions were taking place in the United States. These were in the form of trusts, where companies combined their holdings to form gigantic business entities to reduce competition and control prices in their industries. Only instead of enjoying a smooth ride from benevolent American presidents, as is the case today, they encountered a head-on collision with the White House.

The force behind that collision was Theodore Roosevelt, known as T.R. by friends and foes alike. A blustery, outspoken opponent of the "robber barons" of his age, this Rough Rider hero of San Juan Hill came to the forefront of power through a scenario repeated in a later American election. In the presidential election of 1900, William McKinley chose for his vice presidential running mate the fiery Roosevelt, amazing as many people then as Dan Quayle's vice presidential candidacy amazed American voters in 1988. As one antagonist said at the time about T.R.: "Don't you realize that there's only one life between this madman and the White House?"

In September of 1901, the "madman" found himself in the White House after McKinley was assassinated. And one of his first moves was to break up the gigantic corporations that had more or less been running their own show for decades. In 1902, Roosevelt ordered his attorney general, Philander C. Knox, to bring suit against, and ultimately break apart, the Northern Securities Company, a creation of powerful bankers combining the holdings of the largest railroad magnates. The move was such a shock to the corporate powers that the American financier and railroad emperor, J. P. Morgan, actually journeyed to the White House to learn of T.R.'s intentions.

These he learned all too well. In 1904, the Supreme Court ruled 5 to 4 to break up the Northern Securities Company. In 1903, Roosevelt had created the Bureau of Corporations under the new Department of Commerce and Labor. The Bureau's mandate involved investigating companies conducting interstate commerce, and one of its first successes was the breakup of the beef trust in the case of *Swift & Company* vs. *United States*. Other prosecutions included those of the "oil trust" and the "tobacco trust." However, the Bureau, and T.R.'s support of it, didn't stop giant companies from combining, or seeking to monopolize and control markets. But it did put corporate America on notice that, from now on, its actions would be scrutinized—and, if need be, prosecuted—by the president of the United States.

In looking at the 1980s, it is apparent that the Republican presidents in the White House have taken a more kindly view toward mergers and acquisitions than their Republican counterpart at the turn of the century. Moreover, it is the Securities and Exchange Commission that busies itself with scrutinizing takeovers and mergers, not the White House or its officers. As with all cycles, the age of mergers may phase out, giving way to other forms of business that prove advantageous to corporations and those who control them. But for the foreseeable future it will be smooth sailing for companies wishing to expand by leaps and bounds through merging and acquiring. Eighty years ago, it was much more of a rough ride . . . thanks to a person called T.R.

THE CRASH OF '87 AND THE FRENCH REVOLUTION

The consequences of the 1987 stock market crash still have not come into focus. The post-panic prognosis points to a need for changing existing trading practices, from the hard-disk whirls of program trading to the standardization of margin buying for the purchase of stock-index futures and stocks. The report of the special presidential commission on the market's tumble was long in recommendations, but short in realistic ways to implement the needed changes. Nor is there consensus on what should be done, since no one is absolutely sure why the crash happened in the first place. One thing, however, is apparent to insiders and outsiders alike: It was panic that swept across the trading floors of the world, and it was panic that pointed the high-flying bull market into a growling, bearish nosedive.

Panic arises from fear, be it real or imagined. That is exactly what happened on Wall Street in 1987, and two years later in October 1989, when the market plunged 191 points on Friday the 13th. The fear that the end of the bull market was near—it wasn't—became a self-fulfilling prophecy. Some two centuries ago a panic known as the Great Fear swept across France. It, too, was self-fulfilling, since people made the fear real, and therefore reacted to "reality." The only difference was that it led to a revolution and the overthrow of the established government.

France in the late 18th century was a country of contrasts: well-fed aristocrats, starving peasants, well-off merchants, poor vagrants. Riots were not uncommon, but underlying any protest of economic and social conditions was a fear that brigands were roving the countryside, ready to descend upon innocent victims and decimate everything in their paths. Truth had little to do with this fear. People felt it was inevitable, hence they expected it and brought it into reality. In 1789 the fear began in Estrees-Saint-Denis, spreading into Flanders before heading south to Paris, where dissension had become commonplace. The fear then moved from Burgundy to Dijon and into Normandy and Brittany. There were no telephones or nightly news reports. Rumors were carried by vagrants roaming from town to town, enlarging upon stories they themselves had heard. Monks, priests, and other members of the clergy were good sources of gossip, and local officials and even the country gentry spread the word of impending attacks by roving outlaws and thieves. As one historian noted, "the terrors spread because there was no means of verification and because unbelievers easily became suspects."

The fall of the Bastille on July 14 was but the most visible wave in this sea of fear crashing across the land. Here the rumors included the movement of thousands of troops, amassing to attack the Parisians. Although that didn't happen, the resulting panic forced the takeover of the Bastille—not to free the prisoners (there were only seven) but to release the fear and anger of the crowd. The brigands, as it turned out, were imaginary. The revolutionaries blamed the nobles for starting the panic, but this hardly washes since it was the nobles who ended up with burned mansions and devastated lands. The nobles blamed the peasants for spreading a rumor that led to revolt, but the peasants had repeatedly asked to be kept neutral in the political turmoil of the day. The Great Fear underscored what was already taking place: a movement of change that ended in revolution.

No such revolution was in progress at the time of the stock market panic of 1987, but there must be changes to prevent the self-fulfilling prophecies that tend to drift through Wall Street. Perhaps a special day each month should be designated Market Day, when traders, brokers, and investors get together to discuss current rumors and real facts—and how to distinguish between the two. It would be one way to avoid a Great Fear—a fear that becomes too large to stop once it gets going.

THE SEASON OF THE WITCH

Panic and its kindred spirit, superstition, are not merely the products of medieval minds and ignorant people. Indeed, people today are hardly so sophisticated and secure that they do not knock a little wood or avoid an open ladder now and then. In the stock and futures markets, traders have always cast a wary eye toward potential disasters (or successes) as signs of good (or bad) things to come, depending on what particular position they find themselves in. And we have already explored our dependency on those great prognosticators, the economists (Chapter 3).

One recent superstition of sorts carries an ominous moniker: the triple-witching hour. To the uninitiated, it may sound like a trick-or-treat assault plan for Halloween. In fact, it refers to a certain Friday each quarter, when futures contracts on stock indexes come due, and options on those indexes and on individual stocks expire. Spooky things are supposed to happen during a triple-witching hour—and they often do. On one triple-witching, 52 million shares—or 20 percent of the day's total—were traded during the last minute of the day, pushing up the Dow Jones industrial average a quarter of its gain for the day. On one December witching hour, the Dow flipped from a modest loss to a 16-point gain and its volume doubled at the end of the session. Although the Securities and Exchange Commission has tightened its rules on close-of-the-day trading—the three sets of instruments no longer expire at exactly the same time—traders continue to worry about the very uncertainty they helped create when the triple-witching was noticed in the first place.

If Halloween has hit Wall Street, it has sung a familiar note: fear of the unknown. The Druids of ancient Britain created the same problem when they began celebrating their new year, November 1, on the evening before. And it became a night that could, well, rattle your bones. The Druids thought that maybe the dead could come back to visit the living on that night, leading people to dress up like ghosts to avoid the wrath of such "night visitors." Another of their New Year's Eve superstitions has since been fostered by economists and newsletter writers: the ability to foretell the future. In Scotland, a girl could throw a nut into a fire to ascertain the identity of her future lover. Contrary to stereotype, cats could be very useful. If a feline sat beside you it meant good fortune; if it rubbed against you, it meant good luck; and you were thrice blessed if it jumped into your lap. Arbitrageurs might trade in their lucky rabbit feet and Valium for a good lap cat.

Christians adopted the Druid New Year celebration and called it All Hallows Day to honor the saints. All Hallows Eve, or Halloween, thus became an important night. It also took on all the old superstitions and acquired a few more, including the fun-loving aspect of goblins and ghouls playing tricks on people—today's trick-or-treat theme.

On Wall Street, the triple-witching superstition—like the panic leading to the 1987 Crash—may have become a self-fulfilling prophecy. Despite the new rules to limit volatility, there have been major stock market swings linked to futures and options on other days, possibly because of fear of the triple-witching effect. Perhaps it all comes down to how much we are willing to believe in the phenomenon in the first place. It recalls an old Halloween joke: Is it bad luck to have a black cat cross your path on Halloween? Answer: It depends on whether you are a man or a mouse.

GREECE, ROME, AND SHORT-TERM CRASHES

Lost in all the debate about the Crash of '87 is a fundamental observation: the crash was one loud thud, and not the beginning of the end. True, the crash of 1929 appears to have ushered in a decade of economic depression cured only by the remedy of World War II. But a closer look at that and other historical crashes suggests that what happens after a crash is usually long in coming: One thud does not a major catastrophe make.

It might do well to look at the Athenian Empire of the 5th century B.C., which began with the impressive defeat of the Persian armies and navies by Athens and her allies. By the end of the century, Athens was in disarray and suffered defeat at the hands of a rival city-state, Sparta. Many have linked the decline of Athens with the death of Pericles, the charismatic leader of the Athenians who died of the plague only one year after the war between Sparta and Athens began in 431 B.C. Herodotus, who chronicled this war, believed that after the death of Pericles, his successors strayed from the war effort. He also noted that "private ambition and private profit led to policies which were bad both for the Athenians themselves and for their allies." But in fact, Athens' fall was due to a 40-year policy of trying to dominate other Greek city-states, not the death of one man. And it earned Athens the epithet of "tyrant city." The situation eventually boiled over, Athens lost many of its allies, and Sparta waged a war lasting a generation after Pericles' death, ending in the defeat of Athens and its imperial policies.

The fall of the Roman Empire has a convenient date: 476 A.D. It was at this time that the Roman emperor, Romulus Augustus, was deposed by a Germanic leader, Odovacar (or Odoacer). Yet it is certain that no distant crash would have been heard throughout the Roman Empire. For one, Rome had been declining and falling for centuries, mostly from within. The economy had become static, Christianity represented a threat to Roman law and order, and Germanic tribes moved from being foreign invaders to free-wheeling members of the Roman army. Hence, the year 476 is really the symbol of a long-term march towards decay and ruin.

Another "crash" that never happened was William the Conqueror's conquest of England in 1066. For while the year represents the invasion of Saxon England by Norman adventurers, the conquest went on for decades and well into the next century. Indeed, 20 years after the invasion, in 1086, William finally received an accounting of exactly what he had conquered, in a survey known as the "Domesday Book." (See Chapters 7 and 9.) Moreover, the Saxons were not amused at the changing neighborhood, and they resisted the new laws, language, and the Norman way of life. It was from this situation that the legend of a Saxon Robin Hood was born, robbing the Norman barons to feed the Saxon poor.

So the meaning of the 1987 crash should not be sought in what happened on that day, but in what it represents over time. We can feel secure that economists will keep predicting and historians will keep explaining, but all bets are off that the crash made a long-lasting sound. Only time will tell why the noise was made, and what it meant in the first place. And it is the underlying situation that is significant; noises come and go in the wind with ease.

HOW TO AVOID A STOCK MARKET CRASH

History cannot predict the future—the 1929 crash did little to tell us what would happen 58 years later. But it can suggest what *options* might occur, or how a course of action might proceed. The previous discussion on the Shah of Iran and his son described a possible option. Although the New York Stock Exchange has had a remarkable recovery in the months following the 1987 crash, large investors and institutions still view economic indicators with watchful eyes to see what the future might bring. And the small investor/saver continues to keep money in banks, in money market funds, or just plain under the pillow. Yet while special commissions and not-so-special "specialists" have declared various and sundry reasons for the crash, Americans—and therefore much of the world—were perhaps spared a potential depression in 1987 because people worked their way through the crash. True, billions of dollars were lost on paper, and out-of-work stockbrokers faced retraining for alternative employment. But the United States kept its people working, with very little volatility in the unemployment figures. Keeping employment levels high may be the option needed to avoid a depression brought on by a volatile stock market.

More than a century ago, another American "crash" didn't work out quite that way. After the Civil War ended in 1865, a boom occurred, stemming from an increased demand for goods and heavy investment in manufacturing and industry. Such rapid expansion caused rises and declines typical of a free market economy, and the period 1868 to 1873 witnessed the biggest boom of all. But there were hints of trouble. During the six-year period, American bank loans had increased seven times faster than bank deposits, and in the early 1870s several thousand businesses failed, due in part to the devil-may-care attitude of willing debtors—today we call them credit-card holders!

Then two disasters struck in a short period of time that spelled doom for the boom and the beginning of a depression. In 1871, the Great Chicago Fire cost insurance companies $200 million in claims—imagine the cost today, taking inflation and price increases into account! A year later, a fire in Boston added an additional $73 million in payouts. On September 8, 1873, the New York Warehouse and Securities Company went bankrupt, followed a week later by the prestigious banking house of Jay Cooke and Co. Shock set in among investors, and the New York Stock Exchange stopped trading for 10 days on September 20 to try to quell panic trading.

Things went from bad to worse. Railroads—the runaway transportation industry that helped fuel the expansion—stopped construction, forcing defaults on their bonds. This led to a halt in production for related industries, throwing half the factory work force in America into unemployment. The levels of unemployment rose higher than at any other time in American history as thousands of skilled and white-collar workers were forced to live off charities. Not everyone suffered, of course. The wealthy few looked upon the crash as an opportunity to gobble up failing businesses at a discount. One businessman, the industrialist Andrew Carnegie, put it this way: "The man who has money during a panic is a wise and valuable citizen." He was also in a position to increase his fortune.

As government officials and economists watch current economic conditions and the rise and ebb of the dollar abroad, it would be "wise and valuable" to take realistic readings of the number of Americans out of work. That reading may tell more about our economic future than another one-day plunge in the stock market.

"GAMES OF CHANCE": SOME OBSERVATIONS

From the noninvestor perspective, those that rode the bulls over the 2700 mark on the New York Stock Exchange in 1987 were also riding on a gamble—one that promised either greater profits or the collapse of irrational expectations for a market already out among the stars. And perhaps it is only with the stars that one can ever know when to sit and when to quit. Paul Chatfield, the early-19th-century English verse writer, saw only one sure bet when he wrote "there is but one good throw upon the dice, which is to throw them away." The problem with such an investment strategy, of course, is that you cannot reap what you haven't sown.

Yet the difficulty in entering the market is measuring one's greed quotient: how far one is willing to gamble away winnings. Human nature perhaps excludes such self-control. The first president of the United States, George Washington (1732–99), noted that such gambling is "the child of avarice, the brother of iniquity, and the father of mischief." Playing the stock market is not for everyone: It takes not only capital but nerve, a little expertise and the willingness to ride out bad times long enough to reach good times or to buy and sell at the right time. The 17th-century English Bishop Richard Cumberland wrote that "games of chance are traps to catch school-boy novices and gaping country squires, who begin with a guinea and end with a mortgage."

Part of the game of nerves involves an investor's view of the future. It may be true, as noted by the 19th-century American writer Christian Bovee that "when all else is lost, the future still remains," but the trick is to work out a way not to lose before reaching the future. Some investors simply follow their own predilections and adhere to the dictum of the great physicist and philosopher Albert Einstein: "I never think of the future. It comes soon enough."

But for many, that strategy was not very useful when the market crashed 508 points. Indeed, numerous traders on the Chicago Board of Trade were forced to sell their seats to cover losses, and an army of investors lost great sums of money, on paper if not during the selling binge. It is easy to pontificate from on high, tossing out pithy Old Testament headshakers such as "How are the mighty fallen!" (II Samuel 1:25) But in the end, it becomes an individual's task to examine what exactly happened and what course to choose. It might therefore be an inspiration to investors and traders in the coming years to post a sign on the trading floors of the world quoting a rather prodigious investor in words, William Shakespeare:

"Wise men ne're sit and wail their loss, but cheerily seek how to redress their harms."

THE JAPANESE AND THE
LOUISIANA PURCHASE

It should be clear that the 1987 stock market crash, while affecting not only investors but businesses and workers alike, was a single event, tied perhaps to a trend we cannot as yet perceive, and born from the fears and concerns that humans carry with them throughout their lives. Another area of "fear" in the United States and other parts of the world is that certain cash-rich countries, mainly the Japanese, are buying up real estate globally and will soon be everyone's landlord. It is true that the Canadians, the British, and the Japanese alone have poured billions of dollars into the purchase of American real estate, hotels, office buildings, and retail centers, and that they are willing to pay premium prices. What Americans seem to forget, if they ever knew it to begin with, is that the United States grew to its present geographic size because the U.S. Government invested in North American land owned by other countries. The United States was actually the "foreign" investor!

When learning history was deemed useful, every schoolchild knew the story of how the early Dutch settlers wangled Manhattan from the Indians for what today would be the price of a pair of jeans. But even with that bargain in hand, the Colonists were always aware that the lands beyond the Eastern seaboard were divvied up by the likes of Spain, France, and Russia. And although the American Revolution gained the Colonies independence from Britain, the result was a country on the fringe of a continent owned by others.

The first big land purchase came in 1803, when President Thomas Jefferson paid $15 million for the territory of Louisiana, stretching from New Orleans to the Rocky Mountains. Jefferson had long wanted to annex the territory from Spain so that "our population can be sufficiently advanced [in numbers] to gain it from them piece by piece." Unfortunately, the French dictator Napoleon got the territory by a secret treaty in 1800, and

Jefferson had to deal with the "little corporal." Negotiations were long and tedious, and often mistaken—Jefferson thought he could try to get the Floridas from Napoleon as well, although they were still owned by Spain! When the deal was finally struck for the Louisiana Purchase, it was so vague that Jefferson was not quite sure what he had bought. Napoleon's chief negotiator, Talleyrand, was not too worried for the American president. If the boundaries seemed uncertain, he wrote, "I suppose you will make the most of it."

Beginning in the early 19th century, the United States gained the Spanish territories and the young nation began settling its northern and western borders. It was a slow process, and when treaties failed, war was considered a viable option, as in the case of Texas. Perhaps the most interesting acquisition of foreign-held American soil was that of Alaska. In early 1867, the Russian ambassador actually offered to dump the costly territory. Secretary of State William H. Seward leaped at the chance and signed the deal at 4 A.M. on March 30 of that year. Many Americans, however, were less enthusiastic about the $7.2 million purchase. The press labeled it "Seward's Folly," but the significance of the deal was not entirely unappreciated. Senator Charles Sumner, the Massachusetts Republican who helped carry it through the Senate, stated that the purchase would at least remove "one more monarch from this continent"—namely the csar of Russia.

So while we watch our real estate get gobbled up by foreign investors, we might take cheer in the knowledge that we started the whole thing. All will be well until the hotels start carrying Japanese names and warning signs are written in German. Then, as the oft-quoted catcher for the New York Yankees, Yogi Berra, purportedly said, it will be déjà vu all over again.

INTEREST RATES AND LOMBARDS

It is not only our behavior in the markets that mimics the activities of our ancestors; even our daily terms and routines owe their existence to the past. For example, let's take a circumstance that occurred soon after the 1987 stock crash to see if any "survivors" from the past surface:

The U.S. Federal Reserve Bank increased the money supply to maintain liquidity in the economy after the October stock market crash. This attempt to keep U.S. exports cheap and attractive to stave off a recession is being met with similar behavior abroad. [So far, sounds like a normal, jargon-filled news entry—which it is. Read on.] Britain's big banks recently cut their base lending rates, as did the Swiss and the Dutch. This, hopefully, will cushion the effects of lower rates on a very weak dollar, which has been sliding in value to post-World War II records. The Deutsche Bundesbank, West Germany's Central Bank, has also taken a seat on the interest rate roller coaster ride downhill. The falling dollar is a threat to the export-oriented German economy, causing the Central Bank to lower their Lombard rate.

Lombard rate? Well, in its simplist form, this refers to the highest short-term rate charged by the Central Bank for supplementary borrowings by other banks. But the roots of this anachronistic term go back over 1,000 years, as does much of our financial "behavior."

The Lombards were a Germanic people who conquered Italy in the 6th century A.D. Their empire didn't last long, but a region in Northern Italy became their center for commercial activity and still bears their name: Lombardy. By the 13th century, the Italians from Lombardy were the leading bankers in Europe. They were allowed to mint coins and solicit collateral for loans. Indeed, a Lombard loan in Britain or Europe today involves securing bonds and shares as collateral for a time loan, as opposed to a demand loan such as a check payable on demand.

The Lombards also finagled a way around the church's ban on charging interest for a loan: They simply bought and sold bills of exchange payable in foreign currency. The goal of the lender, of course, was to make a profit on the exchange rate that would equal the amount of interest he would have charged for the loan. Although the bill of exchange dated back to the ancient Babylonians and the Roman Empire—showing that the Lombards, much like us, engaged in practices invented long ago—the Lombards made it an integral part of business transactions. But this did not preclude issuing normal loans. In fact, in the 14th and 15th centuries, lenders could charge two pence on the pound, giving the Lombards a healthy interest rate for a loan.

The very name Lombard became a generic term for finance

and banking. In 1553, a London writer noted "if he have not one Lombard's touch, my luck is bad." Lombard Street became a hub of banking activity in London, and today the street figuratively refers to the world of London finance. Paris also had its "Rue des Lombards," and the term Lombard rate flourishes at the Deutsche Bundesbank.

Most of us will not lose sleep wondering what the Lombard rate will do tomorrow. But it is important to know that much of how we manipulate our modern financial system stems from practices and people long dead. The Lombards of old would have been honored. They might have even figured a way out of our economic plights.

"BENCH-BREAKING" AND GOING UNDER

Closer to home than the Lombard rate is another practice we act out daily that comes from the past: going under, or bankruptcies. One disparaging trend in the late 1980s was the large number of Savings & Loan failures in the United States, to say nothing of the steady flow of bankrupt businesses and personal bankruptcy. Whether through bad loans, overextension of debt, bad investments, or a swindle or two, this staunch money institution is not a happy camper on the American economic campground. Lending money and providing monetary assistance for members of a community are old concepts. What most people don't realize is that the hardships facing banks and S&Ls today have been faced before. Moreover, many of those past problems actually led to the formation of the modern banking institution.

The direct ancestor of the modern lending system can be found in medieval Italy. Our word *bank* comes from the Italian word *banca,* which means bench. It was upon benches in the marketplace that Italian moneylenders sat, setting rates and lending money to merchants and landowners. Should a moneylender go under, the people of the village or town broke his bench, effectively putting him out of business. This led to our word *bankrupt*—broken bench. Unfortunately for the Italian moneylender, there was no Chapter 11 to hold off creditors: When you lost your bench, you lost your livelihood.

The work of the moneylenders developed into the institution of the banking house, and by 1350 some 80 were operating just in Florence. Italian families usually ran these houses, the most famous being the Medici, who opened offices throughout Europe. The banking houses viewed money as a commodity, not merely a medium of exchange. Currencies were bought and sold, and fortunes were made and lost, depending upon the prevailing political and economic winds: a situation completely current in today's money markets.

By the 16th century, the leading bankers were the Fuggers of Germany. Besides lending money, they sought investments similar to those of modern-day merchant bankers. Loans to the Hapsburg dynasty were secured by granting the Fuggers a virtual monopoly on the mining of precious metals in Spain and Central Europe. But as with the Italian moneylenders, the Fuggers were vulnerable to defaults. In 1607, the Fuggers went under after Spain defaulted on its loans for the third time: no doubt a few benches were broken across Germany.

Because large resources were needed to protect against defaults, governments began to charter public banks, beginning with the establishment in 1609 of the Bank of Amsterdam. These banks began converting currencies into bank money to facilitate trade. At the same time banks were developing across Europe, double bookkeeping was replaced by the single entry accounting method. Banks began listing transactions as "those who owe" (*debit*) and those the bank "believed" would fulfill a promise (*credit*). Both banks and businessmen could now readily ascertain where they stood with regard to profit and loss.

Although the present era of banking encompasses unprecedented technological advances in transaction processing and sheer volume of work, the basic principles of banking remain much the same as in centuries past. Only in 1300, when you had your bench broken, you took the pieces home and went scouting for another profession. Today, the government glues the bench back together and lets you return to the marketplace. One wonders if the medieval practice made more sense in terms of business and the procedure of letting a failing business fail. For without a guardian angel to come to the financial rescue, you had to know what you were doing in the world of finance. Perhaps "knowing what you're doing" has lost its importance at the end of the 20th century.

OLIVES, SILVER, AND FAST-FOOD CHAINS

One trend taking place in the United States that can have a profound effect in the near future is nonetheless rooted in the past, with all the warnings and red flags for us to understand, and perhaps to observe in future activity. It involves a once-great industrial giant in the New World doffing its hard hat in favor of a suit or uniform. *Translation:* the United States is shifting from a nation of industries to a nation of services, with more and more of its citizens going into nonproducing or nonmanufacturing occupations.

Although some industries, notably steel, have made a go at recovering from the disastrous 1970s and early 1980s, it is clear that the United States is becoming heavily dependent on external goods and materials. At the same time, an increasing number of man-hours will be spent in office buildings and fast-food chains, not in factories. There is a danger in all this: relying on a major source of wealth—service industries—rather than striving to maintain a diversified economy. It could spell economic collapse if needed external resources are cut off—most of us recall what happened during the oil embargo of the early 1970s. More important, it could mean political and social decline as the nation's wealth diminishes for lack of salable products.

Another great democracy with a claim to world leadership faltered because it focused its fiscal attentions on a narrow source of wealth. That power was ancient Athens, and the sources of prosperity were olives and silver. By the mid-5th century B.C., Athens held sway over other city-states in the Mediterranean world. It also became a major exporter of olives. Although probably first cultivated as a cash crop by the wise ruler Solon (early 6th century B.C.), olive trees dotted much of the countryside in and around Athens by the year 500 B.C. Olive trees require 16 years before first bearing fruit and another 25 years to reach maturity, and the Greeks found numerous uses for olives, including pressing for oil that could be eaten or burned as fuel. Olives became the main product of Athens, and its export trade was taken over by the state as a monopoly. In return, olive exports helped pay for the grain Athens had to import.

The mines at Laurium provided another important industry for Athens: silver. The Athenian government as well monopolized silver mining and large profits helped build the Athenian fleet. By the mid-5th century B.C., this "fountain running silver," as the dramatist Aeschylus wrote, became the main source of wealth for the Athenian treasury.

Then in 431 B.C., as we have seen, Athens and its rival city-state Sparta became embroiled in what was known as the Peloponnesian War. It was a devastating war for both sides, made more so for Athens by the destruction of its main sources of wealth. The militaristic Spartans were not unaware of Athens' economic superiority, and one of their main targets was the silver mines of Laurium, which they eventually captured. But this was only the first spigot of Athenian wealth shut off by the Spartans. During the course of the war, most of the Athenian olive orchards were destroyed, robbing the city of a generation of needed exports. Sparta won the war in 404 B.C.; its removal of Athens' major sources of wealth ensured that the noble city would never again become a world power.

It is hardly likely that foreign invaders will destroy the office buildings and quick hamburger havens of America, thrusting its population into economic despair and unemployment. But it is important to keep a balanced economy that can weather the uncertainty of geopolitics. The Athenians found out the hard way.

TOUGH BOSSES LIVE BY THE "REGULA"

We move from the world of economics and high finance to those who control much of the business world. And it is interesting to note that the people at the top are not all that different today than the bigwigs of long ago. This was made apparent (Chapter 2) in the wonderful world of wealth. In business, top executives everywhere do little more than carry on an old tradition of being in charge. They try to move the business in a direction that benefits them and, hopefully, those directly or indirectly affected by that business.

When we talk about a corporate culture, more often than not it reflects the perspectives and modus operandi of the founder. Digital Equipment Corporation, founded by Kenneth H. Olsen in the late 1950s, has had a culture not unlike the work habits of its founder: entrepreneurial, informal, receptive to take-charge ideas and people, and so forth. Leaders influence not only the bottom line, but the atmosphere and environment that employees share and contribute to every day. Some cultures are conducive to success; others are more apt to breed failure, rapid turnover of employees, and lackluster performance in the marketplace. Perhaps the most difficult environment to work in is one where rules and regulations are writ in stone, with any deviation from the norm being tantamount to cursing at the altar: it's just not done, and if it is, the SB ("Supreme Being") is likely to be very upset. In business, the SB happens to be the boss.

When we think of such work places—assembly lines in factories are obvious, but there are numerous examples in service businesses—we might wonder if the day-to-day tedium belies a 20th-century development: work for work's sake, with little room for creativity. Not so. We need only explore a time and place when almost no room for variation occurred, making our 9-to-5 experiences positively recreational. This was the era of the monasteries, which had their heyday during the thousand years between the fall of the Roman Empire and the coming of the Reformation (c. 500–1500 A.D.). Those spending their lives in a monastery lived by a rule, or *regula,* and thus were called the regular clergy to differentiate from the more worldly, *secular* clergy of bishops and priests.

One of the toughest bosses for monasteries was St. Benedict of Nursia, who founded a monastery in Monte Cassino, Italy, in 529. He wrote a regula to serve as a primer for how to set up the monastic life, and it was received very well throughout the religious community. Benedict wrote that "idleness is the enemy of the soul and for that reason at certain times the brothers ought to be occupied in manual labor; at other times, again, in sacred study." And he made sure that his fellow brothers had every hour accounted for, each day and night. From Easter until October, the monks were to rise early and spend three hours tending to their necessities and chores for the monastery. The next two hours were spent in study, followed by two hours of silence for meditation or reading. The remainder of the hours until evening involved doing chores and manual labor, when they could be "busy by themselves with harvesting the crops." Meals were wedged in between work.

Benedict shifted the workload from October until Lent, but the day included study, work, and prayer. During the days of Lent, the assignment was monumental: "Let them have all the single books in the library that they are to read in entirety, in sequence." The brothers were not to be trusted to follow Benedict's work plan on their own: "Let one or two elders be deputed to patrol the monastery at the hour when the brothers are studying and see whether by chance a lazy brother is found idling or telling stories"—the modern equivalent to extended coffee breaks and chatter in the restrooms. Those who were caught received two warnings, after which "he should be subjected to correction according to the rule, to inspire the others with fear."

While it is true today that many jobs include repetitive tasks, there is some latitude regarding breaking up the monotony where feasible, and enlightened top management usually encourages such diversity of activity. In Benedict's workplace, the rule was the name of the game, day in and day out. Strict rules may work for a cloistered life where the only competition involves trying to "out-holy" the other person—something that would nonetheless be discouraged. But in the secular world, executives must continue to realize that creativity requires some loosening of the assignment to bring out the best in people. Otherwise, it would be difficult to compete in a world where abstract thinking is both salable and required for success. Few chief executive officers would smile at the possibility of being accused of keeping the same company as "Benedict & Brothers, Inc."

FLATTERING THE BOSS NOT A "PRINCE" OF AN IDEA

Whether a good boss or a bad boss, it's tough *being* a boss, especially when that special time arrives once a year known as "The Raise"—or Let's Make a Deal, corporate-style. Moreover, the other 364 days are usually spent by the rest of management and labor trying to impress upon their respective bosses the belief— real or imagined—that they are a "hard worker" or a "brilliant strategist" or a "team player" or a "good manager"—pick a label and the boss has heard it before. Yet what's a deserving, or undeserving, person to do? Should they write out a list of achievements? Bring in samples of work? Or how about telling the boss what a terrific boss he or she is, that there's no one better person to work for, that *whatever the boss does is simply marvelous?*

A manager must measure what is said against what is meant when a compliment comes flying into his or her office. Worse, when a boss earnestly asks for an opinion, how is it possible to tell if the answer spouts forth from honesty or simply from the desire to say what the boss wants to hear? In other words, how does the person in the control seat know in whose best interest the advice is: the boss's or the speaker's? Wading through flattery and fluff to find some useful advice is not a modern problem for managers and those at the top. In fact, it was addressed some 475 years ago by that great Italian management consultant Niccolo Machiavelli in his famous book, *The Prince.*

Machiavelli warned the guy in charge that flatterers were everywhere, and that he needed to be on his guard. Or as he put it, "Because men are so easily pleased with their own qualities and are so readily deceived in them, they have difficulty in guarding against these pests, and in attempting to guard against them, they run the risk of being scorned." So what's a manager to do? In a rare discourse on "the truth," Machiavelli advised fostering just that: "For there is no way of avoiding flattery except by letting men know that they will not offend by telling the truth."

However, giving carte blanche to truth-telling has its downside: "if every man is free to tell you the truth, you will not receive due respect." Since both then and today respect is generally viewed as a necessity for effective management, Machiavelli had a way of solving the problem: being selective. He advised the prince to surround himself with a few wise and learned men, giving them the freedom to tell the truth—but only on certain matters requiring opinions. Hence, executives should seek the truth selectively, from certain people and on certain subjects. Moreover, the chief honcho should let his advisers know that he can be trusted with their opinions: "He should treat these councils and the individual advisers in such a way as to make it clear that their words will be the more welcome the more freely they are spoken."

And what if a manager or top executive lets his guard down and starts listening to advice from all quarters? After all, everyone wants the top guy's ear to advance their own careers and make a mark in the company. Machiavelli believed that such a willing listener would lose his credibility. He noted that "many people believe that some princes are reputed wise, thanks rather to their wise counselors than to their own natural gifts." Therefore, the more advice—legitimate or through flattery—the less likely the boss will be respected, for "a prince who is not wise himself cannot be wisely counseled." And that means taking the opinions of few and making his own decisions.

Machiavelli concluded that while flattery had to be avoided, good advice should be taken only at the discretion of the prince. He wrote that "good advice, no matter where it comes from, ultimately derives from the prudence of the prince, and the prudence of the prince does not derive from good advice." The ladies and gentlemen in charge today need to remind themselves of this early-16th-century advice: beware of too much flattery and too much good advice. The former will be of little use; the latter of little benefit to their reputation.

DANGER AT THE TOP: THE DOOMER

Surviving flattery and advice is one thing, simply surviving is a more fundamental challenge. And in recent years it has been noted that many top executives, especially in Japan, have been, well, dropping dead. Some of the key corporate executives at All Nippon Airways, Seiko Epson, Kawasaki Steel, and Mitsubishi died of heart attacks, pneumonia, and other ailments. While death comes to those both high and low, it has been suggested that the stressful situations of senior executives have been made more tense of late by the fierce competition in world markets. High-powered managers in the United States and abroad have succumbed to workplace pressures.

In effect, they were members of an elite known in most developed countries, and here defined with economy of words: Drained Out Overactive Managers, or DOOMERs. When they get overly depressed or feel they cannot cope with their situations, the DOOMERs often contract the ultimate doom: mortality. Throughout history, those burdened with overwhelming responsibilities or challenges have often made fatal mistakes or, perhaps unconsciously, sought death as an end to the misery of futility or defeat.

Young Frederick of Swabia (1123–90), a German province, had two goals in life: to unify the semimythical Holy Roman Empire and to become master of Italy. He did manage to gain the support of the rulers of the empire's many subdivisions when he was crowned Holy Roman Emperor in 1152. But Italy was another story. For more than 30 years and through numerous wars he fought popes and patricians to gain control of the Italian city-states, and many an Italian feared the coming of Frederick Barbarossa, or Red Beard, as he was called. But in the end, he could not gain permanent control, and in 1183, Frederick and the Pope signed a treaty granting self-rule to the Italian city-states.

He also came to realize the impossibility of controlling Europe, with its various factions and conflicting interests. Eventually, Frederick sought to drown his disappointment with a little distraction: leading 100,000 men on the Third Crusade. The Crusade failed but drowning his disappointment succeeded, literally: Frederick Barbarossa drowned while crossing a river in Asia, his heavy armor making sure that neither Red Beard nor the empire would rise again. (For armor, see Chapter 2.)

Scotland had several DOOMERs who muddled through disasters and disappointments unsuccessfully, especially those inflicted by the belligerent neighbor to the south, England. By 1286, King Alexander III of Scotland, who lacked a male heir to his crown, realized that unless he could establish his granddaughter, Margaret, as his legitimate successor, there would be chaos in the kingdom as nobles vied for the throne. He managed to have Margaret, living in Norway, betrothed to the son of England's king, but that was not a guarantee that rival Scottish claimants would support the arrangement. Subsequently, Alexander went trekking one day and fell off a cliff, leaving 13 claimants to fight over the throne.

A broken heart probably did in one of Alexander's descendants, James V (1513–42). In 1542, James' uncle, the irascible King Henry VIII of England, invaded Scotland. James, recalling the defeat and death of his father, James IV, at the hands of English troops early in Henry's reign, mustered as many as 20,000 men to oppose 3,000 English soldiers. But the English routed the superior force, capturing 1,200 prisoners, among them 500 gentlemen, five barons, and two earls. Three weeks after the battle, the 30-year-old Scottish king died, some said of a broken heart. He left a week-old baby girl, who would become Mary, Queen of Scots, another Scottish victim to the English monarchy.

There are doubtless more desirable ways to handle stress than having a heart attack or falling off a cliff. But in the business world, it might be useful to realize that although the stakes rise at each rung of the ladder, it is rarely worth paying the ultimate price to achieve a goal. Somehow the situation usually follows a logical course, with or without a DOOMER checking out for that Big Boardroom in the sky. Countries and corporations have, and will, survive in spite of such tragedy. They always have.

TAKING TIME OUT: SOME OBSERVATIONS

One way to avoid joining the dubiously honored DOOMER club is to sit back and reflect before flying into hyperdrive. Just as important is the realization that *timing* can be everything, whether in business, sports, or in one's personal life. It is part hard work, part luck, and it rarely allows duplication. Consider the success of the Cabbage Patch Kids dolls—they came out at the right time. Or the success of a mild-mannered, intelligent peanut farmer from Georgia named Jimmy Carter, who became president of the United States in 1976. Timing and events had everything to do with Carter's election—it was in the wake of the Watergate era of scandal—no matter how we would like to believe that relentless, dedicated work made the difference. And yet it was also *how* Carter used his time that shortened the odds that his timing was *right*.

In recent years, the concept of managing the time needed to produce potential successes has become an important aspect of business, one taken up by senior management. A major reason originates from the compacting of time: With computers and telephones, instantaneous communications and opportunities are possible anywhere in the world at any time. Furthermore, because more can be accomplished through our technological wizardry, more time is needed—and demanded—to keep up with the flow of information that is ever increasing.

The 19th-century English politician and novelist Edward Bulwer-Lytton gave the business world a cliché more relevant today than ever before: "Time is money." Add to that the dictum of Lord Chesterfield, the 18th-century English statesman and writer, "Never put off till tomorrow what you can do today," and it has been always clear that people do have some control over what they do at any given time.

Other thinkers have taken time to task, and their observations seem to be as "timely" today as when they were written. Wasting time usually has been universally disdained. Arthur Brisbane, the early-20th-century American journalist, wrote, "Regret for time wasted can become a power for good in time that remains. And the time that remains is time enough, if we will only stop the waste and the idle, useless regretting." The 17th-century English clergyman Thomas Fuller noted that "He lives long that lives well, and time misspent is not lived, but lost." And Johann Wolfgang Goethe, the late-18th-century German poet, dramatist, and philosopher, said: "We always have time enough, if we will but use it aright." The late-16th-century English bard William Shakespeare was perhaps the most graphic in his observations: "I wasted time, and now doth time waste me." How time is spent remains the key. Goethe believed that "It is better to be doing the most insignificant thing than to reckon even a half-hour insignificant." How one uses time also reflects the way a person thinks. Sir Isaac Pitman, the 19th-century English schoolmaster (and the inventor of phonography), wrote that "Well arranged time is the surest mark of a well arranged mind."

Lost time also means lost opportunity in business, as any chief executive knows all too well. Benjamin Franklin, the 18th-century American statesman, inventor, and author, quoted someone notably aware of both time and timing: " 'Improve your opportunities,' said [Napoleon] Bonaparte to a school of young men, 'every hour lost now is a chance of future misfortune.' " Time, of course, has a different meaning to each individual, and some are more successful than others at utilizing it. What appears an eternity to one person may seem a matter of minutes to another. Samuel Johnson, the 18th-century English conversationalist and author, said, "Time, with all its celerity, moves slowly on to him whose whole employment is to watch its flight."

But the last word on time—if there can be such a thing—might fall to the noted 20th-century physicist, philosopher, and father of relativity, Albert Einstein: "When you sit with a nice girl for two hours, you think it's only a minute. But when you sit on a hot stove for a minute, you think it's two hours. That's relativity."

MOBIL OIL AND LORENZO DE MEDICI

Part of the time that chief executives spend is supposed to be on good works for the public—a belief going back millennia and briefly noted in a discussion about the Romans (Chapter 2). Part of the economic thinking that went with the Reagan years involved the role of the private sector in helping communities deal with problems to improve the quality of life, while still maintaining the traditional role of patrons of the arts. The idea stemmed from the apparent belief that the federal government should not be paternalistic—some might think that a contradiction since it could be construed that, indeed, that's why we *have* a federal government. But while many will question this hands-off policy for years to come, especially in light of hands-on federal spending for weapons and defense, it is clear that the former president accidentally stumbled upon a late medieval program, at least in the cultural realm.

Corporations and wealthy individuals have always been

patrons of culture—at one point it was difficult to watch public television without some mention of a sponsorship by Mobil Oil Corporation. Indeed, many donors and contributors have used such "social marketing" as a way of being a good corporate citizen and creating a positive corporate image, the latter a rather useful marketing tool. It also showed that power can be beneficial and, therefore, something that could be trusted. Yet the true heroes of coupling culture with power were the Renaissance princes and popes of Italy. Moreover, they were after the same thing—image-building, good works, and a show of force.

No greater illustration need be found than the powerful Medici family, who ruled Florence for more than half a century by wearing the mask of a family who cared about the lower classes and contributed to the wealth of the city. Their greatest member was Lorenzo de Medici, who held rule over the city from 1469 to 1492. A patron of artists and sculptors, Lorenzo the Magnificent (as he was called) commissioned great works of art, villas, and landscapes, making Florence—and his family—the leading exponent of the Italian Renaissance.

Popes, as well, sponsored artists to show not only their commitment to art and architecture but also their vast power and resources. Pope Alexander VI (1492–1503), whose children (Cesare and Lucretia Borgia) put many a dinner guest in mortal peril, led his Borgia family as a major supporter of great works of art. Not to be outdone, the Medici family, with the same purpose in mind, managed to put two of their own on the papal throne: Leo X (1513–21) and Clement VII (1523–34). One of the most famous papal patrons was Pope Julius II (1503–13), who sponsored many of the famous Renaissance artists. It was Julius who in 1506 commissioned the architect Donato Bramante to replace the old basilica of St. Peter with a new one. Bramante died at the beginning of the project and it was handed over to another giant of the time: Michelangelo. (In Chapter 3 we saw how it was paid for.)

Pope Julius made sure that his beneficence to Rome would be remembered—unlike others whose towering egos barely outlasted their lives (see Chapter 2). At one point, while Michelangelo began painting the Sistine ceiling—a four-year project—Julius brought in a young artist to decorate a series of rooms in the Vatican palace. That artist was Raphael, who along with Michelangelo and Leonard da Vinci formed the triumvirate of the High Renaissance in art, never to be repeated.

It is not known if the large sculptures adorning the lawns of corporations or the marvelous art collections hanging on their lobby walls will outlast the original purpose of contributing to culture and getting credit for it. But rest assured that, today as in the days of the Renaissance patrons and popes, those with money and power will influence culture. Not only are they supposed to, but the U.S. government lately has been encouraging them to do so. Fortunately, everyone wins—something that doesn't always happen when chief executives come to bat.

"DYNASTY," GERMAN STYLE

Wealthy individuals and corporate officers share more than large incomes and commitments to culture: They also strive to appoint their own successors to their accumulated power. This is not new to family-owned companies, who endeavor to keep corporate control in the hands of their kin. Sometimes this works well: Stone Container Corporation has had several members of the Stone family running the business since it was founded in 1926, with its most successful and acquisitive member, Roger Stone, building the company to international preeminence. Other times it doesn't work: The founder of Wang Laboratories tried to establish his son as the next head of the company. But the son wasn't the father—or perhaps never had the opportunity to succeed—and Wang Sr. had to take power back and seek an alternative succession.

Yet we have had Rockefellers and Fords who expanded businesses and brought them to great success and wealth because of family connections. One might even argue that such arrangements over time bring stability and growth. A new idea? Hardly. History has shown that dynasties were viewed as stabilizing forces in society, and every country has had them: the Plantagenets, Tudors, Stuarts, and Hanoverians of England; the Merovingians, Carolingians, Capetians, Valois, and Bourbons of France; the Hapsburgs of Spain and Austria; and the Romanovs of

Russia, to name a few. Ancient Athens had its ruling families, among them the Pisistratids and the Alcmaeonids.

One dynasty that took a small area of land in South Germany and expanded it into an empire over time was the Hohenzollern. And each head of state left his mark on the empire that he helped create, as corporate heads hope to do when they are passed the torch. The castle occupying land in Zollern in Germany at the beginning of the 15th century was hardly noticed in Europe. But through the seizures of church lands, a conversion in religion, and expansion across boundaries, by 1600 the Hohenzollerns had carved out a large landholding to be reckoned with among rival barons.

The great Prussian state was actually created by four Hohenzollern rulers, each with the same goal in mind. Frederick William (1640-88) fought back a Swedish invasion and decided to build a strong army to protect his lands. His armies began mopping up foreign invaders, and with a newly formed civil service the Hohenzollern dynasty maintained strong borders and an efficient state. Frederick's son, Frederick I (1688–1713), took the title "King in Prussia" and began annexing lands that collectively were now called Prussia. His son, Frederick William I (1713–40), more than doubled the size of his grandfather's army and made it the most efficient in Europe—as it remained down to the 20th century, with unpleasant results in 1913 and 1939 (*aka* World Wars I and II).

A by-product of empire-building was strict obedience to authority. Frederick William I made it clear to his people what was expected of them when he said, "No reasoning, obey orders"—he was undoubtedly a kindred spirit of St. Benedict! This led to a complete subordination of the individual to the state, and control from the top into every aspect of life. Indeed, one of the king's favorite lines was "salvation belongs to the Lord, everything else is my business." His son, Frederick II (1740–86) at first seemed to be going in a different direction, what with his love of philosophy, music, and art. But his father would have been pleased once his son took over, for Frederick the Great, as he was later called, became the best soldier in his century and a totally autocratic ruler.

Prussia had grown into a major power from its days under

Frederick William. The army increased from 8,000 to 200,000 in less than 150 years, and land expansion had increased the population from 750,000 in 1648 to 5 million in 1786. No matter what judgment history has placed on Prussia and the rise of Germany, it is clear that the objectives set by the Hohenzollerns were met, regardless of how we view the methods and means. And it was through a dynasty that those objectives could be accomplished. Most corporations groom people for the top spot in much the same way as dynasties of old, hoping to pass on not only the experience learned but the philosophy and vision for how the company should be run. Corporate dynasties are not intrinsically bad— the problem is knowing when an heir in the family is not the right heir for the company, and keeping a close eye on him or her.

SUCCESSORS CAN BE A CLAN OF WORMS

Many successions work nicely and continue the momentum of success as with the Hohenzollern. Walter Cronkite at CBS favored Dan Rather as his successor on the nightly television news broadcast, and Dan so far has survived intact, along with the broadcast. At other times, successors don't live up to expectations—Messrs. Wang Sr. and Junior have already been mentioned. Still, most of the major corporations in America today are too young for a judgment call: IBM and Exxon and McDonald's haven't had centuries under their belts to tell us if the succession is working. But the truly amazing thing about successions is that quite often, even with the proverbial turkey at the top of the corporation, institutions can survive in spite of their inept leaders.

Take the Gordons of Gight Castle in Scotland, a fortified tower house built in the 16th century. The first Gordon, laird of Gight, died in the battle of Flodden Field, previously mentioned, against the English, along with 10,000 other Scots and King James IV of Scotland. One of the laird's sons followed in the father's footfall, dying at the battle of Pinkie in 1547 when the English, under Lord Protector Somerset, once again felt it time to tame the recalcitrant Scots. If that weren't enough, one of the first laird's sons-in-law was murdered, as were three of his grandsons, one being, for a short time, the third laird Gordon of Gight. To round off the grandsons, another one drowned, another died fighting in Holland, and another bit the dust in Flanders. One granddaughter's husband met the fate of a son-in-law: murdered at the hands of his own brother-in-law.

The Gordons of Gight continued this merry dance through disaster from generation to generation, and still Gight Castle survived, even if its successors did not. But it was a female descendant of the first laird—the unlucky 13th in line to be exact—that was the unfortunate undoing of the dynasty, and it wasn't her fault. Lady Catherine Gordon married a gentleman by the name of "Mad Jack" Byron, and then gave birth to a son. In 1787, Lady Catherine was forced to sell Castle Gight to pay off her husband's gambling debts, thus ending the rule of the Gordons. As if some consolation were needed for the finale of 300 years of Gordons at Gight Castle, Lady Catherine's son went on to become the poet Lord Byron.

It is possible that such bad luck for the Gordons was a stroke of fate, if you believe in that sort of thing. The Scottish seer and poet Thomas the Rhymer (c. 1220–97), in one of his prophetic rhymes, had written that "when the herons leave the tree, the laird of Gight shall landless be." As it so happened, the herons did depart from Gight in 1787, to settle in a neighboring tree.

There is no way to predict how a successor will fare once the chief executive hands over the reins of power. Many forces are at work, not the least being economic conditions, competitive conditions, and just plain *timing* that can humble the most brilliant of executives. But it is also evident that a less-than-brilliant corporate head can rule the roost without damaging the company beyond repair, at least for a while. Still, as in the case of the Gordons of Gight, it might not be a bad idea to watch the 13th chief executive carefully—or at least the birds sitting in the tree outside the boardroom window.

BOETHIUS AND THE RETIRING CHAIRMAN

The testimonial dinner. The naming of a chair at the company's favored business school. The oil portrait commissioned for the boardroom. The touches are nice when a company's chairman—

who also may be the chief executive officer, president, or even founder—is graciously put out to pasture, allowing the leading boys (and girls) a shot at the top seat if he hasn't filled it on his own. But unless an alternative route from Mt. Olympus to the Elysian Fields is in the offing—such as the ambassadorship to Britain or the chair of a special governmental commission—it is downright difficult to live only for memories of past glories: Being a hero in your own mind can be very lonely.

The switch from having it all to having nothing at all is an old tale. It was recognized by Boethius (475–524 A.D.), a minister to the Ostrogothic monarchs who ruled over parts of South-Central Europe, and author of several works on philosophy and life. One such work, *De Consolatione Philosophiae* (The Consolations of Philosophy), written while he was in prison awaiting execution on a treason charge, became a virtual textbook on philosophy for medieval scholars, students, and rulers alike. Indeed, it is believed the book may have been translated into Old English by King Alfred the Great, whom we met up with trying to transform England into a literate society (Chapter 3).

Boethius' lament for life rings true for today's departing leaders. He began by noting:

Lo! I sing cheerily in my bright days,
But now all wearily chant I my lays [stories];
Sorrowing tearfully, saddest of men;
Can I sing cheerfully as I could then?

The medieval writer also believed, as well our chairmen emeriti might, that where once there were many stories to tell of success and achievement, there followed a fading of memory, with many triumphs lost to time:

Many a verity in those glad times,
Of my prosperity taught I in rhymes;
New from forgetfulness wanders my tongue,
Wasting in fretfulness, meters unsung.

Perhaps the most relevant part of Boethius' observations concerned the false security brought about by wealth. Chairmen generally make lots of money but often have little time to enjoy it. On the other hand, much of the enjoyment comes from making the money, and it is a hard pill to swallow when the means to accumulate wealth are removed. As Boethius saw it,

> Worldliness brought me here foolishly blind,
> Riches have wrought me here sadness of mind;
> When I rely on them, Lo! they depart—
> Bitterly, fie on them! Rend they my heart.

Now it might be said that most people would not mind swapping a little misery for a wagonload of money. But that is not the point for retiring chairmen. To them, power was the wealth they sought. It is the loss of that particular kind of wealth that hurts so much for one who wielded it. Boethius realized that as well:

> Why did your songs to me, world-loving men,
> Say joy belongs to me ever as then?
> Why did ye lyingly think such a thing,
> Seeing how flyingly wealth may take wing?

A wealth of power—unlike money—can be fleeting. It is part of the reason that the person at the top tries to hand-pick his successor, creating a dynasty of sorts, both to carry on his program and to vindicate his actions as head of the pack. (Ronald Reagan was able to accomplish this with the election of his vice president, George Bush, to the presidency. Parts of the Reagan agenda will no doubt unravel, but the philosophy behind the program remains intact.) Those in business who run their companies need to understand that the power is there for the occupant of the chair, and not a given right of the person who happens to be sitting in it. Once you leave the chair, you leave the power that remains. Boethius understood that very well.

"CAPTAINS OF INDUSTRY": SOME OBSERVATIONS

Ask any little boy on the block what he wants to be when he grows up. Chances are the word *businessman* doesn't come rolling off his tongue. After all, since children inhabit a world where heroes are an essential ingredient, it is more likely that a profession such as policeman or doctor or fireman satisfies the goal in life. (Several youngsters, however, have told this observer that growing up to be He-Man, Pac-Man, Mario & Luigi, Papa Smurf, or a California Raisin might have its advantages.) Although visions of one's future change with age, the image of the businessman—which here includes businesswoman—hasn't attained the degree of respectability found in childhood goals. Indeed, many view such an occupation as merely a means to an end, namely money; and reaching the pinnacle of power in business doesn't carry much glamor or style with it. Because of this, businessmen have received varying critiques over the years. The 19th-century British historian and essayist Thomas Carlyle called them the "captains of industry," a phrase not lost to our present era and those who would be CEO. Others have had thoughts on being a businessman.

Walter Bagehot, the 19th-century English writer, thought that businessmen were most successful at guessing, but not necessarily at thinking things through. "Men of business," he wrote,

> have a solid judgement—a wonderful guessing power of what is going to happen—each in his own trade; but they have never practised themselves in reasoning out their judgements and in supporting their guesses by argument: probably if they did so some of the finer and correcter parts of their anticipations would vanish.

Here's what Thomas Edward Cliffe Leslie, an Irish contemporary of Bagehot, had to say on the subject: "So far, indeed, are men in business from knowing the conditions on which future prices and profits depend, that they are often ignorant, after the event, of the causes of their own past profits and losses."

The great 20th-century English economist John Maynard Keynes also had few kind words for the man of business. He wrote, "Regarded as a means [the businessman] is tolerable, regarded as an end he is not so satisfactory." And yet the businessman is usually totally dedicated to his work, often to the benefit of others. One might even argue that the very beginnings of civilization included the art of buying and selling, an art practiced by the first businessmen. The 20th-century American economist Frank H. Knight did in fact place the businessman on a higher plane than some of his predecessors when it came to motivation and drive: "The businessman has the same fundamental psychology as the artist, inventor, or statesman. He has set himself at a certain work and the work absorbs and becomes himself. It is the expression of his personality; he lives in its growth and perfection according to his plans."

But while the businessman can give of his time to good causes, donate money to help the less fortunate, and contribute free counsel and advice to those in need, respectability still has been long in coming. The 20th-century American editor, author, and critic, H. L. Mencken, noted that the businessman "is the only man who is forever apologizing for his occupation." Perhaps a new bumper sticker for the car is in order: "Have You Hugged A Businessman Today?" Or maybe we should just let one take us to lunch.

LANGUAGE OF BUSINESS A LAUGHING MATTER

Just as science or history or mathematics have their own languages, so too does the business world. From *econometrics* to *random walks* to *sell in* and *sell through,* the words and phrases of business are wrought with meaning that often boggles the minds of the uninitiated. But despite the serious nature of business— money is involved, right?—those of lesser business sense but greater wit have poked fun at the terms and words that make business possible. For example, when we think of a bank, we think of a place that lends money or invests capital. Perhaps. Robert Frost, the American poet, defined a *bank* as "a place where they lend you an umbrella in fair weather and ask for it back when it begins to rain." The 20th-century American comic Bob Hope said a bank was an institution "that will lend you money if you can prove that you don't need it"—many of us have experienced that one.

There are a plethora of business *experts* today advising on everything from how to manage people to how to acquire companies. An early-20th-century U.S. educator, Nicholas Murray Butler, saw an expert as "one who knows more and more about less." The 20th-century Danish physicist Niels Bohr put it succinctly: "An expert is a man who has made all the mistakes which can be made, in a narrow field." (We will run into advisers and consultants in the next chapter.) *Time management,* as we have seen, is also an important concept in today's business world, especially when priorities often defy getting all the work done on time. The 19th-century English philosopher Herbert Spencer noted that time was "that which man is always trying to kill, but which ends in killing him."

Conferences and *committees* are part of the business culture today, and seem to be pretty dry and unassuming activities. Milton Berle, the 20th-century American comedian, defined a committee as a "group that keeps the minutes and loses hours"— too true. And the late American comic and radio personality, Fred Allen, described a conference as "a gathering of important people who singly can do nothing, but together can decide that nothing can be done." Yet conferences and committees are part of a process known as *long-term planning,* which defines company goals and establishes educated guesses on what the future will bring. Ambrose Bierce, the 19th-century American author, thought the future was a convenient place to exonerate present situations when he defined it as "that period of time in which our affairs prosper, our friends are true and our happiness is assured." (We might also add "and when the check arrives in the mail.")

Of course, the purpose behind all this language and the activities that accompany it is to be profitable and successful in business, on a personal level and for the company. Yet not everyone takes kindly to the success of others, especially the one that makes it to the top. Ambrose Bierce again had the last word: *success* is "the one unpardonable sin against one's fellows." And that's a situation found in any profession, and in any language.

SHAMASH, PIRATES, AND ETHICAL BEHAVIOR

No discussion of the view from above in business should close without a notion of ethics, that elusive marble-like sculpture of truth and righteousness that changes meaning depending on who is viewing it. (See Chapter 9.) But if one person's ethics is another person's curse, can it ever be said that common ground can exist for a mode of behavior that harms no one and raises the esteem of those striving to be ethical? Clearly, the temptations are ubiquitous in the business world to throw ethics and honor out the high-rise in favor of a quick buck or a well-placed knife in the back of an enemy. But it should be known that the dilemma of living the ethical life has been around as long as civilization—long enough to establish some strong opinions on what is right and what is wrong.

The scandal among traders at Chicago's Board of Trade and Mercantile Exchange in the late 1980s pointed to a complete lack of ethical conduct. Moreover, coming as it did in the wake of indictments and guilty verdicts on and around Wall Street, it is disconcerting to note that people do not fear jail or the destruction of a reputation—they just work harder at not getting caught. Even for people who grew up in an ethical environment, it seems difficult to apply those teachings to business. True, thinking about stealing a candy bar and thinking about pocketing a million dollars have inherently different risk-and-reward factors. But if ethics are universal, so, too, must be their applications—a notion well-known to the ancient world. For while wheeling and dealing have always led to less than noble business practices, people of long ago subscribed to codes of ethics and justice that would humble the most self-righteous televangelist and corporate executive.

One such code was found in the Shamash Hymn, a 200-line missive to the Mesopotamian god of justice, Shamash. Several versions of the hymn survive today and may have been composed as far back as 4,000 years ago. Its message to our century is of interest. For example, bribery was a definite no-no in the ancient Near East, and was subject to punishment. The hymn noted that "[He]" who accepts a bribe and . . . lets justice miscarry [must] bear his punishment." The other side of the coin was a reward for honesty: "He who receives no bribe but takes the part of the weak, it is pleasing to Shamash, and he will prolong his life"—not a bad reward at all.

How one made investments was also placed into this code of ethical behavior, and it sounds strikingly modern. The hymn asked rhetorically, "What is he benefited who invests money in unscrupulous trading missions? He is disappointed in the matter and loses his capital." That loss occurs by getting caught, and the hymn praised "a circumspect judge who pronounces just verdicts." Much of what ancient businessmen did involved trading goods based on weights and measures, which in turn could lead to unscrupulous practices. The hymn chastised "the merchant who [practices] trickery as he holds the balances, [and] who uses two sets of weights." The judgment here was "the curse of the people," which undoubtedly referred to harsh punishment. But for the "honest merchant who holds the balances [and gives] good weight, everything is presented to him in good measures."

It is becoming increasingly difficult to teach young people today the virtues of leading ethical, honest lives when so many others—usually showcased in the media—throw ethics to the wind in order to make money at all costs. And while religions have certain ethical tenets that go back to "Thou shalt not steal" from the Ten Commandments, the fear of God hasn't worked as a self-policing practice when there is big money to be made on the trading floor or in the boardroom. But to some extent it did work long ago, and invoking a god in the name of justice carried enough weight to make people think twice. Perhaps we need to rethink what a good reward might be for being honest. For the ancients, it was very clear: If you were honest and avoided unethical behavior, the god of justice would promise that "like the water of a never failing spring [your] descendants will never fail." And that means being remembered for knowing right from wrong.

That brings us to a short story: The writer Philostratos described an incident in the life of Apollonios, a holy man and traveler of the ancient world who died near the end of the first century A.D. At one point in his life, Apollonios was captain of a ship during a time when "pirates were infesting the Phoenician Sea." Apollonios learned, to his dismay, that "pirates' agents discovered there was a rich cargo on my ship, and taking me aside they asked me how big my share of the cargo was." He told them that his share was one thousand drachmas, at which point the pirates asked him if he had a house. "A wretched hut on the island of Pharos" was his reply.

The pirates then asked Apollonios if he would like to have "a landed estate instead of the sea, a house instead of your hut and ten times the value of this cargo, as well as escaping from the thousands of misfortunes that assail captains on the surging seas." No doubt running into pirates and their agents was one of those "misfortunes"! Apollonios answered in the affirmative, but noted to himself that he had "no intention of turning pirate just when I had reached the peak of my expertise and had won prizes for my skill." The pirates continued to up the ante, including a bonus of ten thousand drachmas and the right to save the life of any man in his crew he chose, along with his own life. All Apollonios had to do was to "ride under the promontory behind which the pirate ships were stationed." He decided to go along, but he made up his mind not to sell out to the pirates: "I thought to myself that it was not safe to raise objections . . . [and] I therefore promised to render the assistance they wanted."

Apollonios told them to leave, "and I seemed to them all the more convincing as I discussed terms regarding the money, and it was agreed that it would be paid me in cash as soon as they captured the ship." But after the pirates left, this honest captain "doubled the promontory and made straight for open sea." Why didn't he give in, with the promise of a better house and great riches? One answer might be that he didn't trust the pirates or believe that they would keep their end of the bargain. But here is how Apollonios saw it: "I think it took a combination of many virtues for a mere sailor to rise above money and refuse to sacrifice people's lives or hijack the merchants' cargoes."

Combination of virtues: not a bad creed for the business world, especially for those who view it from above.

5

ON BUSINESS: THE VIEW
FROM BELOW

No, it's not pleasant to think of everyone other than top executives as below the realm of high finance, corporate muscle, and other economically elite environments. But quite sincerely—if you are not in the captain's seat, either you are out on deck trying to keep dry or you are climbing the rungs of the ladder, all full of hope. There's nothing wrong with that. In fact, of the billions of people who have occupied the planet since treetops went out as a dwelling-place, most of them have simply gone to work and made the best of their lives. Perhaps that's why it is important to understand how those before our time conducted their *work lives,* since we are talking about "the majority"—it never goes away. At the top, we must admit, the air is still rarified and few are able to breathe it.

THE BISHOP OF ROSS, THOMAS CROMWELL, AND OTHER CONSULTANTS

We might begin just outside the executive suite with those who advise the leaders. These people help the movers and shakers, and seek to stand in the glow of their success, if not on their payrolls. It's a dangerous game. The Watergate scandal during the period 1972–75—which we will explore in Chapter 9—brought down many an aide and adviser to the president and his minions: The glow of power became a blackout rather quickly.

Still, being near the top as a substitute for sitting on top is a very old story. Indeed, consultants have risen to key roles throughout history in business, medicine, education, and government. For while leaders in each field must be proficient in dealing with diverse problems in a variety of areas, the consultant is supposed to be an expert on specific topics. Such advisers rarely surface to the pages of history, but it is not hard to guess what happened when their advice went awry.

In the *Odyssey,* Homer says the famed Trojan horse "was the strategem great Odysseus filled [with] men and brought to the upper [walled] city, and it was these men who sacked Ilion [Troy]." Fine, but who advised to let the horse in? Here's how it happened: The Greeks boarded their ships and pretended to leave Troy; they also left behind the great wooden horse. Homer said the Trojans sat around the horse and "talked endlessly, and three ways of thought found favor: either to take the pitiless bronze [swords] to it and hack open the hollow horse; or drag it to the cliffs' edge and topple it over; or let it stand where it was as a dedication to blandish the gods." Well, we all know what course they took, and one can only guess what happened to the most vocal supporter for dragging the horse into the city. That night, Odysseus and his warriors emerged, opened Troy's gates, and let the awaiting Greek warriors inside. A little more thought about why the Greeks had left a horse and less concern with cheering up the gods might have given the story a different ending.

Some unsung consultants made out fine. Whoever advised Peter Minuit, director general of New Netherland, to plunk down $24 for the island of Manhattan clearly had the consultation coup of the century—any century.

Then there were consultants who made slight miscalculations, often with unfortunate results. No better example exists than Thomas Cromwell. He was the principal minister of King Henry VIII of England (1509–47), a colorful CEO if there ever was one. Besides orchestrating much of the Reformation in England in the king's name, Cromwell also involved himself with what he thought to be a politically strategic marriage for his monarch. The year was 1540, and Henry was hankering for a new wife (No. 4). Cromwell looked to the Protestant lands of Northern Europe and learned that Anne of Cleves was available.

He considered that such a marriage would provide his king with a firm buttress against the Catholic enemies of England. Henry's court painter, Hans Holbein, created an overly flattering portrait of the king's prospective bride—Henry had yet to meet her—and the happy monarch agreed to Cromwell's recommendation.

Once Anne arrived in England, however, the king was not amused at reality's version of the queen-to-be. The "Flemish Mare" (her new nickname) was quickly divorced and sent packing into retirement. Cromwell, who underestimated Henry's penchant for pretty queens, lost his head the same year. If the king had thought about it a moment, he might have seen that it made more sense to behead Hans Holbein, the court painter.

Bad advice has never been an uncommon feature of what experts might offer, nor has their fate been much different than Cromwell's. In 1276, the king of Thomond in Ireland, Brian O'Brien, was routed from his lands by Sir Thomas de Clare. After building a stone castle on his newly acquired property, the victorious Sir Thomas learned that another O'Brien, one called Turlough, was gathering forces for an attack. The defeated king of Thomond went to his conqueror, Sir Thomas, seeking an alliance against Turlough, since they now had a common enemy. It seemed like good advice to Sir Thomas, and the alliance was made. Well, it was a bad idea. The alliance soon collapsed and Turlough defeated Sir Thomas. In anger, Sir Thomas had his "ally," the king of Thomond, arrested and dragged to death by horses. Bad results brought a bad end to Brian O'Brien.

Inappropriate counsel occurred at another Irish castle called Carrigadrohid ("the rock of the bridges"). The castle was, according to a legend, built in the middle of a stream at the whim of a beautiful maiden named Ann O'Carroll. In 1650, during the English civil war, the castle was held by the Royalists and was soon besieged by Parliamentary forces led by Lord Broghill. During the siege, the Bishop of Ross was captured and Lord Broghill asked the cleric to advise the castle to surrender. The bishop had other ideas. Not only did he refuse to advise surrender, he told the castle defenders to hold out to the death. While perhaps a heroic move on paper, in reality there was little practicality in the bishop's actions. Lord Broghill had the bishop hanged on the spot, and the castle surrendered anyway.

It was not a rare occurrence for bad advice to cause a war. In the 6th century, the followers of St. Finian claimed to own a copy of a book made by St. Columba from his own psalter. St. Columba's followers also claimed the copy as their own, and the case was brought before Dermot, king of Meath. The king clearly did not have a grasp of the situation, nor did he realize that St. Columba—nicknamed "Wolf"—was as ruthless as he was pious. Dermot supposedly decided the case by saying "as to every cow belongs a calf, so to every book belongs its copy." Eyebrows probably ascended when this strange muttering came forth, and soon the "Battle of the Books" commenced between the followers of each saint. When it was over, 3,000 of Finian's disciples were dead, or so the story goes. Because of Columba's ruthlessness, he was sent to Scotland to convert the heathen.

Today, consultants and advisers often fear losing their fees or retainers if things go wrong based upon their expert judgment. But at least they can walk away from the situation alive. It wasn't always so, and both adviser and advisee must realize that the expertise proffered today comes from the same source as in ages past: a human being. And regardless of the sophistication of technology to aid our judgments and tighten our margins of error, it will be the human factor that, in the end, is the deciding factor as to whether the advice was wise, or correct.

THOMAS GRESHAM ADVISES THE QUEEN

Advisers offer expertise to leaders in government as well as in business, and they have become increasingly important. One example is the chairman of the Federal Reserve Board in the United States, who sets monetary policy to stabilize the economy and help government and business function effectively. When Paul Volcker took over the chairmanship of the Fed in 1979, it was a time of financial crisis in the United States, with inflation spiraling upwards and the economy falling into one of its greatest slumps since the Great Depression. Through sheer force of will and strong convictions about money supply and prices, Volcker let the world know that he was going to rein in inflation—at all costs. These were many. As he tightened the central bank's grip on the growth of the money supply, inflation continued to rise, with the prime rate passing 21 percent at the end of 1980. The economy continued to slide, as did the chairman's reputation. Businessmen and politicians alike blamed Volcker for worsening economic conditions, but he held firm. When he walked away from his job eight years later, double-digit inflation was all but a memory.

In an earlier era, another shrewd adviser held strong to his beliefs and influenced the way a government controlled its monetary policy during a time of high inflation and economic depression. He was Sir Thomas Gresham (1519?–79), one of Queen Elizabeth I's most able financial ministers. Gresham began his career as a shrewd businessman, accumulating a fortune from the woolen cloth export trade. His accounts from 1546–51 show that he was making a net profit of 15 percent annually, or doubling his capital every five years. In 1551, the booming English cloth trade collapsed due to overproduction, a saturation of cloth in the leading northern European port of Antwerp, inflation, plague, religious persecution, and an exchange rate out of kilter from the addition of base metals to gold and silver coins. It was not a happy year.

Gresham pulled out of trade; others did not and went bankrupt. It became clear to him that England could no longer rely on one export (ancient Athens missed this realization) nor on one market. Moreover, he saw that to establish good credit in international markets, the country had to instill confidence in its currency and in its government. In 1560, with Queen Elizabeth I newly installed on the throne, Gresham warned her in what is now a famous phrase, that "bad money drives out good." He observed that coins with an honest content of metal is hoarded or exported; coins that are debased and cheapened are used for everything. And that included taxes, meaning that the state would in fact be "paid in its own coin."

The currency had been debased during the reigns of Elizabeth's relatives: father, Henry VIII; half-brother, Edward VI; and half-sister, Mary. At Gresham's urging, the coinage was restored. It did not cure inflation, which continued (as we saw in Chapter 2) because population growth and importation of gold and silver outpaced production of goods. But it brought stability to the currency and higher ratings for England in the international markets. Gresham also saw the need to establish an institution where ownership of shares or goods could be exchanged, as well as the sale and purchase of commodities. Using the financial institutions in Antwerp as a model, he founded the Royal Exchange in 1566. Seventeen years later, the Exchange issued the earliest insurance policy. (A gilded grasshopper—Gresham's crest—can be seen on the building today.) The bold moves of Thomas Gresham helped pay off most of the heavy government debts accumulated by previous reigns; he also helped balance the budget.

Paul Volcker's achievements and Thomas Gresham's sterling reputation are the result of the advisers' working against the conventional wisdom—or safety—of their historical times. When such recommendations work out well, so much the better for the advisers' standing in the history books.

"TO CREATE LAWYERS":
SOME OBSERVATIONS

There is another group of professionals who, with their cousins the consultants, hover around corporations and the beltways of governmental and corporate headquarters and power centers: lawyers. They, too, vie for top dollars from potential clients, but in their case a credibility problem exists: Lawyers get minimal respect from the public, least of all from those who have had to retain one in order to enter that legal arena known as the *court of law*. We can guess that the profession will continue to elicit the ire of those who see lawyers as overpaid, underworked, and out to win more for themselves than for their clients.

Unfortunately, lawyers have never had it good, at least outside of court, and the law students of the world need to take note that there is little hope the profession will ever be smiled upon favorably. When the 13th-century English philosopher and scientist Roger Bacon wrote about the degeneracy of his society, he included among his list of evil influences the "wily lawyers who destroy everything with their counsels." And when Shakespeare wrote about Cade's Rebellion of 1450 in *Henry VI (Pt. II)*, his suggestion for establishing a better England came from a character who said: "The first thing we do, let's kill all the lawyers."

Others of greater or lesser fame have taken potshots at legal eagles. In her book *The Mill on the Floss,* the 19th-century English novelist George Eliot described the devil as "a being powerful enough to create lawyers." Hell seems to come up frequently when thinking about those who plea before the bar. Robert Burton, the early-17th-century English philosopher and writer, wrote that "our wrangling lawyers are so litigious and busy here on earth, that I think they will plead their clients' causes hereafter, some of them in hell." Ever since the Watergate scandal of the mid-1970s in America, when lawyers were breaking the law in droves, doubts continue to linger as to how honest a lawyer can really be. One anonymous saying explains it: "A lawyer must first get on, then get honor, and then get honest." Unfortunately, the last part of this equation too often gets put on hold.

It is the lawsuit, of course, where the lawyer finds his life's blood. But it is this same vehicle that plays havoc with defendant and plaintiff alike. Our previously quoted friend, the 19th-century American journalist Ambrose Bierce, looked at a lawsuit this way: "A lawsuit is a machine which you go into as a pig and come out of as a sausage." Once in court, Bierce felt that lawyers were merely those "skilled in the circumvention of the law." Jeremy Bentham, the 18th-century English professor and philosopher, believed that lawyers brought contempt upon themselves because, win or lose, they still got paid and were never responsible for their actions. He wrote: "Lawyers are the only persons in whom ignorance of the law is not punished."

Money, of course, is the obvious cause of consternation among clients who often pay astronomical fees with the hope of obtaining justice somewhere among the bills. And the longer a lawyer practices his craft, the higher his fees become—presumably because his knowledge of the law, and of how to win cases, has increased over time. Not everyone buys the argument. Benjamin H. Brewster, the early-20th-century American clergyman, supposedly wrote a saying about such increases in fee: "A lawyer starts life giving $500 worth of law for $5, and ends giving $5 worth for $500." But when all is said and done, as long as there are laws to be made, obeyed, or broken, there will be those who must write them, prosecute them, and defend them. Fortunately, some kindness has been found for the lonely lawyer amid past thinkers. Charles Lamb, the 19th-century essayist, noted: "Lawyers, I suppose, were children once."

No doubt some would argue that even this requires the burden of proof.

MALPRACTICE IN MESOPOTAMIA

The medical profession, once the mystery of the few and the object of universal admiration and respect, now is confronted with its own problems, notably the high cost of insurance premiums. And where obstetricians once could expect a good living as long as the human race endured and insisted on replicating itself, they now are deserting the field because of enormous malpractice insurance premiums and million-dollar lawsuits. Where doctors tried to use their knowledge to save lives, they now order numerous tests to provide documentation should they be sued.

When has it ever been worse for the frustrated physician? Try about 3,500 years ago, when a Bablyonian ruler named Hammurabi (c. 1792–50 B.C.) instituted a series of almost 300 laws that he said came from the gods. These laws—which were set down to remove numerous social, political, and economic abuses—covered a wide range, from irrigation and trade to marriage and justice. While Hammurabi's code is usually known today because of his infamous "eye-for-an-eye" law, he also had several rules covering the role and practice of medicine. Current physicians' hardships pale beside Hammurabi's requirements.

Doctors today pretty much increase their fees without fear of losing their clientele, especially with health insurance covering much of the expenses. When addressing how much a physician should charge a patient, Hammurabi was perhaps the first ruler to codify the notion of "payment based on worth." He wrote, "If a physician make a deep incision upon a man with his bronze lancet and save the man's life, he shall receive 10 shekels of silver." The fee, however, was not across the board. "If it were a common man, he shall receive five shekels. If it were a man's slave, the owner of the slave shall give two shekels of silver to the physician." The same held for other ailments, thus regulating a profession in a way that would be unheard of today, despite our government guidelines on medical charges.

But what about those multimillion-dollar lawsuits with which modern medicos must contend? How did Hammurabi handle real or imagined errors in medical judgment? Our current docket of doctors should be thankful that all they have to lose is their money and perhaps their licenses, harsh as that may sound. Hammurabi was blunt on this point:

> If a physician make a deep incision upon a man with his bronze lancet and cause the man's death, or operate on the eye socket of a man with his bronze lancet and destroy the man's eye, they shall cut off [the physician's] hand.

It should be mentioned that, despite this punishment, there was a legal code to prevent myriad lawsuits for deliberate malice or manslaughter: "If a man accuse a man, and charge him with murder, but cannot convict him, the accuser shall be put to death." Furthermore—and modern lawyers are not going to like this—a judge could end up paying 12 times the award if he reversed his decision in a case. The judge could also lose his job. So while a physician may have gained comfort in the knowledge that it was risky to accuse him of misdeeds, he nonetheless had to be wary should a patient die or be injured during his ministrations. And once convicted, there was little room for appeal and no reversal of judgment.

Despite the current problems besetting our physicians, it might be reassuring for them to know that once upon a time, a slip of the scalpel had consequences much more serious than the loss of a bank account. Hammurabi ended his laws this way: "My words are weighty, my deeds are unrivaled; only to the fool are they vain; to the wise, they are worthy of every praise." Perhaps the biggest fool in Babylon would have been a doctor seeking appointment as the court physician!

ANGLO-SAXON INSURANCE

Speaking of insurance premiums and payouts for doctors, we should recognize that across the board everyone has been hit with the rising cost of insurance, especially in the areas of personal injury. True, the plight of the doctor is well known because of headlines relating megabuck malpractice lawsuits. But businesses large and small, as well as individuals, are faced with hefty premiums as personal injury lawyers continue plying their trade, seeking injured clients willing to cash in on their misfortunes before courts of law—the fee for the lawyer can be one third of the take. Gimmicks such as no-fault insurance have been tested to reduce the prodigious costs of a litigious society bent on profiting from physical mishap. But until the judicial system moves to change a culture run amuck in court cases, insurance premiums will remain at a premium.

Trying to gain redress from a grievance is as old as Cain and Abel, and we have seen Hammurabi's code and its attempt to set a sliding scale of compensation on wrongdoing, including actions at law against physicians. One interesting approach to the problem of compensation was also found among the Germanic tribes of Western Europe during the early medieval era. These warlike peoples—the Angles, Saxons, and Jutes—filled a void left by the disintegrating Roman Empire in the 5th century. Since a warlike nature could often result in harming or killing a fellow warrior, these Anglo-Saxons came up with a system of reparation: the *wergeld*.

Wergeld was literally a person's worth—his value in money should he be wounded or killed—to be paid to him or his family by the injurious party. Worth was determined by one's position in society—a notion touched upon by Hammurabi. The ruling Saxon chieftain or king and his family had the highest wergeld. In the Anglo-Saxon kingdom of Wessex in England this was around 1,200 shillings per person, an enormous sum in the 8th and 9th centuries. The Anglo-Saxon nobility consisted of a class of wealthy knights owing service and allegiance to the king. These knights, or thegns, each had a wergeld of 600 shillings. At the bottom of the scale of freemen were ceorls, who owned land and served a lord. Their wergeld was 200 shillings. Finally, slaves had no wergeld, but that did not mean they were moving targets. Slaves could be valued at eight oxen, giving them a value that made ceorl and thegn think twice before bumping one off.

The wergeld was a legal definition that allowed a court of law to rule in cases of injury or death. This lump-sum penalty could ruin a guilty party; on the other hand, it was a fixed amount and not the astronomical numbers today's lawyers seek for their clients. To the modern mind, this system of worth based on class may seem barbaric and antidemocratic. After all, most civilized nations promote the ideal that all people are created equal under the law, regardless of wealth or advantage. Still, there might be merit in setting rates for particular injuries or circumstances of death—these apart from penalties of incarceration. Lawyers may not be ecstatic at the prospect of fixed rewards, but judges and juries might find immediate benefit in trying cases that would last several days instead of several years.

The Anglo-Saxons used the system for five centuries. It may have been a high price for swift justice, but no complaints have come down to us about costly, 9th-century insurance premiums.

GOING TO WORK: SOME OBSERVATIONS

Let's face it, not everyone is a lawyer, doctor, or consultant (although most of us have some kind of insurance). For the majority of humans meandering about the planet in the late 20th century, the name of the game is simply going to work, and it makes sense to explore the very aspects of work and labor we partake in each day. Work, as well we know, can often be tedious, tiresome, unrewarding, and downright burdensome. Sir James Barrie, the turn-of-the-century British dramatist and author of *Peter Pan,* quipped that "nothing is really work unless you would rather be doing something else." Peter seemed to always have something else to do in Never-Never Land.

Since it is a fair guess that most people would indeed "rather be doing something else," going to work does not rank high on the list of praiseworthy activities by those humans so employed. Nevertheless, work is what most people do in order to survive, whether they like their occupations or not. Some people have actually found it a worthwhile endeavor. The famous 19th-century poet and artist William Morris saw work as one of

the two virtues of life: "Give me love and work—these two only."
Other thinkers have pondered the meaning of work. Joseph
Conrad, the Polish-English author, noted brusquely: "A man is a
worker. If he is not that he is nothing." The American clergyman and poet of the 19th and early 20th century Henry Van
Dyke saw work more as one's lot: "Heaven is blessed with
perfect rest but the blessing of earth is toil."

But if work is a given, what exactly does it give? To some,
work has represented a noble activity for mankind. Calvin
Coolidge, the 30th U.S. president, was not so silent when he said
"Work is not a curse; it is the prerogative of intelligence, the
only means to manhood, and the measure of civilization."
Benjamin Franklin, the 18th-century statesman, philosopher,
and scientist, would have concurred, and he saw work as
nobility itself: "A ploughman on his legs is higher than a
gentleman on his knees."

Work—hard work—also has represented the road to
achievement. The turn-of-the-century American inventor of the
light bulb and moving pictures, Thomas A. Edison, pinpointed
the reason for his success: "I never did anything worth doing by
accident, nor did any of my inventions come by accident; they
came by work." Just doing the job will always find acceptance,
but not among those like Edison who strive for greatness. Elbert
Hubbard, the late-19th-century American author, saw it this
way: "Folks who never do any more than they get paid for, never
get paid for any more than they do."

The alternative to working, of course, is not working, but
this has rarely been viewed as a desirable goal, even among
those who look for fortune and freedom from financial worry.
Edison said that "as a cure for worrying, work is better than
whiskey," while the 17th-century English bishop Richard Cumberland observed that it is "better to wear out than to rust out."
Perhaps simply viewing work as a necessary part of the human
experience is the easiest way to cope with the day-to-day grind
that must go on if people are to make their way in the world. Or
maybe there is some very old ground for common agreement—at
least since the time Adam kissed his wife good-bye and went off
to the fields—as expressed by the turn-of-the-century English

humorist Jerome K. Jerome when he wrote: "I like work; it fascinates me. I can sit and look at it for hours."

CATHERINE THE GREAT AND THE RIGHTS OF WORKERS

Throughout history, there has been a steady struggle between those who work for a living and those who live off the working. Even in the 19th century, when the union movement brought forth the promise of employees having a say in the workplace, the iron hand of management always made its mettle felt, especially around payday. Workers nonetheless still feel the need to organize. When President Reagan fired more than 11,000 members of the professional air traffic controllers organization, he no doubt hoped the control towers would be free of organized labor. The president may have been miffed to learn later on that the nearly 13,000 replacements put together, of all things, a union.

History has seen hundreds of revolts by peasants and workers longing to improve their lot and gain more control over their lives. More often than not, armed conflict became the only recourse—witnessed numerous times in Britain, the United States, and various other parts of the civilized world. One interesting manifestation of the worker-manager conflict was the Pugachev revolt during the reign of Catherine the Great, Empress of Russia from 1762 to 1796. What made the revolt notable was that the great lady may have helped sow the seeds that grew up to try to supplant her.

By 1765, Catherine—who assumed the throne after her unpopular husband, Peter III, was deposed and murdered—realized the Russian economy consisted of an agricultural base mired in medieval feudalism, with lords owning serfs and any incentives for increased productivity all but nonexistent. (This should not be confused with the situation today; the Soviets still lack incentives though there are no serfs—in name anyway.) Because of the power of the nobles, Catherine proceeded slowly to aid the serfs, sharing the aristocrats' fear of a disrupted economy should the workers be freed and allowed to migrate to the cities. She did forbid serfdom in the towns she founded, and she outlawed the purchase of serfs for factory labor by resurrecting an edict of Peter III. Yet Catherine gave numerous land grants to her favorite generals, administrators, and lovers, and while she tried to curb cruelty to serfs by their landlords, she also forbade serfs to petition her with their grievances.

The workers may have been encouraged by her moves, but clearly she did not move far enough. Between 1760 and 1769, 30 landlords were killed by their serfs, and at about the same time there were 40 peasant revolts. Finally, in 1772, a disaffected cossack named Emelyan Pugachev proclaimed he was Peter III, that he had not died, and that he wanted his throne back. About 20,000 serfs, escaped prisoners, forced laborers, and peasants throughout Russia rallied to his cause and marched toward Moscow, killing and plundering along the way to make the point stick. At first, Catherine did not take him seriously, but as Pugachev gained followers and victories, she allied herself with the nobles, who soon repressed the rebellion. Pugachev and his lieutenants were executed, and the revolt actually strengthened the alliance between Catherine and the aristocrats she so often challenged.

Russia remained a feudal state until the 20th century, although the vestiges of the past, combined with a noncompetitive economic system, have kept the country close to its 18th-century progress in production. Had Catherine allied with the peasants rather than the patricians, Russia might have emerged with America as the second 18th-century experiment in rule by the people. That, however, could not have happened under Catherine the Great. As her contemporary, Germany's Frederick the Great, observed: "If Catherine were corresponding with God she would claim at least equal rank." No inferiority complex there.

As Russia, China, and other countries emerging into a 20th-century economy struggle with the changing role of workers, it will become increasingly important to understand the relation between work and productivity. A country's wealth directly correlates with the output of its workers, and that means figuring out how to keep them happy, secure, and worth their effort. It will be a challenge for all countries as technology puts more demands on certain skills and abolishes many manual tasks traditionally performed by humans. The trick will be to discover the correct balance without the need for walkouts or revolts. Violent solutions have always been short-lived; those people directly involved have been short-lived, too.

THE NFL AND "BREAD AND CIRCUSES"

It has been observed that workers have the need to organize since they share similar plights, and what might be unfair for one is probably unfair for most. In the United States, there are organized groups for every imaginable type of work, from pilots and plumbers to doctors, dentists, and dockworkers. Some fields of work are more dangerous than others: sweeping streets may carry less risk than topping off the television antennae on a high-rise apartment building. Such high-risk workers usually have greater demands because of their work, which one might argue is understandable given the odds of injury or a shortened career. But such rights are a modern phenomenon; in earlier times, it mattered not what you did for a living, only that you did it efficiently and without complaint, with any just rewards coming in a heavenly life, not an earthly one.

The strike by National Football League players in the United States in 1987 might be viewed as a case of high risk and no rights. The football players' position centered not only on the rights of players but their wages. True, many of the players made more in one game than the average U.S. citizen earns in a year, but the sport had become increasingly popular and players felt they could assert themselves. The argument seemed to run that since the average "playing time" of an NFL player is about four years, it was essential to cash in while they were on the field. The owners felt that the players were pampered pups voluntarily joining a profession they knew carried high risks, high rewards, and no dearth of replacements. No one forces someone to become a football player.

We can observe all this from a lost era where a public also enjoyed violent sport, high-paid athletes, and endless chatter about "the games." Only in that world, the stakes were not the starting position versus the injured reserve list. The stakes were life and death.

The Roman poet and wit Juvenal (c. 55–127 A.D.) would have found late-20th-century America a familiar place. His ultimate reproach of his own Roman citizens—that they only cared about "bread and circuses"—is not far from our own weekend, even nightly, preoccupation with sports and food. In his day, it was the gladiatorial games that commanded the interest of emperor and plebeian alike. There were other games besides gladiatorial ones—charioteers competed driving teams of horses and could reap fortunes if successful—but it was the spectacle of watching men and beasts kill each other that became part of daily Roman life.

Today, we have the NFL players union. Almost 2,000 years ago, there were the troupes of gladiators (*familia gladiatoria*) run by a manager. A troupe would contract with the rabble of society to became gladiators, with the promise of wealth if victorious. But these killers had no rights. They traveled wherever the manager arranged a contest, fought when and how they were told, and about half of them died in any given contest. In Rome, it was worse. Gladiators were chosen from prisoners and condemned men. They usually fought to the death, although an enthusiastic crowd could ask the emperor for a "thumbs up" on a brave but fallen warrior.

Our players today say a prayer for victory before the game, with after-game plans already made once the contest is over, win or lose. The Roman gladiators saluted the emperor and yelled "Hail, Emperor, those who are about to die salute thee!" Post-contest plans were hardly considered. The emperor Augustus Caesar (27 B.C.–14 A.D.), in a list of his accomplishments, tells us that he sponsored eight gladiatorial games in which 10,000 men fought. He also staged 26 wild-beast shows in which 3,500 animals were killed.

Football players today can retire when they want to, depending on their contracts and health. The Roman gladiators could only survive the arena by winning a wooden sword: an honor that meant liberation. Few did. Some aggressive gladiators—perhaps the forerunners of our linebackers—actually refused it. A gladiator named Flamma turned the sword down four times. Gladiators who contracted with troupes or for their cities could also receive pensions, but in a very different way than our own pigskin professionals. Pensions were based on merit and what a gladiator achieved when he was active. Thus, one Aureliuim Leucadius, in a manuscript from 267 A.D., asks for a pension based on "the victory and crown which I won at the sacred Iselastic Games . . . 180 drachmas per month [for 48 months]."

Our NFL players should thank their lucky stars they can at least get out of their sport alive; getting out rich is another story. Yet it reminds us that workers and their organizations have come a very long way from the days when rights were few and the state controlled the lives and destinies of its people. This unenviable status was in spite of the fact that some workers engaged in activities that were popular with their fellow citizens. Today it is easier for us to accept large salaries given football and basketball players than the income levels of lawyers and politicians: We get more enjoyment out of watching the former, less benefit out of observing the latter.

MANAGEMENT BY MUSSOLINI

We have already noted that there is natural tension between those who work and those who own. Even with the enormous gains achieved by the century-old modern labor movement, conflicts arise over who rightly deserves the fruits of corporate success. This struggle in turn has led to differing economic theories and the political framework they engender. Although in the United States the theories run from equal opportunity and equitable proportioning of earned wealth to governmental intervention, the bastion of capitalism maintains an ideal that tries to accommodate both the demands of labor and the concerns of capital.

Communists view private capital with hostility (at least in theory) and the result of a political system dedicated to destroying the labor class. There has been a softening of late— Marxism is experiencing difficulty in putting bread on the shelf— but the theory is still preached to the masses, although less and less are listening. The Soviet Union was established as a labor state—indeed, labor is the state. But a middle ground was also proposed around the time of Lenin, the theory of the *corporate state,* which strives to abolish the inherent war between capitalism and labor to establish a cooperative effort. This partnership sounds interesting, almost reasonable; it is also the foundation of Facism and in practice it has obtained mixed reviews.

When Benito Mussolini (1883–1945) began organizing his groups of "fasci"—from the symbolic axe-and-rods *fasces* symbol of authority in ancient Rome—his goal was to capture control of the government during the economically depressed years following World War I. By the end of 1923, Mussolini was in charge of Italy, taking the opportunity to put into effect the capital–labor partnership. Following the syndicalist theory of creating a confederation of unions or syndicates to govern the state, Italy was divided into 13 of these so-called corporations: six from labor, six from management, and one for professionals. Through these corporations all labor disputes were to be settled, including wage scales, prices, and working conditions. Strikes were outlawed.

The results of the system were less than successful as a long-term plan. Economically, Mussolini wanted Italy to be self-sufficient, and his campaign to expand the wheat crop resulted in an increase of 70 percent. He also instituted slum clearance programs, set up child welfare clinics, and gloated over the fact that the proverbially late Italian trains now ran on time. But there was a downside to the corporate state: The system was dedicated to preparing for war. Since the state was now the focal point of society—not the individual—it was inevitable that nationalism would foment a belief in Italy's destiny as a world power. That in turn would lead to setting up other fascist states, whether the targeted countries wanted to be such or not.

To keep the state at the center of life, most individual rights were suspended and censorship became a way of life. Economic output was now geared toward rearmament, and the new creed taught all citizens "to believe, to obey, and to fight." The capital–labor partnership worked only for the good of the state. And the economic theory ended up being a fake and a fraud. While on the surface Italy looked prosperous, in fact it was the large landowners and industrialists who made out like bandits at the expense of their labor "partners." Italy was poised for having its own Pugachev revolt; however, Mussolini was no Catherine the Great, and it was World War II that ended fascist Italy.

Today, strikes and labor disputes in democratic societies continue to cause concern among citizens and governments over the rights of workers, managers, and owners. But those very confrontations perhaps are a safety valve, guaranteeing that workers can be heard and even force owners to remedy the problems. Labor crises will not be condoned by management, nor are they desired by most workers. But it means a democratic system is working—imperfect and noisy. We should remember this de spite the inconveniences and harsh words of labor and management during disputes. The trains sometimes run late, but there is also the opportunity for all of us to complain about it.

ST. BERNARD AND THE
THREE-MARTINI LUNCH

Matched against the problems at work, of course, is fun at work and the perquisites that go with a job. Whether it's vacation days, coffee breaks, a company car, or free dental checkups, those who work try to take advantage of the benefits that may come with their employment. One near-sacred activity that has taken on the proportions of a summit meeting is the business lunch, *aka* "power lunch" (*c.* 1985–??), paid for by the company and yearned for by those employees fortunate enough to find a home on a corporate expense account.

Alas, the times they have changed. Gone today are the days of the three-martini business lunch and the big meals and desserts. But it should be noted that while the new tax laws reduced the deductible amount for business entertainment, something else has been at work to curb alcohol and six-course intake: shaping up. It is now a normal practice to take gym bag in hand to work for a daytime workout; business people crowd the pre-dawn streets in jogging outfits and designer earphones, and fitness centers overflow with overflowing figures attempting to pare down—or die in the attempt. In other words, in the abundant land of America at least, its citizens are doing a better job on their bodies to get the job done better.

But avoiding gluttony and the ill effects of gorging and chugging can hardly be attributed to a sudden awareness that pigging out is bad for your health and your livelihood. Medieval monks had problems that mirror any executive's voracious appetite. It was Bernard of Clairvaux (1090–1153), the well-known medieval churchman, who decided to broadcast the problem of gluttony that was currently besieging the holy orders of monasteries. He wanted his readers to remember that monks were supposed to spend their days "with hungry stomachs but not hungry minds," so they could concentrate on the tasks of the monastic life. (His predecessor St. Benedict, seen earlier, would have bought into that as well.) Such abstinence, however, was no longer the case, and Bernard felt that monks had forgotten their role.

"When you come together into one place," he wrote, "this is not to eat the Lord's supper." To his dismay, he saw prayer and study replaced by "nonsense and laughter and words poured forth to the wind." Worse, Bernard observed that "in dining, the ears are fed on as many rumors as the mouth is on food. Completely absorbed in this, one knows no limit in eating." With contempt he observed that "dish after dish is set before one; and in place of meat, those who abstain are served double helpings of fish."

Most business people are aware that heavy meals make it difficult to function, let alone think and remain semiconscious. Imagine the studious monk, trying to work after reaching critical mass at lunch. Temptation was always at work here, according to Bernard. "Everything is prepared with such care and skill by the cooks that, after four or five platters are eaten, the first dishes do not impede the last ones, nor does satiety diminish the appetite." He concluded: "The belly is loaded without knowing it, but variety dispels disgust." Overzealous cooks apparently were just too much for the munching monks. Bernard said that "the exterior appearance of these foods is so treated as to delight the eye as much as the taste"—today we demand such visions at finer restaurants! He went on to say "and when the stomach by frequent belchings announces repletion, still curiosity is not yet satisfied."

Bernard also noted that monks were overusing wine:

> One may see at one meal a cup served half full, thrice and four times; so that, as different wines are more sniffed than drunk and not so much drained as sipped with intelligent relish and quick appraisal, the one that is stronger than the others is finally selected.

Food and wine were pleasures that should not be enjoyed by religious monks, according to Bernard. And the results of overindulgence have cursed both monks and managers. "When the veins are gorged with wine," he wrote, "throbbing in the entire head, to a person thus rising from table what other pleasure is there except sleep?" Next time you go out for lunch during work, be sure to take a copy of St. Bernard with you. It is possible you may still fall asleep, but you won't wake up bloated or with a headache, at least not without a great deal of guilt.

EMPLOYEE REVIEWS BY ONE OF GOD'S CHOSEN

Behavior on the job provides a measurement for where an employee is headed in the company. Most large companies have some type of formal review process whereby the performance of employees is judged against a set of acceptable standards. These reviews often form the basis for future raises and advancement—or demotion and dismissal. Scrutinizing the work of employees from the top to the bottom of any organization is not new. More important, some unexpected things can turn up once a little digging begins to uncover exactly what it is that people do all day long.

It should be no surprise that the review process is an old one, and that we once again turn to one of the greatest organizations of medieval times: the church. This administrative behemoth was supported by bishops and archbishops who managed their territories and provided guidance and counsel to the rulers of principalities, cities, and countries. Part of that management responsibility was the visitation, when a bishop or archbishop would visit a church habitation to find out what problems existed, how the books were being kept, and what needed attending. Beginning in January 1248, a series of visitations took place by Odo, the archbishop of Rouen in France. And the book he compiled on that trip, the *Registrum Visitationum,* is testimony to the observation that even in the most efficiently ordered organizations a few bad apples cling to the branches.

Odo and his entourage first visited the priests of the deanery of Buris. Odo noted "we found that the priest of Pomerevalle is notorious and his bad reputation persists on account of his frequenting taverns; he does not make confession to a penitential priest." It's a good guess the priest was not long in his job. And another priest named William Mesnieres had an "evil odor for his business dealings, possessing farms that he visits so often that divine service is curtailed in his church"—his counterpart today may be found in the employee whose outside interests get in the way of his work. Odo and company also learned of a priest from Basinvalle, "notorious in connection with a woman: Although rebuked by the archdeacon, he persists, taking her to the marketplace and frequenting taverns." (Sounds like the taverns did a brisk business in the 13th century.) Yet another priest, this time from St. Rheims, was found to be "notorious for drunkenness, does not wear a cassock [floorlength garment], plays knucklebones, frequents taverns and often fights there."

The review process must have been dreary for Odo, especially upon learning of the bad behavior of his flock: a priest at Petra Ponte "drinks and plays knucklebones;" Master Walter, a priest of Grandis Curia, "is notorious for excessive drinking;" Robert, a priest of Campenoiseville, "has no cassock." And we shouldn't leave out the priest of St. Martin in the Woods, who "is fond of lawsuits and is a wanderer"—there's a modern equivalent in there somewhere.

But personal behavior wasn't the only problem. Poor management also plagued church establishments, much to Odo's dismay. At the priory of Villacelle, the prioress was a no-show for the visitation, but Odo met with all 22 nuns. There were only supposed to be 20, according to his books, but the prioress had brought in two extra for good measure. Although the nuns thought they had enough food for the winter, it became apparent that they underestimated their needs. Odo also observed that "they did not know how much they owed and were rather ignorant of the state of the nunnery."

Today, reviews are deemed necessary because they provide a snapshot of an organization, showing its strengths, weaknesses, and where improvements can be made. But it's a painful process, often bringing out the worst as well as the best. Come next review, it might be useful to have a good record of achievement that doesn't carry any unwanted surprises. And that means staying away from the taverns and wearing the right cassock.

THE BOSS AND THE DISTURBANCE AT OXFORD

Keeping a clean record is one thing; behaving yourself in front of the boss quite another. Most people put on their best behavior when the boss comes to town or enters the room—after all, survival of the fittest doesn't just refer to blue-footed boobies or Galapagos tortoises. And you would think that people would be extra careful of what they say and do when the "big man" or "big woman" enters through the portal. Often a job could be riding on how one deports oneself or on avoiding a situation that would anger the boss. Unfortunately, such amiable visits don't always materialize despite the best of intentions, and some people go so far as to throw discretion to the winds, especially if the boss and his entourage make it difficult to be polite. Quite often, however, the winds come howling back to blow the indiscreet off their feet.

An example of an unpleasant visit by the boss comes to us from Matthew Paris, one of England's greatest historians (d. 1259), who told of a slight disturbance at Oxford. It seems that the papal legate—a man of great authority representing the Pope and the Roman church—visited Oxford and was entertained at a nearby abbey by the residents. Before breakfast, a group of clerks brought meat and drink to the legate's room and sought entrance. Well, like some protective administrative assistants of this century, the legate's porter "saucily refused admittance to them all, with haughtiness and abuse." The clerks were not overly content with the situation and forced their way in, starting a brawl with the legate's attendants.

While this scuffle was taking place, a hungry Irish chaplain visited the abbey's kitchen seeking food, which was customarily given to him by the monks. Unfortunately, he ran into the legate's chief cook, who not only became angry at the request for a free handout but "threw in [the chaplain's] face some boiling water drawn from the cauldron where fat meat was being cooked." One of the abbey's clerks watched the whole affair and yelled out, "Shame on us to endure anything like this!"—whereupon he grabbed a bow and shot an arrow into the cook, killing him on the spot.

The papal legate heard these various altercations and decided that discretion was the better part of valor—he ran to the church tower and bolted himself in. After sundown, he mounted a horse and with several of his assistants crossed the river and headed for the king of England. The papal legate left behind him a group of angry Oxford clerks, who cried out, "Where is that simoniacal usurer, that plunderer of revenues and thirster for money, who perverts the king, subverts the kingdom, and enriches foreigners with spoil taken from us?"—apparently these were disenchanted members of the organization. The legate and his group finally made it to the king, who was appalled to hear of the events at Oxford. The king quickly sent an armed troop to the abbey, where the clerks were arrested and thrown into jail at a nearby castle. The legate also excommunicated them for good measure.

Self-control is a difficult thing when the boss arrives, especially if you find particular faults with him or believe he doesn't know how to do his job. And while many would love to run him out of town, other ways must be found so that your career isn't jeopardized and the company can continue to keep good people, rather than lose them because of a bad manager. It is a very old situation, but going to the extremes found at Oxford in the 13th century will not work today. Unless, of course, you're good friends with the king.

HEZEKIAH'S TUNNEL

The past and the present differ little when it comes to who wins the accolades for success. Lee Iacocca has been credited with bringing out the Ford Mustang, but obviously there were others more intimately involved with its creation and perhaps more worthy of the praise bestowed upon the former Ford executive. It has always been this way: The Great Pyramid of Cheops (or Khu-fu), king of Egypt some 5,000 years ago, is in truth probably the Great Pyramid of some brilliant architects, planners, masons . . . to say nothing of the tens of thousands who worked on it. And for centuries, Henry VIII of England (1509–47) got credit, whether good or bad, for the Reformation in England—never mind that his chief minister, Thomas Cromwell, and numerous court and county officials, masterminded the whole affair.[1]

Put another way, George Washington may have been the "Father of His Country," but it was numerous "children" who founded the republic and kept it going.

One piece of evidence from long ago comes down to us so we can hear what the actual workers accomplished: a monumental project known as Hezekiah's tunnel. Although Hezekiah was, in fact, the king of Judah in the late 8th century B.C., we have the words of a worker who helped build the tunnel, although he and his mates never reaped the glory of their creation. According to the Old Testament, Hezekiah ordered a tunnel built at Jerusalem to carry water inside the city walls. He received full credit for the feat: "[Hezekiah] made the pool, and the conduit, and brought the water into the city." (II Kings 20:20) And again, "This same Hezekiah also stopped the upper spring of the waters of Gihon, and brought them straight down on the west side of the city of David." (II Chr. 32:30)

Today you can follow the tunnel, which runs over 1,700 feet from the Virgin's spring to the pool of Siloam. It was an engineering marvel, using pickaxes and hammers to chop solid rock in complete darkness, starting at both ends and meeting in the

---

[1] You will recall that Cromwell also masterminded Henry's marriage to Anne of Cleves, thus cutting short his career as a mastermind altogether.

middle. Fortunately, in 1880 a young boy discovered a partially worn inscription some 20 feet inside the tunnel near the pool. Written in classical Hebrew, it tells the worker's side of the story, with nary a mention of the king. The inscription was carved soon after the two work teams met, and begins "This is the story of the piercing through." According to the writer:

> While [the stone-cutters were swinging their] axes, each towards his fellow, and while there were yet three cubits to be pierced through, [there was heard] the voice of a man calling to his fellow.

If this is accurate, one team apparently heard the other team digging nearby.

Eventually, the teams met. "On the day of the piercing through, the stone-cutters struck through each to meet his fellow, axe against axe." The writer was clearly proud of their accomplishments: "Then ran the water from the Spring to the Pool for twelve hundred cubits, and a hundred cubits was the height of the rock above the head of the stone-cutters." A cubit is about 18 inches.

So we have a message from the people behind the accomplishments, some 2,700 years ago. Maybe we should have similar inscriptions for the modern-day implementers of our dreams and schemes, rather than just the plaque naming the mayor and his commissioners. It seems only fair.

FLIPPING BURGERS AND THE 12-HOUR SHIFT

As the population grows older and the ranks of the young thin, employers worry about a contraction in the work force. After all, planning for the vitality and future of a company means nurturing and training younger employees. Coupled with this demographic reality is a social reality: Many of the young want money, comfort, and leisure, but are not really keen on earning it. Moreover, entry-level jobs are not always viewed as opportunities to learn and grow, but mere drudgery with low pay and long hours—Hezekiah's tunnel diggers would probably agree, but there wasn't much they could do about it.

A quick jump into the past may enlighten our young workers who believe they have it rough and tough flipping burgers and bagging groceries. It is a lesson that perhaps suggests we have given ourselves so much protection from abuse and hardship we have forgotten what working hard truly means. To begin, most historians agree that the industrial revolution began in England, and was going full force in the 18th century. Expanded markets, new technology, uninvested profits, an available labor force, and a government that smiled upon business were the winds that fanned the flames of industry. But to keep those flames burning workers were required, especially those of the unskilled variety, to maintain the factories. This meant reaching into the total population for labor—men, women, and children— and the latter two suddenly found themselves driving England's industrial revolution.

Child labor was not new to England or Europe, especially in the areas of agriculture or trade apprenticeships. English children were considered useful workers, and no social stigma—or pangs of conscience—was attached to their working in factories. And work they did. Once machines were simplified for easy use, children as young as five were employed. Local authorities strapped for money to keep orphanages running welcomed the chance to ship children off to factories, sometimes 80 or 100 at a throw. Some orphanages also demanded that employers take one idiot (their term) for every 20 youngsters—a cruel version of our equal-opportunity laws. Children worked 10 to 14 hours each day. They usually lived in groups, and since factories tried to keep 12-hour shifts going, beds were occupied around the clock. Discipline involved beatings and, along with disease, took many a youth's life. Children were maimed or deformed by factory accidents or the strenuous nature of the work they performed. Some actually committed suicide.

The direct beneficiaries of this system were factory owners, who reaped handsome profits as their enterprises cranked out products. The laborers, however, remained as poor in 1800 as they were in 1700. Alcoholism increased dramatically, and pauperism spread rapidly as workers were dismissed if they could not keep up with the vigorous demands. England did develop a conscience, and reformers succeeded in passing child labor laws that have brought us to a reasonable state of affairs today for the young who work. But the primary difference between today's youthful worker and those children forced into hard labor centuries ago can be found in the word "opportunity." There was little hope for the young worker of the industrial revolution who eked out an existence for his family or himself. Each day brought him closer to nothing other than a broken body and the possibility of the poorhouse.

Today, the young are able to start at jobs that can provide direct benefits for future career opportunities, if they are willing to learn, ask, risk, and work hard. Working at the fast-food restaurant or a department store isn't the same as running a billion-dollar corporation. But companies that succeed usually are run well from bottom to top. And those workers who do well at the bottom have nowhere to go but up. That was rarely the case 200 years ago.

HOT SUMMERS AND DUST BOWLS

Perhaps the oldest occupation—which gave birth to civilization—is farming. It is also one of the most precarious jobs, since not only can markets determine a good or bad year as with other businesses, there is also the uncertainty of Mother Nature and her ability to destroy a livelihood in a matter of days. The summer of 1988 will be remembered as one of despair and devastation for many of America's farmers—a tragedy that occurs frequently around the world but was brought home to Americans because it happened in their country. The months of June and July brought constant 100 degree-plus temperatures (F) and little or no rain to much of the grain belt. Cattle were slaughtered because they could not be fed.

The plight of the farmer has been an ongoing struggle with the land, the environment, and the government—a struggle many believe cannot be won. When crops fail, loans cannot be repaid, seed and machinery cannot be purchased, and farm ownership becomes jeopardized. It is easy to overlook this situation when grabbing a loaf of bread or an ear of corn off the supermarket displays. But perhaps unknown to the post-war generations in the United States, this kind of hardship occurred during the lives of their fathers and grandfathers. And the panacea then was not more rain—it was more government.

By the 1920s, farmers were stuck with huge debts from overexpansion during World War I and a market of depressed prices for their products. Nominal net farm income from 1919 to 1928 fell from $9.5 billion to $5.3 billion. Yet President Coolidge refused to grant aid to the farmers, twice vetoing relief bills. "Farmers have never made money," he said. "I don't believe we can do much about it." The Depression in the 1930s made matters worse. Markets dwindled, debts mounted, and evictions were an everyday occurrence. To make matters worse, a large area of the Southern Great Plains became a dust bowl as winds eroded the topsoil and forced thousands of families to move.

Today we have "Farm Aid" concerts—peaceful, thoughtful gatherings to raise money for beleaguered, yet law-abiding, farmers. In 1933, Edward A. O'Neal, head of the Farm Bureau Federation, told the U.S. Senate: "Unless something is done for the American farmer we will have revolution in the countryside within less than 12 months." He was not far off. Farmers fought evictions and often gathered in mobs to assault officials and bankers. The farm community was on the brink of nationwide violence. But then a new wind blew over the barren plains—FDR and his "New Deal." President Franklin Delano Roosevelt and his administration set up the Agricultural Adjustment Administration (AAA) in 1933 to deal with the farm problem. By cutting back production, the AAA hoped to raise prices and create domestic need. Farmers were paid subsidies to take acreage out of production, a practice inherited by today's farmers.

On first glance, it might have seemed heartless for a government to cut food production at a time when a large proportion of the country's people were going hungry. But as Secretary of Agriculture Henry A. Wallace said, "Agriculture cannot survive in a capitalistic society as a philanthropic enterprise." Although other laws were enacted to help the farmer, millions of families had to be resettled. Farmers were not to prosper for any length of time again until the onset of World War II.

Few would take issue with the farmers' need for help today. But it would be useful to work out peaceful solutions rather than to wait for another war to lend a helping hand. And that means getting help from a government which prides itself on wanting to end poverty, feed people, and keep them healthy. The alternative is to create a monopoly (already in the works) of a few megafarms controlling most of the production and market for food. In this way, prices could be hiked when disaster strikes on the farm. It would mean the end of the small farmer who helped found this nation, but as is too often the case, emotionalism doesn't solve the problems at hand. Much depends on how a government views itself: Is it a protector of the ideals of the country, or a dispassionate implementer of what works best for the country? Tough choice.

THE FARMS, THE FORESTS, AND CHARLES III

As mentioned above, many countries have suffered disasters on the farm, at which time there is usually a hue and cry to set things aright and keep the population fed. This is a reactive approach to agricultural problems—we all eat what the farms produce, but farming is not a hot enough topic in governmental circles until the weather makes it hot. Then it's too late. But there have been times when governments tried to solve agricultural problems beyond the bandage approach of bureaucratic decision-making. We might explore such an instance to see what happened.

During the waning years of the 18th century when America and France waged revolutions for greater freedom and equality, Spain was struggling to rise out of its past stagnation—and shed the tattered glories of colonization—in a bid to join the modern world. The plight of the farmer in Spain found a friend in the enlightened king, Charles III. This Spanish monarch (1759–88) put in a full day's work, rising at 6 A.M., working until lunch, meeting with ministers and dignitaries, hunting in the afternoon, continuing to work, eating dinner at 9:30 P.M., and heading off for bed after prayers. Charles was faced with an agrarian nightmare when he mounted the Spanish throne. Much of the land in Spain was owned by titled families or ecclesiastical houses, who jealously guarded their rights. At the same time, there was very little incentive to work in Spain—begging was a chief occupation. Successive Spanish governments also unwisely deported those who did work—Moors, Jews, and Moriscos—effectively ensuring a stagnant economy for centuries.

But Spain awakened under Charles III. Where Spain had once been gold-rich and grain-poor, Charles now imported grain and seed for areas of Spain that had become inhospitable to agriculture. Through his ministers, Charles also lent money to farmers at low interest rates, using his revenues from vacant ecclesiastical lands—money known as *montes pios,* or pious funds. Noting the great expanses of waste that had once been forest, the king ordered communes to plant a certain number of trees each year, a move that led to an annual holiday known as Arbor Day, which is still held in various parts of the Western world. Charles also moved to break up the old landed estates, creating new farms with built-in incentives for growth and increased production.

To populate vast areas of unclaimed land, Charles imported foreigners, creating some 44 villages and 11 towns that prospered over time. He also commanded that canals be dug from rivers to irrigate arid land, and new roads were built to link Spanish towns—and their ensuing trade—together. With this improvement in industry and trade, the Spanish economy rebounded after centuries of decay. As money poured into the royal coffers, the benefits of such wealth became apparent—Charles was able to have water directed from Spanish mountain ranges into 700 fountains, for use by local residents. Yet despite reforms, the poor remained poor and the middle classes gained in wealth and power (an old story with most reform movements implemented by well-meaning governments). Nonetheless, Charles left Spain in a far better state than it was left to him.

Farmers have never had it good over time, with the dust bowl of the 1930s serving as a prime example. Charles III of Spain recognized the uncertainties of living off the soil and tried to help his agrarian people. In the heat of other state and international problems, he never forgot the farmer. We might consider his agenda as we begin to enter the last decade of our own century, with more people to feed than ever before in the history of the planet.

MONEY, MONEY, MONEY: SOME OBSERVATIONS

What all this boils down to—this working day in and day out regardless of personal goals, lack of any goals, or in utter abandon—is *money*. Not just the accumulation of wealth for all it can bring, as we saw in Chapter 2, but the necessity to earn in order to survive. The early-19th-century English clergyman Caleb Colton noted that "the secret of making money is saving it," and he went on to say that it didn't really matter what one's income was, "but the relation of his expenditures to his receipts, that determines his poverty or wealth." Today, when it comes to personal spending, Americans are as adept as homing pigeons heading home. Indeed, Americans are about the worst savers of their money in the industrial world, putting aside a paltry 3 to 4 percent of their income, while their exporting cousins in Japan and Germany set aside around 15 and 13 percent, respectively. It could be argued that America has become a self-indulgent society with a rather Epicurean view that today is what matters: Tomorrow will just have to take care of itself.

Irresponsible? Frightfully myopic? A lot of past commentators on frugality and wise spending would respond with a resounding "Yes!" The English editor and literateur Edward Parsons Day wrote a century ago: "To acquire wealth is difficult, to preserve it more difficult, but to spend it wisely is most difficult of all." Most people, of course, would jump at the chance to make lots of money, and not a few live and spend as if they do. State lotteries that anoint instant millionaires and fuel the burning desire to attain sudden wealth form the 18th-century English dramatist Edward Moore's penultimate vision: "I am rich beyond the dreams of avarice."

One of the hardest things to do is to plan for retirement—a time when income could be scarce or nonexistent despite the desire to maintain an acquired standard of living. Samuel Johnson, the 18th-century English lexicographer and author, put it quite succinctly when he wrote, "the first years of man must make provisions for the last." The 17th-century English divine Thomas Fuller had an earthier way of saying it: "It is better to have a hen tomorrow than an egg today." Investment for the future does more than sustain a particular way of life; it allows a freedom from wanting the bare necessities. Agesilaus, the 4th-century B.C. king of Sparta, noted that "by sowing frugality we reap liberty, a golden harvest": something to consider when the golden years creep up.

Knowing what to do with money—controlling the temptation to unload it—is not an easy skill for anyone to acquire. No doubt there is a bitter pill to swallow when someone who makes a lot loses a lot: The poor have already been there, but the well-off are ill-prepared for such a loss. The 17th-century English bishop Richard Cumberland put it thusly: "Abundance is a blessing to the wise; the use of riches in discretion lies; learn this, ye men of wealth—a heavy purse in a fools' pocket is a heavy curse." Hanging on to the heavy purse requires the exercise of a human proclivity not always fully developed by adulthood: self-control.

CREDIT CARDS IN THE COLONIES

Self-control: hardly a hopeful goal at the turn of the 20th century when you take one quick look at how consumers make purchases. For one might quickly conclude that the world is turning plastic. The credit card has become such a way of life that currency—both paper money and metal coins—is more a burden than a boon. This dependency on credit cards, of course, has turned many clear-headed people into unknowing debtors, caught between the ease of purchase and the crunch of monthly finance charges. But one thing is certain: The options of making purchases now or in advance are too strong to change, regardless if there is cash-on-hand to cover those purchases. Moreover, currency is figuring less and less in the daily transactions between parties. At most, it has become a very temporary medium of exchange.

Witness the person who cashes a $50 check in the supermarket, fills a basket with groceries, and pays for them with the $50 in cash. The shopper probably held onto the actual currency less than an hour.

Back in Colonial times in America, hard currency was the desired medium for exchange. It was also a means to get out of debt; credit cards today have the reverse effect. And it was the desire for currency among the populace—especially the rural population—that caused frequent fighting with the representatives of the British crown who were the ruling administrators in each colony. One colonial group affected by cash crunches were the farmers, who were usually in debt for their land but also for supplies and other items impossible to manufacture at home. The only way to repay these debts was with paper money, but supplies of currency were either scarce or undervalued when in abundance. And when money was in short supply or worth little at all, taxes, rent, and loans went unpaid. It was then that many a tax collector would be tarred, feathered, and ungraciously escorted from a village or town.

One battle over currency occurred in 1741 in the Massachusetts colony. Many farmers were in debt and they tried to establish a land bank to service their finances. The governor, aware that it was election day and fearing rebellion with so many people in the streets, arrested several of the leaders before they could march on Boston. The day was uneventful, but it was soon learned that most of the voters favored a land bank. The British Parliament intervened quickly, declaring land banks illegal. This not only widened the rift between rural New Englanders and their rich urban cousins, it helped alienate the farmers from Parliament.

A decade later and learning little from this and other experiences, Parliament passed the Currency Act of 1751, making new land banks illegal in New England and putting time limits on when currency had to be called in and reissued. The insensitivity of Parliament and the colonial rich helped sow yet another seed that would soon shoot up in total rebellion against the crown. In 1764, 12 years before the Declaration of Independence, Benjamin Franklin warned the British: "I wish some good angel would forever whisper in the ears of your great men that dominion is founded in opinion." Clearly, the British were of the opinion that no opposing opinion was required in matters concerning their colonies. It was a position that proved their downfall in 1776.

The same would be true if the U.S. Congress were to decide to outlaw credit cards. Plastic has become the opiate of the middle classes. Removal of the cards would send shivers through suburban houses and department store aisles alike, although savings and loan associations might enter a renaissance of sorts if cash came flowing in—there would be no credit cards to help it flow out. It is the stuff dreams are made of.

THE ROMAN WHO WANTED TO WORK

Sending sons and daughters to college, paying off the car loan, keeping food on the table: These are some of the financial worries most people have on their minds as they go to work. In recent years, *financial planning* has become a buzz phrase for preparing for the future while meeting the fiscal demands of the present. But medieval account rolls from manor houses, and personal account books, tell us that keeping track of making and spending money was an integral part of everyday life long ago. Moreover, we have the story of an ancient Roman that stands out as perhaps the ultimate example of someone dedicated to financial planning, because keeping to the plan meant risking his life!

The source is the *Gesta Romanorum,* a compilation of semi-historical tales written down in the 13th century. The story takes place in Rome during the reign of the emperor Titus (39–81 A.D.). One day, Titus decreed that the birthday of first-born sons should be held sacred, and that whoever worked on his own birthday would be put to death—Romans had a way with penalties for disobeying the most innocent of laws. The emperor, however, could not figure out how to enforce the decree and decided to do what most managers do when confronted with an overwhelming dilemma: He went to a consultant, the wise man Virgil. After a bit of thinking, Virgil came up with a solution, which to modern minds is obviously a fable. He created a statue with the power to speak the names of anyone who violated his birthday by working. Needless to say, lots of Romans lost their lives on their birthdays when the statue started naming names.

A certain carpenter named Focus needed to work every day and, therefore, decided to confront the statue on his birthday. "I vow to my god that, if you accuse me, I will break your head," he told the statue. He then went to work. The statue was probably made of marble but he was no dummy. When the emperor's men came to see if anyone had cheated on his birthday, the statue refused to say. Titus himself went before the statue and got it to talk—in return for protection—and soon Focus the carpenter was hauled before the emperor of Rome.

"Why did you break my law?" the emperor demanded.

Focus was brief and to the point. "For I am obliged to obtain every day eight pennies, which, without incessant labor, I have not the means of acquiring." This intrigued Titus, who now wanted to know why the carpenter needed eight pennies a day.

"I am bound, each day, to repay two pennies to my father; for, when I was a boy, he spent that on me each day and now he is poor and needs my help," Focus replied. "Two other pennies I lend to my son, who is pursuing his studies." This, the carpenter said, was an investment, since his son would repay him in his old age for support, as he was doing for his own father. "I lose two pennies every day on my wife," Focus continued, "for she is contrary, willful, and passionate. Because of her ways, I account whatever is given to her as lost. The last two pennies are needed for my meals."

Titus was impressed and after his death, according to the story, Focus became emperor. Further, when Focus died, a bust of him—with eight pennies on his head—was placed next to the other emperors. We never do find out what happened to the statue that turned in any violator on his birthday.

Personal finance and accounting have become a little more complex nowadays, but the diligence required to manage well hasn't changed since the days of Focus. The challenge is to exercise self-control and use your head—at least you don't have to worry about having it removed.

We have spent some time exploring work, business, and spending and saving from the perspective of the past, since these aspects of life are what surround most of our waking hours. It is time to move on to other expressions of our present world to see how much of it we can discover—and learn about—from the past. It should have become clear that virtually all our actions and reactions are but old pieces on a new chess board: The game is the same; we just have an updated playing field. And while we may not always win, we can at least gain a better understanding of what the game is all about.

6

ON TRADE AND TRAVEL FOR FUN AND PROFIT

People travel from place to place, and never more so than in the late 20th century. Thanks to some old technology (roads, the wheel) and some innovative approaches to moving people (automobiles, trains, planes), the world at the end of this century is a world on the move. Yet ever since tribes and groups of prehistoric people were forced to give up their familiar hunting grounds in search of new ones, moving from place to place afforded not only new opportunities for food-hunting but an outlet for the human spirit—to explore, to analyze. Or to mimic a late-20th-century television program about the future, "to go where no man has gone before."

This was even true once civilization took root in the soil of an agrarian society no longer dependent on following the herds for food. Not only did people want to know what lay over the next hill, they recognized that trading with neighboring societies and cultures could be both economically and politically rewarding. It was mentioned earlier that primitive Greek sculpture looked similar to Egyptian statuary, and we know that there was trade between the two cultures. Such cultural borrowing became offshoots of the desire to exchange goods and seek alliances against common enemies.

Trade and travel—they occupy their own sections in newspapers around the world, with trade falling under the aegis of business and travel unto itself as a desirable activity for human experience. Yet both have developed from the need to move goods and people from point to point, and it is therefore with the roads that we first look at our own world from the perspective of long ago.

THE ROAD TO BABYLON

It is easy to take for granted the importance our roads play in everyday life beyond a means of traveling for pleasure. So much of what can be purchased and consumed is made available to the public because of the interstate and highway road systems that criss-cross countries, carrying transports packed with goods. Of course, this system began as a hazardous venture, with engineers surveying unknown landscapes for possible routes, often at their peril. Indeed, it is really the 20th century that has seen the opening of roads from border to border; in the United States, the interstate highway system was a child of the post–World War II era and has only recently reached completion.

In ancient times, progress was often curtailed because there was no easy access from one country to another, or even between cities. Worse, piracy and highway robbery often discouraged traveling with goods for fear of theft, if not loss of life. (We saw a little piracy on the low seas regarding Apollonios and the pirate agents in Chapter 4.) But goods were ready for export nonetheless. Even at the beginning of recorded history in Mesopotamia the potter's wheel and the weaver's loom were spinning away pots and cloth. Other staples known to our own world were available: grapes in Mesopotamia, peaches in Persia, cherries from the Black Sea, and milk in the Near East. The impediment to commerce was therefore not any lack of invention or of product, but of distribution.

Local transport five millennia ago was basically accomplished with a wheeled cart drawn by mules. The horse, which first appeared in written records about 2100 B.C., was called "the ass from the East," a reference to Central Asia. Because of this initial form of horsepower, trade expanded throughout the ancient Near East. This in turn encouraged the building of roads to facilitate inter-city commerce.

Babylon became a commercial center and was one of the first

ancient empires to create a road system. Its greatest ruler, Nebuchadnezzar (605–562 B.C.), boasted, "I have turned inaccessible tracks into serviceable roads." Where all roads were later to lead to Rome, some of the earliest caravan routes ended in Babylon. Soon the Babylonian marketplace became one of the largest in the known world. This was helped along by a new discovery: the observation that straw-mixed clay bricks left in a fire were harder, and formed at a faster rate, than laying them out in the sun to dry. It was a quick step to inventing a kiln, and buildings dotting the Babylonian skyline could be seen for miles around.

Many of the wealthy citizens built their homes on the outskirts of town to escape the hustle and bustle of city life: the ancient beginnings of suburbia and the commute to work. A surviving letter from a Babylonian suburban businessman to King Cyrus of Persia (late 6th century B.C.) reads as if it could have been written yesterday: "Our estate seemed to me the finest in the world, for it was so near to Babylon that we enjoyed all the advantages of a great city, and yet could come back home and be rid of all its rush and worry."

So the next time a large, noisy semitrailer truck barrels by on the interstate highway, it might do well to offer a thanks instead of a curse. Milk and peaches are rather basic items to modern thinking, but they don't appear magically on the grocery shelf. Nor are roads for a driving vacation the gift of the earth to the humans who inhabit it. Rather, Babylon had something to do with it.

ALL ROADS LEAD TO ROME

When Ronald Reagan was president he grimaced a bit upon receiving an $88 billion price tag for the Highway and Mass Transit bill, especially since he was never a fan of excessive spending in areas not near and dear to his heart, like defense. (This attitude will have its price—one estimate for repairing U.S. roads to the condition they were in during the early 1980s is $315 billion, with another $72 billion for bridge repair.) Unfortunately, the president missed not only the historical significance of keeping roads safe and functional, but how the highway has become part of our way of life. And if he was unaware of Babylonia's upkeep of the roads, surely he might have run across the case of the Roman Empire, which had perhaps the most prodigious road-building program the world has ever seen.

After conquering a country, the Romans usually made it accessible by building roads, much as the United States opened the West with railroads and, later, highways. When the Roman Empire was at its zenith, its legions could march from the Euphrates River in the Middle East to the Rhine. The Romans even built 16 routes over the Alps—only in the late 19th century could Europeans construct roads that made the mountains more accessible. It should be noted that the original purpose of the Roman roads was military: They were the best way to move legions across the empire. But the roads also were used for commerce and for travel. The same pattern is true of highways in the United States. When the interstate system was planned in the 1950s, during the Cold War with Russia, it was officially called the National System of Interstate and Defense Highways— something no doubt missed by families traveling along Interstate 80 into South Dakota. This meaning soon was lost as it became clear that America would not be rushing troops along the road to fight invading Russians. But many of our manufactured goods and food came to be trucked over these highways.

The Romans, of course, needed to build and maintain their roads for their legions as well as for trade, and famous roads were built by important citizens, usually when in office. Perhaps the most familiar route was planned by Appius Claudius, a censor, or one of two Roman officials who kept the census, awarded contracts, and supervised matters involving public works. In 312 B.C., he began what is known today as the Appian Way in Rome. Emperors were particularly interested in keeping the roads in working order. A roadside inscription in North Africa from 123 A.D. reads:

> The Emperor Trajanus Hadrian Augustus, grandson of the deified Nerva, son of the deified Trajan Particus, Pontifex Maximus . . . had the road from Carthage to Theveste paved by the Legion III Augusta under the command of Publius Metilius Secundus, imperial legate with rank of praetor.

Roman roads, like those in America and abroad, were expensive to build. Augustus Caesar (d. 14 A.D.) and later emperors encouraged triumphant generals to build roads instead of throwing costly exhibitions. As the Roman historian Suetonius put it, Augustus "assigned the rest of the highways to men who had been honored with triumphs to pave out of their spoils money"— we might consider that for our own triumphant wealthy. Landowners close to the roads had to contribute to their upkeep, as did provinces and towns. And, as the inscription above indicates, the army was used to build and maintain the roads through a series of detached posts commanded by junior officers.

It might be inspired to suggest that we get our armed forces to maintain our highways—and at the more than $262 billion a year to keep American men and women in uniform alone, we might seriously consider the possibility. It also would be interesting to propose that those who become enriched by the highways of the world spend a portion of their wealth repairing them. Taxes alone cannot keep millions of miles of roads functional and safe. Unfortunately, most people don't think about a road until they hit a bump. Roads aren't sexy; they don't give us warm and cuddly feelings. But like many of the flora and fauna of the world, roads can become distressed and, ultimately, extinct. So when next you travel along the highways and byways of your city, state, or country, realize that you are following a concept first proposed thousands of years ago to open communications, trade, even adventure. And their importance has never declined.

JAPAN AND THE SEARCH FOR PRECIOUS METALS

The roads, of course, are also *symbols* of trade—moving goods from one country to another, whether by land, sea, or air. And when we think of a trading empire to rival Rome or Babylon, we might look to a group of islands that miraculously rose phoenixlike from the ashes of World War II to dizzying heights of economic success: Japan. The Western world is both in awe of, and angry with, the Japanese. This stems in part from Japan's success as an industrial nation, and in part from its incredible capacity to export goods globally. Where awe turns to anger is in their system of trade. Although the Japanese have large numbers of products in need of foreign markets, they are loathe to open their own country to any significant number of goods from other exporting countries. Japan wants to bake its cake and make others eat it, but refuses to sample rival bakeries.

This is hardly a half-baked situation concocted by Japan to anger its Western allies. Rather it is born out of a sense of necessity from a country reliant on foreign energy to run its industries and an economy based on the ability to dispose of its manufactured goods. It is also reminiscent of *mercantilism,* a system of trade developed by, of all people, the Europeans who at the moment are suffering the most from Japan's dominance in world trade. Mercantilism is an economic theory that emphasizes the need for a government to intervene in trade activities for the benefit of its country. And the relationship it required and was developed for consisted of the Mother Country and its colonies.

By the 16th century, countries such as Spain, England, France, and Portugal had established footholds in the New World: North, Central, and South America. Once colonies were founded and local economies established, it became clear to the mother countries that their offspring could be exploited by forcing exports upon them. Since the colonies provided ready markets for homeland products, each European country could regulate its trade so that exports outnumbered imports: a neat surplus. This, in turn, led to the heart of mercantilism: accumulating wealth as calculated by precious metals. Spain could export wines and finished products to its New World colonies in exchange for gold and silver. Moreover, Spain banned her colonies from producing goods that would compete with those manufactured in the mother country.

Japan, it could be argued, today views Europe and the United States as colonial markets for its products. Further, Japan has accumulated billions of dollars and other currencies from this relationship, which it turns into investments in the United States and other countries. In the 16th and 17th centuries, this doctrine of uneven, controlled trade had devastating effects for the mother countries. For example, Spain, dependent on agricultural and other goods from its colonies, never fully developed these products at home. Once the colonies slipped from her grasp, this major power declined economically, never to recover her glory days, despite attempts to become self-sufficient. (See Chapter 5 regarding Charles III.) Mercantilism was also one of the thorns in the side of the American colonists, who eventually decided to create not only their own markets but their own nation.

Ironically, the Japanese resisted contact with Europe during this colonial period. When Portuguese ships arrived in the 1540s, the Japanese rulers grew suspicious of the strangers' intentions. The Japanese had already witnessed the missionary work of the Jesuits and were not impressed. Now they saw European arrivals exploiting Japanese workers to acquire inexpensive products. Japan soon kicked everybody out and isolated itself from the rest of the world. Although the Dutch were allowed to keep a small outpost at Nagasaki, Japanese islands remained cut off from European contact well into the 19th century.

Colonies are rare birds to locate today, and global trade has become more complex and intermingled. If the Japanese want to remain an economic power, they will have to learn to cooperate in a global marketplace that cannot tolerate imbalance of trade for too long, let alone the notion that a country is trying to become a Mother Country. Otherwise, Japan will be locked out, something neither the East nor the West really wants to have happen.

A CRUSADING WE WILL GO

Problems with Japan have, indeed, caused reaction from other nations, including the United States, where sanctions have been voted upon several times as a result of the enormous trade imbalance between the two countries—an imbalance favoring the Japanese. For while the United States sees Japan as an important Free World force to counter Russian and Chinese influence in the Far East, the Japanese also have become the major economic rival to the West. Worse, the European community also feels the threat of Japanese economic dominance in trade, although allies are now distracted by a new potential rival: a unified Germany.

The situation with Japan—an ally yet a rival—is reminiscent of another confrontation between allies in the face of a common enemy: the Crusaders. By the 12th century, the Seljuk Turks—fanatic converts to Islam—overran the Middle East and seized Jerusalem. Although this presented difficulties for Christians visiting the holy city, those Christians living in the East had been dealing with the Moslems for centuries with little hardship. The Moslems were great traders, selling their wares on three continents. There were no tariff barriers to inhibit trade, and many joint-stock companies and branch banks prospered—concepts that sound modern but actually existed long ago. Despite this working relationship between Moslems and Eastern Christians, coexistence was not always easy. One Islamic caliph, Harun Al-Rashid (786–809 A.D.), sent the following message to the Byzantine emperor:

> From Harun, commander of the faithful, to Nicephorus, the dog of the Greeks. I have read your letter, you son of a she-infidel, and you shall see the answer before you hear it.

Harun was not one for beating around the bush, and he proceeded to ravage lands of the Eastern Roman Empire.

While Byzantium and the Moslems were rivals of different cultures, a more ironic conflict arose between the Eastern and Western Christian empires. Despite Rome's call to arms against the infidels in Jerusalem, a greater holy war took place between the two allied empires run from Rome and Constantinople, with trade a key issue. The important commercial centers of the West, especially Genoa and Venice, had stiff competition from their Eastern brethren, whom they felt monopolized trade in the Byzantine Empire. For its part, the East had little love for the West. Anna Comnena, a 12th-century Byzantine princess, wrote, "The West stands for wars and exploitation; it is incurably tainted by its Roman roots; Rome—West Rome—is Babylon, the mother of all wickedness." No doubt many hard-line communists still feel this way about the West.

When Pope Innocent III called together the Fourth Crusade to free Jerusalem (1202–04), it was a perfect opportunity for the West to intrude on Eastern Empire trade—never mind that both empires were Christian and supposedly against the infidel in the Holy Land. Whether the Western Crusaders would make it to

Jerusalem was a moot point at best. The Venetians, headed by the old doge we previously met up with (Chapter 2), encouraged the Crusaders to capture the Christian town of Zara (a trading rival) on the Adriatic Sea, and then induced them to attack the Eastern capital, Constantinople. This economically inspired act came despite the fact that the Byzantines were fellow Christians, and that the Crusaders wore the cross to defeat the Moslems in Jerusalem. In 1204, Constantinople was sacked and pillaged. Thousands of Eastern Christians were slaughtered by their Western Christian "brothers," and the Crusaders set up a Latin Empire. Genoa and Venice soon gained a monopoly on trade in the East and in Western Europe. The Crusaders never did make it to Jerusalem.

The enemy, of course, lost little from the Fourth Crusade, and was eventually replaced by an even crueler lot, the Ottoman Turks, who outlasted both Christian empires.

So while we take potshots at Japan because of economic rivalry—one of our prerequisites for war—we might remember that in the long run we have more to gain by working it out than by knocking each other off—especially since it's not all that clear who the next infidel will be. Crusades just don't work, even when stamped with holy approval. Better to express differences at the table than on the battlefield.

OLD EMPIRES AND THE DECLINE OF AMERICA

There is, one might guess, another side of the coin dealing with Japanese rivalry in trade: the uncertain position of the United States in geo-economics. For as the trade deficit in the United States continues to border on the unbelievable, it is becoming evident that the country has lost its luster as a nation in control of its economic destiny. Of course, there are many underlying factors that have contributed to the economic decline of a nation that, according to President George Bush, seeks to become "kinder and gentler" in spite of its balance sheet. But until credibility is reestablished and trade reaches equilibrium, the United States will have difficulty vying for economic leadership.

When one gazes back in time to other nations and empires that dominated their historical eras, it becomes clear that economic stability plays a major role in maintaining that dominance. Perhaps the greatest example of this dictum—one that lasted more than a thousand years—is the eastern half of the Roman Empire just discussed and centered at Constantinople. For before its slow decline after the Fourth Crusade, the Eastern Empire truly dominated the world.

After the Roman emperor Diocletian (284–305 A.D.) split the empire in two, the West entered an economic decline while the East rose in stature and wealth. One major reason was the continuous existence of a money economy in the East to encourage trade and pay a standing army. In the West, where a barter economy was a way of life, no such economic and military stability could be maintained. The East had a sound gold currency, one that became the international exchange for more than 700 years, longer than any other currency in history. Constantinople became the trading center of the world and carefully balanced its export of weapons, hardware, wines, and textiles for furs, fish, caviar, beeswax, honey, and amber. The empire also controlled its economy through a guild system that held all tradesmen to specified wages, profits, and working hours. Prices also were controlled.

A surviving handbook from Constantinople on trade noted that such control was needed "so that men, being well directed thereby, should not shamelessly trample upon one another and the stronger should not do violence to the weaker." There was also a balance between agricultural output and urban consumption. This helped maintain a steady population growth throughout the Eastern Empire at a time when population declined in the West.

The empire anchored in Constantinople, like the Western Empire, was beleaguered from constant invasion by various armies, many of which threatened its very existence. By the 10th century, rapacious nobles began seizing the lands of free peasants, thus weakening a large class of citizens who were largely responsible for paying the taxes and supplying the men for war. At the same time, rival trading cities—notably Venice and Genoa—threatened the economic dominance of Constantinople.

And as we have seen earlier, the Fourth Crusade involved the sacking of Constantinople (1204) and the disruption of its trade. Although weakened, the Eastern Empire crept along until its eventual demise in 1453 at the hands of the Ottoman Turks. As the walls of Constantinople were breached, its last emperor—named after the city's founder—met his death crying, "God forbid that I should live an emperor without an empire! As my city falls, I will fall with it!"

The United States has a way to go before historians begin clanging the death bell and writing tomes on the nation's decline and fall. But if the country is to continue to dominate world affairs, it will have to clean up its economic act soon, especially in the area of trade. The choice is between acting like the Eastern Empire that stayed the course, or the Western one that skidded off the map of history. Even the Roman roads couldn't help; indeed, they are all that remains of that past glory.

GORBACHEV AND THE MAURYAN EMPIRE

Japan has made its mark in the world, and the world looks in wonder at the strides this small, defeated island has made in less than half a century. From creating "Made in Japan" products that signified something cheap, shabby, and disposable, Japan now produces products and technology on the cutting edge of what any country has to offer. But there is a sleeping giant that the Western world has mainly viewed as a political enemy and threat, not an economic one: the Soviet Union. The current changes occurring there, thanks to the openness fostered by Mikhail Gorbachev, will first benefit Western countries already competing heavily for new markets for their products: the great flagship of Western decadence—McDonald's—now graces Red Square, to the delight of the young and the business-minded, and to the horror of the old guard. Although blessed with natural resources, it will take time for the Soviet Union to modernize to the point where its exports will be salable in foreign countries. Mr. Lenin's great experiment may have fizzled, but old ways die hard.

The Soviet Union's paucity of goods to offer the global

market stems mainly from its political system, which has done little to stimulate economic growth, industrial competitiveness, or product creativity. But a repressive society can, on occasion, become a major factor in world trade, and we shouldn't kid ourselves about the potential of Soviet dominance. The Mauryan Empire in India is an example of a tightly controlled political system that nonetheless became a key player in world trade, and it would do us well to explore what happened.

After the death of Alexander the Great (323 B.C.), the domain he fashioned in India all but vanished. Then a soldier named Chandragupta Maurya gained control of a large state in India, founding a dynasty that flourished for almost 250 years. Considered by some the first emperor of India, Chandragupta ruled with an iron hand, and kept trade open between his kingdom, China, and the West. His lands were divided into provinces administered by state officials and about 30 imperial departments, which managed everything from revenues and public buildings to canal irrigation and trade. At the same time, a well-run war office maintained a large army that kept order and stood ready for war at a word's notice. In a commentary written by Chandragupta's chief minister, it was clear that conquest by any means was the name of the game. For example, the five methods for capturing a fort were "intrigue, spies, winning over the enemy's people, siege, and assault"—this sounds curiously Russian, although some might argue that the CIA wouldn't blanch at such a formula.

As in the Soviet Union now, all lands belonged to the Indian state, with agriculture the main revenue generator. Yet trade prospered in the city bazaars: goods from other parts of India, Asia, China, and the West were available. Products made within the empire traveled caravan routes as far as the Greek city-states, with everything from weapons and farm tools to cotton cloth and silk yarn for sale. Two-way trade was so prosperous that, even after Chandragupta's death, strong ties continued between his empire and the Greeks. A letter from his son, Bindusara, to Antiochus in Asia Minor requested a sample of raisins, Greek wines, and a sophist, or Greek philosopher. Antiochus replied that he would be happy to send the raisins and the wine, but that "it isn't good form among Greeks to trade in philosophers."

Once the rulers in the Soviet Union decide that economic progress demands certain freedoms and better management, their country can enter the world marketplace competitively. For it is apparent that their system of tight state control has contributed to their dismal performance as a producer and world trading power. Yet some 2,300 years ago, an Indian ruler and his successor figured out a way to maintain control and prosper simultaneously. It was an experiment that worked for a long time before the dynasty disappeared. And it proved that certain state controls can work; Mr. Gorbachev need not wait for major political changes before making some key economic ones.

FREE TRADE, 1992, AND LORD PALMERSTON

The biggest change that will occur in the 1990s, and beyond, regarding trade centers is "EC 1992," when the European Economic Community, in theory, will be linked together as 12 countries benefiting each other economically. Although much remains to be ironed out—from resolution of some 300 proposals to the exact membership of the EC and the currency to be used—it is clear that changes have already begun, and that a new economic force is in the making. In the post–World War II era, geo-economic debate in the United States has focused on what exactly global trade means, and how it can be made possible for a country to trade freely and unencumbered by another. The debate often focuses on Japan, perhaps the greatest post-war trading empire, which protects its domestic production by limiting imports. EC 1992 will only force the issue of how free a trading nation can be when dealing with its commercial partner states.

The notion of free trade has been around ever since overland merchants and intrepid sailors began selling their wares beyond their borders. Sometimes the argument for free trade has taken on interesting philosophical arguments. In the mid-19th century, Europe was recovering from the Napoleonic debacle and trying to ensure that, despite imperialistic outbreaks of war, trade could flourish. One proponent of free trade was Henry John Temple, 3rd Viscount Palmerston. A no-nonsense politician—we saw him fight the United States on the slavery issue (Chapter

3)—Palmerston held tenures in the British government as foreign secretary, home secretary, and prime minister. It was in 1842 before the House of Commons that he used the corn laws as an example of the "rights" of free trade.

Palmerston asked the Commons several rhetorical questions:

> Why is the earth on which we live divided into zones and climates? Why, I ask, do different countries yield different productions to people experiencing similar wants? . . . Why are lands the most distant from each other, brought almost into contact by the very ocean which seems to divide them?

His answers were well in hand. "Why, Sir, it is that man may be dependent upon man. It is that the exchange of commodities may be accompanied by the extension and diffusion of knowledge . . . multiplying and confirming friendly relations." Indeed, Palmerston saw free trade as a means to promulgate peace and tranquility, since every nation's best interests were at stake. "It is, that commerce may freely go forth," he said, "leading civilisation with one hand, and peace with the other, to render mankind happier, wiser, better."

Contemporaries of Palmerston agreed that free trade had a strong political benefit. The radical British leader Richard Cobden said that free trade was "God's diplomacy, and there is no other certain way of uniting people in bonds of peace." Perhaps the current world leaders should pick up the baton carried so proudly by the free traders of more than a century ago, especially when we consider the increase in political strife and rivalry facing most trading nations. Clearly, Cobden would have approved of EC 1992 as a step in the right direction, with the hope of bringing about a situation that would "[draw] men together, thrusting aside the antagonism of race, and creed, and language." Time—and events—will tell if we are heading in that direction.

"PERFECT HONESTY ON BOTH SIDES"

When all is said and done, the topic of trade must be reduced to the lives of individuals who make it all possible: the consumers. A fair deal generally is what consumers want when they reach for their wallets or credit cards. But in an age where products are made by the millions and customer service is more delay than assistance, one often wonders if it is possible to get what you thought you paid for at the cash register. Buyers of cars from the "new" Chrysler Corporation may have wondered about this in the late 1980s when they learned of executives allegedly driving new cars and having the odometers turned back before selling them as *new.*

But if the consumer is at the mercy of the seller, then the seller is at the mercy of how he is perceived by the consumer. You can only put out an overpriced or bad product for so long before customers spread the word, which often leads to decreased sales or Chapter 11 bankruptcy protection, as A. H. Robins Company, maker of the Dalkon shield birth control device, discovered. Has the consumer ever felt safe when making a purchase? Commercial relationships have been established over the centuries where the price of a product was usually amenable to both sides, but one rarely comes across a document or story where everyone was happy . . . and willing to talk about it. One example of an almost utopian buyer–seller relationship may raise a few brows on both sides of our current daily retail exchanges.

The story was related by Herodotus (5th century B.C.), the Greek traveler and writer we have encountered before and considered the Father of History. (He told us about the Persians in Chapter 3.) His "History"—from the Greek *historia,* which means "inquiry"—was the first major attempt to research and write about diverse peoples and their origins and customs, using a variety of sources: documents, monuments, oral histories, and eyewitness observations. In talking about the ancient Libyans— a wild, nomadic people who taught the Greeks to "harness four horses to a chariot"—Herodotus related a story told by the seafaring Carthaginians about certain Libyans living beyond the Pillars of Hercules.[1]

Herodotus noted that the men of Carthage, the powerful

---

[1] Known to us as the Rock of Gibraltar and the Jebel Musa in Africa. The story goes that the rock was ripped asunder by the Greek demigod, Hercules, who thus connected the Mediterranean to the Atlantic Ocean.

maritime city-state near modern Tunis, traded with these Western Libyans in an interesting way:

> On reaching this country, [the Carthaginians] unload their goods, arrange them tidily along the beach, and then, returning to their boats, raise a smoke. Seeing the smoke, the natives come down to the beach, place on the ground a certain quantity of gold in exchange for the goods, and go off again to a distance.

This, however, was only the beginning of the transaction, and what followed would make any department store manager mint green with envy:

> The Carthaginians then come ashore and take a look at the gold; and if they think it represents a fair price for their wares, they collect it and go away; if, on the other hand, it seems too little, they go back aboard and wait, and the natives come and add to the gold until [the Carthaginians] are satisfied.

This relationship was a marvel to Herodotus, who no doubt had visited the haggling merchants and vendors of numerous cities in the Mediterranean world. "There is perfect honesty on both sides," he wrote. "The Carthaginians never touch the gold until it equals in value what they have offered for sale, and the natives never touch the goods until the gold has been taken away." The flaw in this harmonious arrangement, of course, is that we do not know what happened if the Libyans felt they had paid enough for the goods and the Carthaginians still wanted more. Had Herodotus stuck around a little longer, he might have learned of the first supermarket boycott, or perhaps the first "All Items On Sale 'Til Midnight" retail promotion. Regardless, we see two sides making an effort to trade fairly. Perhaps we should send a copy of Herodotus to the leaders of the United States and Japan for study. It might just prompt some cooperation that will not only avoid an economic crusade—as we have seen—but initiate an era where the consumer can win; not just those who trade for profit.

CHARTRES CATHEDRAL AND TRADE SHOWS

Of course, one way of looking at what the Libyans and Carthaginians were doing might be to describe the trade process as one big trade show, where goods are displayed and buyers come to browse and consider ordering what they like. In the United States alone, trade shows are a multibillion dollar business, and industries worldwide come to display their wares at hundreds of exhibitions: the Consumer Electronics Show, the Auto Show, the Boat Show, Toy Fair, etc., etc. Unlike individual endeavors by a company to sell its goods or services to target markets, a trade show allows all the players to snoop about their competitors' showcases while hoping to lure current and would-be customers into their own lairs.

The trade show is not a new phenomenon. Throughout history, cities and countries have devised ways to display their wares (or exports) for view and potential purchase. Medieval France represents a good example of such mass marketing, and their international character. In the 12th century, fairs were held at Saint-Denis, Chalons-sur-Saone, Beaucaire, and in towns in the Champagne region. Several towns catered to more than just the country: Cities such as Geneva and Bruges became European centers of trade. In Champagne, it was the local Count who ensured a safe journey to and from the town fairs. The counts also instituted special legal jurisdictions for suits and crimes arising at fairs. This was essential since the frequency and duration of the various fairs meant that one was going on at any given time of the year, a situation similar to our own shows.

The major business deals struck at the fairs centered on the textile industry, Europe's first important trade. England, which did not weave its homespun wool at this time, exported it to Europe where it would be woven in Flanders, Artois, Hainault, Brabant, and other cities; from there, it would reach the fairs. Other towns developed cloth-weaving industries, with about 60 of them in northwestern Europe alone providing finished products for the fairs of Champagne. Fabrics from the Orient via Italy also found their way to the fairs. The very names of the fabrics point to their origins: damask (from Damascus), muslin (from Mossul), and gauze (from Gaza). Much of the capitalization for the fairs was provided by the Italian bankers of Genoa, Milan, Bologna, Venice, Siena, and Rome—when, as we have seen, they weren't "bench-broken." Merchants, craftsmen, and soldiers came from Germany and other countries to visit the fairs, often settling down in nearby cities to practice their professions.

Great European cities held fairs as a means of enriching both the citizenry and the city coffers, much as today. Both church and state could benefit from these trade shows. Chartres Cathedral became the focal point for the four fairs held each year on the festivals of the Virgin. These attracted pilgrims and merchants alike, both eager to be relieved of their money in the hopes of attaining either salvation or a profitable line of goods—as with today, the line between the two could be blurred. And like today, the fairs allowed the little guy the opportunity to show his wares along with the major merchants and trading groups.

It is a costly exercise to companies today: booth fees, displays, transportation and salary costs, entertainment, and the numerous gimmicks purchased or rented to attract a crowd. (Talking robots were big at one time; sexy females long in smiles and short in costumes remain in style, and one wonders if that was the case in medieval France.) The winners, hopefully, are the consumers, who learn about the latest trends and fads right off the trade show floor. It is an interesting, and very old , way of doing business.

AN AWFUL TRIP TO THE EAST

Transportation, travel, trade—moving goods, and people, from various places, usually for profit. But humans like to travel for fun, too, even if there is a business element to their journeys. Moreover, we are not just talking about a trek to the neighboring village: People over the centuries and millennia have braved the hazards of weather and fellow human beings to move across the earth. Our friend Herodotus traveled all over the Mediterranean seeking information about unknown lands and countries. And we mustn't forget that intrepid traveler and salesman, St. Paul, who took his message over thousands of miles of land and sea more than 1,900 years ago . . . with some very impressive results.

There is also another hazard that, while not normally fatal, can nonetheless unsettle the most seasoned traveler: *culture shock*. Americans are world-famous for wandering into a strange land and becoming incensed over the "foreign" language, "foreign" food and, of course, "foreign" customs—never mind that *they* are the foreigners. But culture shock is not new, nor has it just happened to the recreational tourist. We might spend a moment with an international business traveler named Liudprand, bishop of Cremona, who was born in 922 A.D. and often served as ambassador for the Holy Roman emperors. On one memorable trip, which he wrote about at length, he visited the Eastern emperor in Constantinople with several colleagues on behalf of the Roman emperor, Otto I.

In a letter to Otto, the ruffled Liudprand wrote of his unhappy visit to Emperor Nicephorus Phocus. Business began on a bad note: "We arrived in Constantinople on June 4 and, to your shame, we were welcomed insultingly and treated discourteously." The bishop and his party were confined to a building guarded by soldiers, and when they were summoned to the palace, "our breath was taken away not riding there, but walking." Liudprand also complained of the food, especially the wine. "We had the additional worry," he wrote, "that the Greek wine, being mixed with pitch, tar, and gypsum, was undrinkable."

For his first meeting with the emperor, Liudprand and company waited out in the rain before being received. The bishop then had to listen to a speech by the emperor's brother, Leo, which in effect took potshots at Liudprand's boss, Otto I. The bishop finally met the emperor:

> I was taken before Nicephorus, a monstrosity of a man: a dwarf, swollen-headed, with small molelike eyes, a foul short beard, fan-shaped, thickly grown, half tinged with gray, with a neck the size of a finger, rather pig-faced with his long thick hair.

We might venture to say the bishop gained a less than favorable impression of his host. Still, Nicephorus must have spotted something wrong with his guests, for he explained to the bishop that he was not very hospitable to his guests because of a quarrel he had with Emperor Otto: a piece of information Otto might have imparted to the befuddled Liudprand prior to his departure for Constantinople. Liudprand nonetheless defended his master; the Eastern emperor then ended the meeting with a celebration honoring himself, not his guests as the bishop might have expected.

Liudprand was not thrilled with the proceedings. After hearing chants of "Long live Nicephorus," the bishop observed "with how much greater truths should they have chanted 'Come, burnt-out coal; come, slow down, you old woman . . . you Pan-face, you boor, tramp.'" The indignities continued for the visitor. When Liudprand arrived for dinner, he was seated 15th from the emperor, "without a napkin." The bishop didn't like the dinner, either: "[It] was rather prolonged and marked by the usual drunken obscenities, streaming with oil and soaking in some kind of foul fish sauce." Liudprand got into an argument with Nicephorus, and soon after the bishop and his party departed for the West.

Culture shock makes it difficult to do business abroad, to say nothing of enjoying a fun vacation. But enough preparation and understanding of the other's culture can ease the pain and allow for a peaceful, tolerant trip. We are still learning this today; whether traveling for business or pleasure, an American going to London or Madrid or Tokyo or Moscow cannot expect to experience a trip similar to traveling to Chicago or Dallas or New York—although some non–New Yorkers might argue that Moscow could be easier to take than Seventh Avenue or the Bronx.

PARTAKING OF A LITTLE "COCK AND BULL"

Then there are the adventures of travel that have a lasting effect on the traveler, even if the adventure is not quite based in reality. It could be visiting a haunted castle, an estate reputed to be this-or-that, or simply learning of tales or yarns that take on a validity of their own through constant repetition. For those who enjoy such romantic romps (present traveler included), it is essential to visit the quiet Buckinghamshire village of Stony Stratford in England, with its main thoroughfare running along Watling Street, the old Roman road. For several centuries, doing business or simply passing through Stony Stratford meant visiting the pubs and telling stories, especially at the village's two famous hotels, the Cock and the Bull. (More on these later.)

Stony Stratford was built along Watling Street and for almost 2,000 years afforded a resting stop for travelers and troops along the way North from London. In the era of coaches, there was a coaching town with inns for refreshment and overnight stays every seven miles: Bletchley is seven miles south of Stratford, Towcester seven miles to the north. Because of its location, Stony Stratford was always in and out of British history, as it were. When the Roman legions ceased to march along Watling Street, the town was on the route of successive invasions by the Saxons and the Danes. After the Norman invasion in 1066, the nearby forest of Whittlewood became a favorite royal hunting ground, bringing Plantagenet kings and their entourages to Stony Stratford and neighboring towns.

Perhaps the most famous incident in the town's history took place in the early spring of 1483, when the young Edward V stayed the night at the Rose and Crown Inn with his mother's kinsmen en route to London for his coronation as king. There he was intercepted by his uncle, Richard, duke of Gloucester, who escorted him to the Tower of London, where Edward's younger brother later joined him. The two princes, as we learned in Chapter 2, disappeared within the Tower, and the duke proclaimed himself King Richard III.

By the 18th century, Stony Stratford had 52 pubs—"one for every week of the year," according to a local proprietor—and coaches cluttered the High Street to allow their guests time to relax and take meals. Looking down the street today, most of these establishments have archways through them, called coaching arches, and all the rear buildings were once stables. Men would drink their fill and tell stories and jokes. These would be enlarged upon from pub to pub, and such pub-hopping (called "bunny runs") allowed people to get the latest news. It was the coachmen who usually told tales about what happened to them on the highway and then embroidered them so they became more scary and hairy. Stories abounded with specters jumping out of hedgerows and ditches. It was no wonder that by the time the storytellers reached the adjacent establishments of the Cock and the Bull, they were accused of telling "cock and bull stories."

In 1742 a fire damaged the buildings along the High Street, including the Cock and the Bull. Both were rebuilt and today serve business and vacationing travelers from Milton Keynes, a booming new industrial town. Business remains good at the Cock and the Bull, and both proprietors claim that there is no rivalry between them. That may be—or it just might be more cock and bull.

THE ONCE AND FUTURE TRINKET

Since we are in England, we might end our journey about journeys here with some observations concerning a certain legendary king (Arthur, by name) who symbolizes much of what we see on a trip. Every nation, city, or island has its icons—based on real people or pure fiction—that not only bring awe and wonder to the uninitiated, but numerous coins into the coffers of those who would sell the myths to the visitors. It can be a bus tour of Al Capone's Chicago or a guided tour of the life of Bonnie Prince Charlie in Scotland. Legends and heroes sell . . . and that's half of what tourism and travel are all about.

The rockbound castle and monastery in the ancient Cornish village of Tintagel is shrouded in mist and mystery, but the local economy shines. It was here, 1,500 years ago, that the legendary King Arthur purportedly was born, nine months after that persistent Celtic king, Uther Pendragon, accomplished his liaison with a Cornish lord's wife. Since that time, Arthurian lore has helped local economies throughout Western England, where the king is said to have performed many of his deeds. The ruins of the 5th century monastery can be visited today on a jagged island connected to the mainland at Tintagel by a steep land bridge. It is a breathtaking view, hampered only by occasional storms and the admission fee. There are also souvenir shops along the main road in Tintagel leading to the monastery, where everything from T-shirts and postcards to placemats and other trinkets portray the adult image of the village's famous baby—baby, because according to the legend, the newborn Arthur was taken from the stark Cornish coast northwards to be raised by guardians, one being Merlin the magician. The souvenir shops, however, wisely overlook that hasty departure.

Although the marketing of Merlin and his protégé does not in any way detract from the beauty of Tintagel—or dampen the possibility that there could be an historical connection with Arthur here—it should be noted that the heroic king and his legend have been linked with fund-raising throughout history. The most famous incident occurred in the 12th century, when Glastonbury Abbey in Somersetshire caught fire and burned. The abbey was in desperate need of money to rebuild and resume its premier role as England's wealthiest monastery. And it was an interesting money-making operation at Canterbury that got the Glastonbury monks thinking thusly:

Soon after Thomas Becket was murdered at Canterbury in 1170, miracles were attributed to the dead archbishop in and around the cathedral. Coin-carrying pilgrims soon came flowing into Canterbury cathedral, and this practice continued for centuries, immortalized in Geoffrey Chaucer's *Canterbury Tales*. The church officials at Glastonbury no doubt marveled at the cash potential from pilgrimages. Lucky for the monks, the town of Glastonbury had long been associated with the Isle of Avalon, where Arthur, the Once and Future King, is said to have died after a battle with his nephew, Mordred. Not long after the fire, it was announced that the graves of the king and his perfidious queen, Guinevere, had been discovered on the abbey grounds.

Lo and behold, pilgrims and pounds cascaded into the abbey, which was eventually rebuilt to its earlier splendor. Arthur's grave was venerated and moved to a more prominent spot during the reign of Edward I (1272–1307), only to be desecrated and lost during the dissolution of the monasteries under Henry VIII (1509–47). To those cynical folk who later saw the discovery of the graves as a matter of fiscal convenience, it should be noted that a cross commemorating Arthur's death was found in the grave—and that the writing on it appeared to be from the 11th century or earlier, much earlier than when the monks allegedly discovered the graves. While the cross seemed to be too old to have been fabricated by the Glastonbury monks, it was far too new to have been placed in the grave at the time an historical Arthur would have died, perhaps in the early- to mid-6th century. If indeed it was created at an earlier time as a replacement of an original cross, then the discovery of Arthur's grave was perhaps more a stroke of luck than a stroke of genius.

Either way, it pays to have legends. Remember that, the

next time you are offered a piece of chain mail from Robert the Bruce's armor or—dare we say it—a piece of the True Cross. Enjoy the journey, read the legend, fantasize about what might have been . . . and keep the travelers cheques in check when asked to buy part of the legends. When you think about it, legends really aren't for sale.

7

ON GOVERNMENT, DIPLOMACY, AND POINTING FINGERS

Business, trade, travel—little of this could exist without the framework of government and the promise of stability and order that it represents. And though there are many forms of government that repeat themselves over time—primitive democracy, oligarchy, tyranny, radical democracy, timocracy—all attempt to maintain society in an authoritative, workable way to the benefit of many, especially those in charge. The last point is important, for whether you are running a government or running a race, there has to be some payoff in the end to make it all worthwhile, sometimes literally. (It was the humorist Will Rogers who, when speaking of our elected officials, observed that "We have the best Senators and Congressmen that money can buy.") To discover what is taking place in government today and how *modern* it may or may not be, we need to understand not only what governments do but also what people in government do, for better or worse.

"A GREAT STEP FORWARD": SOME OBSERVATIONS

It is easy today for people to be cynical about government and government officials since politics is the name of the game and "the interest of the people" is often taken to mean self-interest, which it frequently is. Yet the organization of a group at the top is a very old, acceptable concept and perhaps derives from the *leader of the pack* mentality required for the survival of many animals on earth. One problem, of course, is that, try though a government may, not everyone ends up happy with the results of governmental action. And many a thinker has taken note of the usefulness of government and what we might expect from it.

An anonymous writer once observed, "Before this government came to power we were on the edge of an economic precipice. Since then we have taken a great step forward." That's not a bad summation of what often happens when the government steps in to solve a problem: It becomes worse or, quite often, unsalvageable. Yet other thinkers have recognized that government is a necessity. The early-4th-century B.C. Greek philosopher Plato understood this when he wrote "a state comes into existence because no individual is self-sufficing, we all have many needs." And the 18th-century American revolutionary Thomas Paine believed that "government even in its best state is but a necessary evil; in its worst state an intolerable one." Clearly the reign of King George III was viewed as the latter.

In recent years, especially under the Reagan administration, the belief has been fostered that less government is good government. This is not a new idea. The 19th-century English philosopher and economist John Stuart Mill wrote:

> In all the more advanced communities the great majority of things are worse done by the intervention of government, than the individuals most interested in the matter would do them, or cause them to be done, if left to themselves.

Some have noted that government can be more a part of the problem than of the solution, and that in terms of economic policy governments cannot be objective parties. The 20th-century economist James B. Ramsey has written that "government should see that the economic game is played vigorously and according to the rules. But the referee cannot also play, for who will then referee the referee?"

Does government do more harm than good in the key areas of business, finance, and economics? Probably not. The 20th-century economist Oskar Morgenstern took the middle road when he wrote, "Wisdom and stupidity in matters of economic policy are not linked with particular forms of government." And the 18th-century Scottish economist Adam Smith noted with relief that "though the profusion of government must, undoubtedly, have retarded the natural progress of England towards wealth and improvement, it has not been able to stop it."

When all is said and done, governments will continue to exist. But when things go smoothly—something within the realm of possibility—it should not be assumed that things are working. Or as the late President John F. Kennedy observed: "My experience in government is that when things are noncontroversial, beautifully coordinated and all the rest, it must be that there is not much going on."

REGULATIONS AND MONSIEUR COLBERT

The Age of Reaganomics will be remembered as a time of deregulation, during which the idea that one should be allowed to go about one's business freely and unbridled has seen the light of day across many industries and across daily lives. But with the loosening of rules and guidelines has come some challenges: avoiding the consequences from the loss of federal aid needed by those unable to take care of themselves, and avoiding the threat of chaos as companies compete for bigger, unrestricted pieces of the proverbial pie. The recent spate of near-collisions and mechanical problems by "free and unbridled" airplanes has actually led to the suggestion that, alas, a few regulations might not be such a bad idea. Free enterprise is possibly too free for comfort.

The government regulation of everyday life, especially in the areas of products and services, happened to be music to the ears of Jean Baptiste Colbert (1619–83), the son of a Reims clothier who became the financial genius of Louis XIV's so-called French empire. Colbert took a foundering economy and brought it to greatness by instituting regulations possibly unheard of before or since. Companies today, who complain about the Food and Drug Administration and other government regulatory agencies watching over their shoulders for standardized quality and safety, would have gagged on the hundreds of ordinances passed by Colbert. The French minister established numerous standards for manufacturing, including color, size, and quality. He also prescribed the hours and conditions of labor. Indeed, Colbert ordered that all industries work through guilds or communes, which, with local boards, checked for defects by local factories.

If a consumer today is impressed by reaching into the pocket of a new suit and finding a tag that says "Inspected by No. 42," imagine the reaction in Colbert's France, where defective products were publicly displayed with the names of the responsible managers or workers attached to them. Workers caught making three substandard products were tied to posts for public exhibition! Employers could punish workers for a variety of violations beyond inferior work—including indolence, profanity, insubordination, concubinage, and indecent conversation. They could even have employees flogged in public for such indiscretions. This was government in its strongest form of intervention into everyday life.

Today's workers often look not only for higher wages but shorter hours on the job. They would not have made a squeak for such things in the reign of Louis XIV under Colbert. Wages then were low and partly paid in kind, not cash. And the typical shift was at least 12 hours a day. Modern union representatives might not be amused to learn that Colbert outlawed strikes and forbade workers to meet to discuss improving their conditions.

Through these governmental regulations, Colbert created an industrial machine that brought wealth to the nation and to the business class. But it also meant that he had to regulate exports and imports to keep trade lanes open for French products. This led to a strict control of imports (shades of modern Japan!) since France could only keep its industrial machine going by exporting or consuming the fruits of its regulated labor. In the end it fell apart—wars and high tariffs undermined Colbert's regulated system of work and economic control, and his program made him one of the most unpopular men in France, if not Europe. Even the businessmen he made rich felt that the plethora of regulations clogged development and expansion. One businessman told the minister flatly: "You found the carriage overturned on one side, and you have upset it on the other." Colbert died on September 6, 1683, and he had to be buried at night for fear his body would be desecrated by the rabble.

More regulations today might help avoid near-collisions in the air, but they also might cause head-on crashes between the executive branch and the executive suite. What we need to question is how to establish a balance between governmental help and governmental suffocation, and the very meaning of what a government is supposed to do. If governments exist to help the people they govern—including the maintenance of a meaningful quality of life, free from internal and external invasion and devastation—then some thinking will be required on how best to spend the money allotted by the people for their own wellbeing. But if governments exist simply to help those connected to the government, then the very usefulness of government must come into question, as it has been in the Soviet Union. Regulations and laws are not new, nor are they intrinsically bad or self-serving. But as Colbert learned with too many rules—and perhaps Ronald Reagan and his disciples will with too few—the key is to define a course where the benefits for all are clearly visible. Running the course is yet another challenge.

JOSEPH II TAKES ON THE THREE T'S

Several battles heated up in the 1980s involving what the government's role should be in certain areas we shall call the *Three T's:* taxes, tariffs, and technology. And in each case, solutions are far from becoming apparent. Although it is true that the United States has new tax laws, it is also true that many find them not only incomprehensible but inequitable, still favoring the few at the expense of many more. What the public can do about it is uncertain, but the laws will undoubtedly fall to newer ones as America attempts to figure out how to keep its wealthy happy and everybody else calm and collected.

The other two T's are tariffs and technology. We have already explored the situation with Japan and other foreign exporters, and the dialogue continues on whether to impose tariffs on trade, and at what political price. Thousands have lost jobs in industries that cannot compete with foreign goods. And despite the decline of the dollar at the end of the decade, making exports more expensive, there are many who want to protect those things "Made in the U.S.A." Then there is technology and the government's role—or lack of a role—in supporting research and development to keep the country competitive globally. When the government readily antes up money, usually it is for military research. That begs an important question: Should the U.S. government get involved in supporting the development of high-tech machinery for nonmilitary use, as do the Japanese and other Western nations who foot the bill for billions of dollars of research and development?

A Holy Roman Emperor, Joseph II, grappled with these same problems but did not bat an eyelash when he made up his mind on what to do. Coming to power in Austria in 1765, he initiated a series of governmental reforms that addressed the three T's with vigor. As an absolute monarch, Joseph had little difficulty pushing through laws. He revised the tax structure to reflect a single land tax paid by all landowners, regardless of wealth or rank. The great winner was the peasant, who now pocketed 70 percent of his income; under the old law he kept 27 percent, with the remainder going to the nobles and the church. The aristocracy, of course, was not overjoyed, fearing the loss of income would deplete their resources. In Hungary, a revolt broke out. But initially, most people could live with the new law.

Joseph also provided support for the manufacturers and merchants. Many were granted honorific titles, and he reduced internal tolls to encourage trade. He also kept high tariffs on imports to protect domestic goods. Unfortunately, the tariffs allowed manufacturers at home to raise prices and produce lower-quality products. The tariffs also produced retaliation: Prussia, Saxony, and Turkey refused to accept Austrian goods. When it came to technology, Joseph discovered numerous restrictions placed upon economic development. But while he encouraged industrial growth, he was against an increase in producing industrial machinery for fear it would throw thousands of people out of work—a similar fear regarding computers in the late 20th century.

The epithet "Enlightened Despot" has been attached to this reform-minded monarch, who died in 1790 at the age of 48. But he instituted reforms his country was not ready to accept permanently. Joseph may have moved too quickly in too many directions or simply failed to gain a majority to support his actions. But it became evident that the citizens of his empire, when pressed to the wall, preferred their old beliefs and customs—including a feudal system where the wealthy ruled supreme. Three weeks before he died, Joseph II rescinded all the reforms enacted since he became emperor.

Citizens may want, unrealistically, a government that solves all their problems in a fair and balanced fashion. But when push comes to shove, new reforms often look worse than the old evils, this being the opposite side of the policy coin of doing little or nothing. It is an interesting perception of the past coming home to roost—one that reform-minded governments must consider before attacking problems for the common good.

DECENTRALIZATION IS AN IMPERIAL IDEA

The opposite of regulation is none at all, and thus a belief that the central government should decentralize its function and allow local governments and municipalities to run their own shows. The national government then exists for guidance, minimal funding of local projects, and the protection of the whole country from outside forces. But is that what a central government is for, and can such decentralization work? Let's look at perhaps the greatest decentralized entity in history, the now familiar Roman Empire, with its vast network of roads, city centers, and administrative districts—all reporting to Rome.

When the empire first began to expand, the idea was to leave in place what wasn't broken, and this seemed to work. An order from Mark Antony in 42 B.C. to the council and magistrates of Aphrodisias in Caria shows the practice of Roman leaders granting autonomy. He spoke highly of the Roman envoy, Solon, who "has handled your public interests most diligently." Solon asked for, and received, documents from Antony showing previous Roman laws "issued for [the city's] benefit." Those documents, from the time of Julius Caesar (100–44 B.C.), noted that the city could "employ its own [system of] justice and judgments, without posting security at Rome pursuant to any resolution or order." They also allowed the citizens to "have, possess, use and enjoy the villages, districts, strongholds, uplands and revenues with which they came to the friendship of the [Roman] people."

To show his support for his right-hand man abroad, Antony noted that "I have conferred upon him appropriate benefactions, judging him a man worthy of honor from us, and I congratulate you on having such a citizen." Thus a decentralized system of government was born, and it continued to thrive. By 25 B.C., under Augustus Caesar, treaties were made to the mutual benefit of the distant towns and the Roman Empire. A decree of the Senate ordered the town of Mytilene to refuse passage of Rome's enemies through their borders, not even by "public decision." In return, Rome promised that the "Roman people shall come to the aid of the people of Mytilene" if attacked. A letter to the envoys of Chios in about 10 A.D. noted that

> the Senate [of Rome] guaranteed the Chians, in response to their representations as to all they had done in loyal support of the Romans . . . that they might continue to employ the laws, customs and legal procedures which they observed when they entered the friendship of the Romans.

Although decentralization made sense as the empire grew, it also meant that consistency in governance was difficult to maintain over vast distances. And all it took for the whole thing to come unglued was the steady influx of foreigners to the empire, who slowly gained power from province to province until the enemy from without became the enemy within.

Europe today, with its various countries bordering neighbors that have been both historic friends or enemies, has more to fear from attack than the United States, which is isolated from Europe and bordered by friendly nations, Canada and Mexico. But aside from the central government's function as a soldier protecting the realm, decentralization can work if local governments are able to solve their own problems and possess the tools to do so. For Western countries, most of the resources—in the form of taxes—go to the national government for its own use, often with inadequate allocations for the hundreds or thousands of cities and towns in need of funds. When the Reagan administration took a hands-off attitude on local affairs while increasing national defense on a prodigious scale of spending, it looked as though the power of Rome was in the offing; the central government provided the military protection for the nation while the local governments fended for themselves.

Time will tell if American federal governments of the 1990s swing back to local intervention and aid, or pursue an imperial course where city and town must find their own way. If the latter policy continues, Americans—who are mesmerized by symbols and slogans—might consider dressing up their 100 senators in Roman togas to pay tribute to their predecessors, the Roman senators. It would be more than a gesture—it would signify a return to the very, very old days, when the central government thought of war and taxes, leaving the rest of life to those living outside the Capitoline of Rome, or now the Capitol of the United States.

THE GOVERNMENT'S DAYS ARE NUMBERED: SOME OBSERVATIONS

We in the modern era have become fascinated with the numbers game—generating and analyzing all sorts of data to prove or disprove a point or plan. The government is a key player, and every day statistics are released on such subjects as employment, gross national product, personal income, retail sales, the trade deficit, new construction and housing starts, the consumer price index—you name it, they've got it. Most interesting of all, both the proponents and antagonists of a particular cause harvest the numbers to bolster their respective positions or arguments. Curiously, each side uses the same numbers to attack the other's position. And the government—and its officials—use numbers liberally and frequently when seeking support for a program, or justifying one in progress or completed.

Many great minds have pondered the plethora of statistics and their usefulness. Some have not been overjoyed with the abundance of numbers and what they purport to signify. The 19th-century American short-story writer O. Henry is supposed to have called statistics "the lowest grade of information known to exist." While cynical, the aphorism points to a greater truth: A number is only as good as its source. One anonymous commentator, quoted by the early-20th-century English economist and financier Sir Josiah Stamp, understood the problem of attaching importance to numbers derived from less than perfect sources:

> The government are very keen on amassing statistics. They collect them, add them, raise them to the Nth power, take the cube root and prepare wonderful diagrams. But you must never forget that every one of these figures comes in the first instance from the village watchman, who just puts down what he damn well pleases.

Moreover, numbers can be seductive. They can suggest trends, a course of action—even moods. The problem lies in verifying interpretations of those numbers. The motto of Britain's Central Statistical Office offers a warning about basing interpretations on numbers: "Any figure that looks interesting is probably wrong."

Yet somewhere within the numbers lie elements of truth about current events and what may happen in the future, or so the government hopes. In 1849, the *Journal of the Statistical Society* defined the statistician's work as a search for the truth: "We are employed in narrowing the circle within which the final truths must lie, rather than in an attempt at once to seize them." Other observers of statistics have noted the danger in relying too much on surveys, analyses, and projects, regardless of how the circle is narrowed. Walter Bagehot, the 19th-century English writer, said that " 'political economy' is in danger of dissolving into 'statistics,' which is much as if anecdotes of animals were substituted for the science of biology." Recent technological advances suggest that all of us, not just the government, will rely ever more heavily on statistics because of our greater capabilities to produce them. The difficulty will be in wading through the mass of numbers to come up with clues to the meaning of a result or a trend, both for the short term and the long term.

But the study and usage of numbers never should be viewed as an end unto itself, regardless of what a government would have us believe. As the late-19th-century author Andrew Lang wrote, "He uses statistics as a drunken man uses lamp-posts—for support rather than illumination." It is still up to human beings to decide what the numbers mean, and what courses of action need to be taken. Governments should be wary about basing their programs or their successes on numbers. It is the people behind the numbers that matter. A reduction of .2 percent in the unemployment "number" means little to millions out of work, and millions more fearing their number will come up next.

HENRY TUDOR AND NEW HEADS OF STATE

When a new president or prime minister takes up the mantle of leadership, it is a trying time as the country wonders what course the new government will take while the person in charge endeavors to hire a new cast of characters and set an agenda for the future. But besides trying to keep campaign promises—or coyly disavowing them when they remain unfulfilled—there is a curious situation that occurs in the short term: The leader will have to assert control over his or her administration even before getting to the task of running the country. For although the leader will work through current government officials as well as the new ones he or she brings in, there will be a certain amount of self-directed activity quite separate from the leader's wishes. The reason: new leaders are usually weak when arriving on the scene of a functioning bureaucracy because they must "create" a power base—they must establish loyalty and respect, and that takes time. Moreover, the officials and executives already in place take advantage of this weakness by running their own show, at least until the chief asserts himself. Should he fail to take charge, then the ship of state goes its own way, quite often crashing on the shoals of indecision and inactivity.

This is what almost happened upon the death of Henry Tudor, crowned Henry VII and the first English king of the Tudor dynasty, who died in 1509. He left an 18-year-old heir to the throne who, until as late as 1502, was destined to become a churchman, not a king. But Henry VII's eldest son and heir, Arthur, had died young, leaving the only other surviving male heir, Henry, to take the throne. So in 1509, young Henry VIII was crowned king among the seasoned ministers and officials of state who had run the government under his father.

The business of kings during the Renaissance was war, and young Henry VIII wanted to jump into the European fray and maybe pick up some real estate, as the past glorious kings of England had done. But that required money, and money was the business of the national treasury, the exchequer. Under his father, who perhaps scrutinized the royal accounts more than any other king—we have his signature on page after page of account books—much of the royal treasure was diverted from exchequer review and deposited in the king's personal chamber. This gave Henry VII money whenever he wanted it, and allowed him to maintain a strong, solvent monarchy. But when he died, the exchequeur officials decided that enough was enough and it was a good time to exercise their ancient responsibilities as debt collectors and keepers of the royal funds—a responsibility that also brought in fees.

This they did, to the dismay of a young king itching for war and trying desperately to secure money expeditiously so he could launch an army on the Continent. Through his father's close ministers he wrote letters and declared orders to have all debts due the crown, and any monies collected, to come directly to his chamber, bypassing the exchequer. The exchequer officials hardly convulsed with joy. Although they began complying with the orders, by 1513 they were once again keeping both the royal debts and the money. But by this time, an experienced king sat on the throne, fresh from a dubiously successful campaign abroad and a desire to run his own show. Together with his father's former dispenser of charity, Cardinal Wolsey, he took both the reins and the fiscal responsibility of the kingdom in hand.

Our new leaders of the world will no doubt want to get down to business and run their governments, and not allow their governments to run them. But it will take time to establish both their agendas and their authority over a vast bureaucracy averse to change. (This has never been more evident than in the trials and tribulations facing Mikhail Gorbachev, and whether he can survive long enough to grab total control à la Henry VIII.) For elected leaders with potentially short terms in office (compared to

Henry VII, who ruled for 23 years, and his son, for 38 years) authority must be established quickly to create a viable government that complies with the new agenda. Otherwise all the positive statistics and far-reaching plans in the world will not save a government where the leader lacks authority, and therefore cannot lead.

WILLIAM THE CONQUEROR COUNTED EVERY COW

One pressing issue of the 1980s involved the amount of information the government should, or should not, have about its citizens. In this age of computer storage and instant credit checks, it is worrisome that so much information about an individual is known to the government and large companies, and that it can be retrieved at the push of a button. What's more, information breeds more information: Should you use the Freedom of Information Act to ask the U.S. government if it has information about you, you are likely to have a file opened up for making the request. If you then discover that no file on you existed, it does now!

Historically, knowledge has always meant power, especially to governments in search of new forms of taxation or military adventures. The United States and the Soviet Union have not been the only ones in the business of snooping into people's business. The ancient Romans gave us our word *census* from the censors who supervised counting the number of citizens in the empire. It was one of the first wide-scale systems of gathering information about a country's inhabitants. The rulers of Rome learned quickly how valuable that information could be, especially for the tax rolls. By 44 B.C. Julius Caesar ordered that the census should be tabulated street by street and building by building. His heir, Augustus Caesar (27 B.C.–14 A.D.), who by now ruled as emperor and not through a popular government, took the census further. According to the Gospel of Luke, an edict went out "for the whole world to register in the census." One Roman complained that the officials "investigate our levels and morals as well as take the census"—a criticism that might apply to recent U.S. Supreme Court decisions about prosecuting private behavior.

If the Romans didn't like being counted or categorized, one can imagine how the Anglo-Saxons felt about it after the Norman Conquest over 900 years ago. William the Conqueror, who earned his descriptive title in 1066 by invading England, decided to find out exactly who it was he conquered and exactly what they owned. In 1086, his officials produced an incredible survey of England known as the *Domesday Book* (pronounced "doomsday"). Domesday was a compilation of information about every person in every shire in England, what village they lived in, their personal worth, and even how many animals they had. William's motive, of course, was not mere curiosity. He wanted to assess the wealth of the country to determine what tax he might levy on the conquered people.

The Anglo-Saxons were less than rapturous at this intrusion into their lives by this Norman king. One Saxon monk wrote: "So narrowly did he cause the survey to be made that there was not one single hide nor rood of land, nor—it is shameful to tell but he thought it no shame to do—was there an ox, cow or swine that was not set down in the writ."

So while it is true that we complain about the government having too much information about us, it gives one pause to realize that, in past years, other cultures also had to put up with the counting of heads (and cows), and often in greater detail. Were William the Conqueror alive today, he would probably complain about how *little* the U.S. government knows about its citizens. It was lucky for the Saxons that William didn't come up with a computer as well as a conquest!

PROTECTING THE PRINCE: WATERGATE

Governments—and those who head them—spend a fair amount of time and energy seeking ways to claim credit for things that go right. After all, their livelihood—and perhaps more important, their reputations—depend on making things happen, and remaining *popular* (a word whose root means "of the people"). But when things go wrong, too often the head of government and his chief advisers circle the wagons and plead innocence. Governments and leaders have always possessed this no-fault posture, which has often bordered on siege mentality because there are lots of *enemies* out there—waiting to discredit the current government and oust it in order to form their own.

An interesting tactical approach to deflecting blame from the top took place in the 1970s with a scandal known as "Watergate." This refers to a break-in at the Democratic National Convention headquarters at the Watergate complex in Washington, D.C., in June 1972, prior to the November presidential election. The incumbent president, Richard M. Nixon, was seeking reelection to the presidency at all costs, and plans were laid to disrupt and sabotage the Democratic party's efforts to get their candidate, George McGovern, elected. Watergate was one of those plans. The culprits, who apparently broke into the Watergate to replace bugging devices previously placed there, were apprehended. But the ensuing investigations by the government, in judicial proceedings, and by the newspapers turned up a nasty trail of deceit and coverup that led directly to the White House and President Nixon. It was to cause him to resign from office.

During the course of the Watergate investigations, Nixon and his cronies came up with an interesting approach to protect both himself and his closest advisers, and to shield them from blame: *executive privilege.* This veil of an unwritten, self-proclaimed privilege employed the notion that the president and his aides were protected from prosecution under a right of the presidency to keep his people above such due process of law. Executive privilege was hotly debated, although examples claiming such privilege dated back to 1886. In the end, however, it failed to keep Nixon and his minions safe from the truth. Numerous indictments and several convictions of top administration officials demonstrated that even if the head of state didn't want the people to know of wrongdoing under his very nose, it was destined to come out anyway, executive privilege notwithstanding.

The U.S. Constitution didn't create a strong executive or executive privilege—a reaction to the rule of King George III. But while Nixon's call for this privilege was not Constitution-based, it found relevance in English customs and traditions . . . for kings. That tradition was the *royal prerogative,* a belief that the head of state could do certain things beyond the law. While coronation oaths were probably sworn by kings since the year 1100 to uphold the common law, monarchs also claimed certain privileges, or royal prerogatives. They did so until a 17th-century crisis brought the practice to a debate that ended in civil war.

In a way similar to the thinking of our emerging Congress in the 19th century, Parliament had felt that it embodied both rights and privileges, and that tradition and law supported these beliefs. Unfortunately for English monarchy, or perhaps inevitably for the development of democracy, the kings at the time, James I and Charles I, held firmly to their prerogatives—and Parliament be damned. James I informed Parliament in 1610 that "it was dangerous to submit the power of the king to definition"—a thought Richard Nixon may have empathized with. Not long after that, Parliament abolished kingship, one reason being "that for the most part use has been made of the regal power and prerogative to oppress and impoverish and enslave the subject."

If a leader of government goes beyond written law to accomplish his proclaimed destiny or to protect himself from blame when people are pointing fingers, it could be viewed as the traditional use of power cloaked in the guise of legality. But conflicts arise when a democratic body sees its own traditions trampled by the leader and his counselors, especially when so-called privileges contribute to hiding the truth or allowing unethical behavior. Then the rulebook is questioned, and the game is played to some resolution, violent or otherwise. We will return to Mr. Nixon, kingship, and ethics in the last chapter.

PROTECTING THE PRINCE: THE IRAN-CONTRA AFFAIR

The Republican administration in the 1980s ran into a problem of illegal doings that reflected poorly on the president: the Iran-Contra affair. When national security advisers John Poindexter and Oliver North departed from their jobs in late 1986, it was really the tip of a very large iceberg that included Swiss bank accounts, weapons, and money siphoned off to aid rebels fighting in Nicaragua. And like Watergate, those working directly or indirectly for the president felt they had to protect their leader from scandal, even if it meant telling less than the truth, or losing their jobs, or facing prosecution. It also meant that the president could claim ignorance—as Nixon had done about the Watergate coverup—with the hope of saving the presidency. President Reagan succeeded; President Nixon failed.

We have seen more than once the actions and activities of the Tudor kings of England to protect themselves, especially the loss of Thomas Cromwell's head after Henry VIII met his fourth wife, Anne of Cleves; Henry was underwhelmed enough to divorce her and shortened Cromwell's career and height. But that was to be expected: Kings historically could do no wrong, unless they were so bad that rebellion was the only alternative. Henry VIII may have figured it out for himself when he gained the throne in 1509. In that year, people were in an uproar over the harsh financial policies of his father, Henry VII, and justice was demanded. The young Henry VIII, although aware that dear old dad did, in fact, spend much of his time relieving subjects of their money, nonetheless sought out scapegoats to take the blame. However, no finger could be pointed at the late Henry VII, only at his "evil ministers." That is indeed what happened, and in August 1510, two of Henry VII's key financial advisers, who did no more than carry out the royal favor, lost their heads on Tower Hill.

If Henry VIII was an astute leader he was also a good teacher, and his daughter Elizabeth must have been taking notes. In 1558, she was crowned Queen Elizabeth I and became a successful leader by pitting advisers against each other, making sure that someone other than herself took the blame when things went awry. One famous example centers on her rebellious cousin, Mary, Queen of Scots, who sought to unite England and Scotland under a Catholic queen—herself. She failed and spent almost two decades under house arrest. After several unsuccessful attempts by Mary to support an overthrow of Elizabeth by her Catholic allies at home and abroad, the Queen of England figured enough was enough. Elizabeth let it be known to her advisers that she *wished* the demise of Mary, and even signed a death order to that effect. But when the deed was done, Elizabeth denied having anything to do with it (today her lawyers would plead duress on signing the warrant), and her loyal secretary, pen in hand, was thrown into the Tower of London. He was quietly released from the Tower once the commotion from knocking off a queen subsided, and Elizabeth went back to work making blameless decrees and pointing fingers like so many thorns on a rose—in her case the Red Rose of the Tudor dynasty.

Ronald Reagan, like Richard Nixon, escaped prosecution relating to affairs that smacked of White House approval and knowledge, although Nixon ultimately resigned his office. Instead, many of their loyal servants went out in front of their chiefs and did what they felt they had to do to protect them— either tell the truth or commit perjury. Yet it should be noted that protecting the prince also means refraining from negative comments about past leaders of dubious character by those newly placed in power: young Henry VIII was very careful not to knock dear old dad. The Soviet Union is a prime example of successive leaders who have had to walk warily when it came to talking about the previous regime. Only with Mikhail Gorbachev has there been a break with this kind of behavior—Stalin and Lenin are now under review and the glimmer from their "achievements" is beginning to fade. Only time will tell if it works, or if he will become the victim of his own changes and suffer defeat and defilement. There will be no one to protect him.

TAKING THE PULSE OF THE NATION

Popularity means survival—there is no way a government can survive if the majority of the people are against it. Even with total control by a military police, governments of such a genre must constantly keep vigil to prevent a revolt. The late Ferdinand Marcos found that out in the form of a quiet lady named Corazon Aquino and 1989 marked the overthrow of governments in Eastern Europe by their people. To maintain their popularity, especially when policies aren't working, leaders try to get out among the people to be seen, heard, and—they hope—adored. If they are out of sight, they are out of mind except for the things they haven't accomplished, which are usually in plain view. Leaders throughout history have known this; the leaders of tomorrow have the incredible tool of television to reach everyone in one fell swoop.

We might go back to the reign of our previously mentioned politician—Queen Elizabeth I of England (1558–1603)—to see how her style of taking the pulse of the people was flawless. It was also the opposite of today's political efforts. Where 20th-century leaders help businesses and towns by visiting them, the Fairie Queen actually brought those towns and hosts she visited to the brink of financial ruin—it was they who paid the bill.

When Elizabeth became queen in 1558 it was not uncommon for the ruling monarch to make annual progresses through the countryside. Elizabeth, however, did it in grand style. Hundreds of carts bore the baggage of the queen and her royal household and entourage. Since the procession could only cover 10 or 12 miles a day, the queen usually spent the night in one of her royal residences or in the home of a nobleman. If a city was chosen to host her, the town leaders were expected to spend big bucks (or rather pounds) to impress Her Majesty. On one occasion when a sheriff met the queen, he had with him 200 gentlemen in white velvet and 300 lesser men in black velvet coats. These were followed by 1,500 serving men.

Towns cleaned the streets, fixed up the houses, and shelled out money to buy gifts for the queen and her company. At the city of Sandwich, the wives of the town magistrates prepared a banquet of 160 dishes on a 28-foot-long table. And at Norwich, after a typical outlay, Elizabeth purportedly departed saying, "I have laid up in my breast such good will, as I shall never forget Norwich." No doubt they never forgot her, either. Although visits to private homes meant that food and furnishings were paid for by the royal household, the host was expected to spend lots of money and put on a good show to impress the queen. Today, it is the politicians who are expected to put on a good show to impress the citizens. Things change.

The shows for royalty included gifts and entertainment and could cost a fortune. In 1577 a four-day stay cost Sir Nicholas Bacon about 577 pounds, a huge sum by 16th-century standards. A 10-day stay at Lord Burghley's abode in 1591 cost more than 1,000 pounds; a three-day visit to Lord Keeper Egerton in 1602—a year before the queen died—ran about 2,000 pounds. One major loser was the earl of Hereford. In 1591, he received the queen for just three days, yet had 300 workmen enlarge the house, erect outbuildings for the royal entourage, and dig a pond to be used as part of a play. When the affair was over the unlucky lord was left to lick his financial wounds. As one historian put it, "The earl was left to foot the bill and count the silver and dishes and all manner of movables, for the passing of the queen's followers was apt to resemble that of a plague of locusts."

So we shouldn't feel put out by our leaders when they pop in to say hello to Pittsburgh or Toronto or Bonn or Poitiers or Manchester or Sidney. The cost to the taxpayer is piddly compared to the personal visits foisted upon medieval men and women. And a baby or two being kissed is harmless when you compare that to their parents having to pay for a play or feed a thousand people 30 meals. Today the alternative is to rely on television, with its makeup, camera angles, and prepared expressions. A little in-person perspective isn't so bad, and it lets us all know that the computers haven't taken over running the government completely. Or at least one hopes.

CHARLEMAGNE AND THE ART OF SPEAKING OUT

Anyone in a state of semiconsciousness during a national election in a Western democracy cannot help but notice the abundance of rhetoric flying forth like so many swallows returning to Capistrano, wanted or not. This represents the ritual known as *speaking out on the issues,* or if we want to be honest, trying to get a job by waxing eloquently and not tripping over facts or gaffs. Once in office, government leaders and senior officials continue this course of oral salesmanship, launching catch words and phrases abroad to show that the government is working. This, they hope, will allow *them* to continue working as well.

Some leaders are very good at it—Ronald Reagan was dubbed the "Great Communicator" because he had a way of saying what people wanted to hear: never mind if it was true or realistic or even intelligible, or that it came off cue cards. Since perceptions have always been more important than the truth, those capable of speaking out successfully will ultimately reach a certain degree of success, be it Reagan, Winston Churchill, Adolph Hitler, or Jim Bakker. This is an old behavioral trait in humans, however—you will note that other animals get their points across with gestures and brute strength.

One leader who hardly needed eloquence in speech but who nonetheless possessed such talent was Charles the Great, or Charlemagne. During his lifetime (742–814 A.D.), he was not only renowned for his prowess on the battlefield but also in the areas of culture, learning, and architecture—a Renaissance man 700 years before the Renaissance! As a conqueror, king of the Franks, and emperor of the West, he followed in the footsteps of his family and gained control of much of Western Europe. He also actively promoted Christianity, and he founded schools and became a patron of teachers and scholars.

In his book, *The Life of Charlemagne,* the 9th-century writer and member of the Frankish nobility Einhard noted Charlemagne's abilities in learning and speech. Charlemagne's teacher was Alcuin, "a man of Saxon race from Britain, the most learned man of his time," Einhard wrote. "Under him he devoted a great deal of time and effort to the study of rhetoric and dialectics and particularly astronomy." Another area of interest to the emperor was writing, which he accomplished on his own. Einhard wrote that Charlemagne "was accustomed to surround his pillows on his bed with tablets and notebooks for this purpose, so that when he had any spare time he would train his hand to form letters." (Many executives, including those in the White House, would not go this far today.) Einhard admitted, however, that Charlemagne "met with little success in these efforts because he had started too late in his life."

But it was Charlemagne's gift as a speaker that helped form the legend of this king: "He had a readiness and richness of speech and a capacity for the most lucid exposition," Einhard said. "Not satisfied with the vernacular, he even took pains to learn foreign languages; he mastered Latin so effectively that he even appeared loquacious." Imagine American leaders today learning the languages of their counterparts in other countries . . . it sounds too logical and productive to come to pass! In one respect, Charlemagne was following a school of thought dating back to the time of Socrates (470?–399 B.C.), where truth could be discovered through questioning and reasoning between two or more people. It is apparent that, to Charlemagne, speaking clearly and effectively was something leaders needed to do, and do well. And part of that skill required extensive study in culture, science, and learning so that what was spoken by the leader would be intelligent and meaningful.

In the late 20th century not many leaders set out on the road of intellectual pursuit. For many of them it is more important to look good and sound good than to have any innate intelligence or extensive knowledge beyond the briefing books and the scripted speeches. In the 1988 presidential election in the United States, the Democratic candidate was accused of snobbery and elitism because of his connection with one of the most prestigious institutions of learning in the world: Harvard. The Republican candidate distanced himself so much from his own impressive academic institution, Yale University, that he could avoid the stigma of being too smart or too knowledgeable.

What has happened here? Why has being intelligent and forthright become a liability for leadership, when throughout history such attributes stood as important qualities, even necessities, for good leadership? It would be easy to blame television, the decline in education, or the rise of a pushbutton society where thinking is not required. But it goes deeper than that. We are obsessed with appearance, not substance, which again defies historical experience. We are almost frightened of an independent thinker: Jury selection by lawyers is based on choosing jurors who can be swayed and cajoled, not on finding 12 objective thinkers who can weigh facts and arrive at a fair conclusion.

Charlemagne would have a hard time finding his equal from among the current crop of leaders in our world. We might also guess that he would attempt to learn everyone's language; few leaders in our world would make the effort to learn his. One wonders what would come to pass if the Frankish king and a late-20th-century world leader were left in a room to write their own speeches on the state of things and the plans for tomorrow. The smart odds-makers in Las Vegas would have little difficulty placing bets on who would come up with the more meaningful speech.

DIPLOMACY, IMMUNITY, AND THE QUEEN OF SHEBA

Diplomacy is the craft of government, whereby leaders spend much of their time trying to avoid warring with their fellow leaders while maintaining an open dialogue to sustain peace. Whatever kind of government comes into being within a country, much of its time will be spent protecting the interests of the country through communications with other countries. (We explored the concept of the summit in Chapter 1). In order to accomplish this activity with friend and foe alike, immunity from arrest for diplomats and elected officials developed when those offices were viewed as essential to the maintenance of international communication and the viable functioning of governments.

The concept is old but not without controversy. The envoy (*envoyer*, to send) was a messenger of one ruler traveling to the realm of another, and though in theory immune from harm, they often had problems—we saw what happened to Liudprand at the court of Nicephorus in Chapter 6! More than 2,400 years ago, two messengers of the belligerent King Darius of Persia traveled to Athens and Sparta to demand surrender. In Athens, the envoys were thrown into a pit; in Sparta, they were tossed down a well—not too hospitable were the Greeks to their Persian enemies! Nevertheless, the sanctity of diplomats did prevail: In Sparta, the leaders asked for volunteers to go to Persia and offer their lives to amend the indignities perpetrated against the Persian envoys. Xerxes, the new Persian king, spared the volunteers' lives, saying he wasn't like the Spartans, who "by murdering the ambassadors of a foreign power, had broken the law which all the world holds sacred"—a view often lost today when ambassadors are murdered.

The rights of officials in the government were also recognized early, although political circumstances could negate those rights. In 44 B.C., a Senate packed with Julius Caesar's friends could nonetheless murder him for exceeding his authority. Fifteen years later, Augustus Caesar could expel 190 "unworthy" senators. Even the dignity of senators was violated when, under

Caligula's rule (37–41 A.D.), they were made to run for miles beside his chariot.

By medieval times, members of Parliament in England had "implied freedom from arrest" arising from a private suit. The rationale was simple: Men were called to Parliament to do the king's business and therefore could not be hindered by actions at law. But violations of immunity were not unknown: On January 4, 1642, King Charles I marched to the House of Commons with 400 swordsmen to arrest five men he felt were undermining his authority. The men were warned in advance and fled, leaving Charles to remark "the birds have flown."

The defense today is that immunity must be afforded diplomats and government officials so they can function without fear of outside interference, but concern about abuse of such protection remains. Diplomatic immunity is a nice cover for spy activities, and ill-doings by government officials sometimes encourage the perpetrators to seek protection under the privilege of their offices (a ploy Richard Nixon & Company tried during the Watergate investigations). But putting aside the internal business of government, it is clear that, in order to accomplish international business between nations, it is important to protect the messengers and ensure that they are not harmed just because they carry bad news. Governments of old recognized this in all corners of the globe; we need to remember it as well.

Then there is the actual practice of diplomacy whereby countries communicate in a friendly way even if they have rather unfriendly thoughts about each other. In ancient times, the way that different peoples interacted was through the medium of gift-giving. Gifts were exchanged as tokens of friendship—or at least a lack of ill will—and thus set up an atmosphere for open dialogue. The Old Testament has many examples of gift-giving, perhaps the best known being the gifts given King Solomon by the Queen of Sheba, from Arabia. After meeting Solomon (10th century B.C.) to see if he lived up to his reputation for wisdom, the queen was so impressed she gave him "120 talents of gold [or about $9 million today] and a very great quantity of spices and precious stones; never again came such an abundance of spices as these which the queen of Sheba gave to King Solomon." (I Kings

10:10) There was undoubtedly a little method to her madness, since Sheba needed to ally with Solomon to protect her trade routes. Not only was Solomon wise, he was also enormously wealthy and owned a good chunk of the Mideast trade industry.

Gift-giving was an important means of interaction among nations and peoples of the Mediterranean world. Among the ancient Greeks, there were no national states, and travelers were dependent upon the hospitality they received from their hosts. This included gift-giving, and those who gave gifts expected to receive them. According to the *Odyssey,* after Odysseus related his adventures following the fall of Troy to the king of Phaeacia, the king thanked him and declared that "intricately wrought gold, and all other gifts" were to be given to Odysseus. The king also enjoined each Phaeacian noble to give Odysseus a tripod and gold cauldron, "and we will make it good to us by a collection among the people"—meaning the taxpayers were about to ante up for a shipload of gifts to send Odysseus packing for home. It was definitely a wise investment nonetheless, since Odysseus, a king himself, started to see his luck turn for the better after 10 years of wandering. Once back on his throne, he would be a powerful ally to have, and a galleyfull of gifts can make the heart grow fonder, especially during times of war.

Today most world leaders and governments fear what might happen to their careers if they receive lavish gifts from foreign countries as tokens of friendship: It looks too much like a bribe. Yet maybe this old custom should be reestablished: Gift-giving would allow governments to spend quality time thinking up impressive presents to bestow upon other countries as remembrances of peaceful gestures, not of warlike threats. Gestures by governments and leaders are powerful symbols, whether they be Premier Nikita Khruschev's shoe-slamming at the United Nations or a wreath placed at the tomb of an unknown soldier. Why not a lasting gesture of peace—couldn't countries allot space wherein to receive special gifts from other governments? Those would be powerful symbols, too—symbols of attempts by different governments to communicate openly, and in a spirit of good will.

POLITICS AND THE DEATH OF THE
OLYMPIC MYTH

Many in the world of sport and disport believe that the Olympic movement is chugging to an ignominious halt because of geopolitics. After all, they argue, the American boycott of the 1980 Games in Moscow was followed by the Russian boycott of the 1984 Games in Los Angeles—clear examples of superpowers spoiling the Olympic ideal of brotherhood and fair play. And since both the Soviet Union and China did not have diplomatic relations with South Korea when that country hosted the 1988 Games, making their participation largely unknown until months before the event, isn't the whole affair a little shaky on its feet, with no place to go but down for the count amid a plethora of political pandemonia?

Further, politics are found not only in government but in all aspects of life—in business, art, news, education—so can't we make an exception and keep the Olympics politics-free, as they are supposed to be? The Olympics, many believe, are where the amateur youths of the world—although many get *paid* to be amateurs—can gather and glory in their physical prowess, supposedly untouched by the world of politics. And it is precisely politics—from prejudicial judges to governmental interference—that is destroying the very essence of the Olympic philosophy.

Well, wishful thinking aside, although the Olympics probably aren't dead yet, the *myth* of the Olympics—that it stands for something pure and apolitical—can clearly be declared null and void. This myth should never have been fostered to begin with, because the Olympic Games have *always* been political. Some ancient examples might prove useful so that eulogies may be kept brief and rational minds can claim to have discounted the myth all along. First the myth:

The earliest recorded Games were in 776 B.C. when the foot-race was won by Coroebus, a cook from the city of Elis near Olympia. Unlike the modern Olympics, which are canceled during times of war, in ancient Greece any warfare in progress during the month of the Games was suspended and an immediate truce effected until the contests were concluded. This no doubt contributed to the belief that war—and politics—were outside the Olympics. The Olympics declined in prestige and honor after the conquest of Greece by Rome, and in 394 A.D. they were abolished altogether by the Christian emperor Theodosius, who deemed them a pagan celebration. They were revived some 1500 years later and here we are today.

How pure and apolitical were the Olympics in ancient times? One need only read our oft-quoted ancient historian, Herodotus (490?–425? B.C.) to see how the Olympics became political as well as athletic arenas of might and power. One observation relevant to the present world situation is the influence the host country might have over the Olympics. Herodotus related the story of the pharaoh of Egypt, Psammis (or Psammetichus II, *c.* 600 B.C.), who received a deputation of Greeks from the city of Elis. The Eliseans were the host city and organizers of the Olympic Games every four years, and they asked the pharaoh if he could imagine any fairer way of running such a contest than the Eliseans managed to do. Before answering the question, the pharaoh's learned men asked if any people from Elis were allowed to compete in the Games. The Eliseans replied that "competition was free and open to members of all the Greek states, including Elis."

The Egyptians concluded that such an organization was not fair at all, "for it was quite impossible, when men from one's own city took part in some event, not to favor them at the expense of the strangers." If the Eliseans truly wanted fair games, the Egyptians noted, "then they should open the various events to visitors only, and not allow anyone from Elis to compete." The Eliseans were not amused. Adolph Hitler would have ignored the point as well, for in 1936 he staged the Olympics in Berlin precisely to gain advantage over other competitors and to showcase his superior countrymen. Unfortunately, der fuhrer didn't count on a black American named Jesse Owens to upstage his self-proclaimed master race.

The Egyptians, like Hitler and other hosts of the Olympics, were astute observers and believed that controlling the Games had its advantages. Some Greeks thought so as well. Pheidon, tyrant of Argos (*c.* early 7th century B.C.), "turned out the Eliseans whose duty it was to manage the Olympic Games and proceeded to manage them himself." Herodotus was upset by this usurpation and called Pheidon's move "the wickedest and most arrogant thing ever done by a Greek." What the Greek historian failed to mention was that Elis regained the Games through armed force with the help of the Spartans. Alliances, prestige, and home-team advantages were never lost to the participating Greek city-states, nor are they today.

All entrants to the Games had to swear they were free-born Greeks or they could not participate. The Olympics were, therefore, far from the international pageant they are today and only celebrated the feats of one extremely ethnocentric people— global brotherhood was never a consideration. Alexander I of Macedon (c. 500 B.C.) wished to compete in the Olympic Games but "his Greek competitors tried to exclude him on the ground that foreigners were not allowed to take part." Alexander subsequently proved his descent from Argos, "and so was accepted as a Greek and allowed to enter for the foot-race." He came in first, and one wonders if rival countries used the Olympic rules to try and keep out a superior athlete, the "foreigner" from Macedon. The recent travails of the runner Zola Budd suggest this conjecture.

The Games were used as public forums for political exigencies. Cleisthenes, "master" of Sicyon (c. 600–570 B.C.), won the chariot race and then publicly announced that "any Greek who thought himself good enough to become Cleisthenes' son-in-law should present himself in Sicyon within sixty days." He then proceeded to hold his own athletic contests to find "the best man in all Greece" for his daughter. The eventual winner provided a strong political alliance with Cleisthenes' powerful Alcmaeonid family, which controlled much of Greece.

Influential Greek families and their followers were the main political forces in ancient Greece, and the Olympics often allowed a means to gain or regain political advantages, even at the expense of what we would call ethical behavior. Herodotus recorded the story of Cimon, a member of the Philaid family. Cimon was banished from Athens by Pisistratus, ruler of the city and a member of the rival Pisistratid family. While in exile, Cimon won the chariot race at the Olympic Games (532 B.C.). At the next Games, he won the prize a second time, "but this time

[he] waived his victory in favor of Pisistratus, and for allowing the latter to be proclaimed the winner was given leave to return to Athens." Cimon actually won the event a third time (524 B.C.) using the same four mares as in the previous two victories—a feat Herodotus said was accomplished only once before. Soon after, Pisistratus died and Cimon was murdered by the ruler's sons, perhaps for fear of his increased standing in Athens.

As if a consolation to this sad ending for an Olympic hero and political savant, Herodotus added that opposite Cimon's grave were buried the four mares that brought him his triple Olympic victory.

It is interesting to note that commercialism was never part of the ancient Games, as it is today. At the time of the battle of Marathon between the Persians and the Greeks (480 B.C.), Xerxes, king of Persia, heard that the Olympic Games were being held. Upon learning that the Greeks competed for a wreath of olive-leaves, one of Xerxes' governors blurted out, "Good heavens! What kind of men are these we are to fight against—men who compete with one another for no material reward, but only for honor!" This was no doubt a bit of pro-Greek propaganda on the part of our storyteller, Herodotus. Nevertheless, the historian recorded that Xerxes branded the governor a coward and the lesson, at least, is not entirely lost. Our athletes today compete for the honor of victory, but the Persian governor no doubt would have felt vindicated upon learning of the post-Olympian successes found on cereal boxes, on athletic gear, and in television commercials.

Regardless of how athletes or governments perceive the meaning of the modern Olympic Games, it is clear that the Games always will be a focus for politics and diplomacy. The important thing is to recognize that the myth is dead, and perhaps for the better. The Games allow for superior athletes to compete, and for their respective countries to reap whatever political glory and advantage they can harvest. If we are going to have Olympic Games in the future, they should be held in full view of human behavior, and that includes politics. It's a very old story.

8
C H A P T E R

ON RESEARCH, TECHNOLOGY, AND STEALING IDEAS

The term *modern era* refers to recent years, sometimes centuries, that are somehow different from the rest of recorded history. Most often, that difference is found in technology, where advances in the 20th century alone seem to dwarf all that has gone before it. Our present journey to this chapter has shown us that nothing is truly new, and that to understand what we see around us we must look back to similar situations, because we have been there before. This is also true of technology and ideas: despite our ability to go quicker, faster, farther, stronger, longer . . . we still are merely improving upon some very basic activities first tried and tested by the earliest humans. Whether recording three notches on a clay tablet for three bales of wheat, or sending such information over a telephone modem from Maryland to Melbourne, the purpose and need are the same.

ROGER BACON AND THE RESEARCH OF THE MIND

If necessity is the mother of invention, then apparently the 20th century has had many needs. In nearly every dimension of life—transportation, communication, instruction, medicine, construction, food processing, manufacturing—new inventions have come to our attention almost daily. Most inventions have been tied to economics: Machines that are either labor-saving or cost-saving. One invention also tends to spawn another. The canals of America and Britain, for example, demonstrated an easy way to ship goods but were short-lived when railroads began rolling across the landscape for the same purpose. Further, inventions are modified to be less expensive and more efficient. Witness the computer, which 30 years ago took up a whole room. Today, a desktop model can do more, in less time, than its growling, key-punched grandfather did way back in the ancient 1960s.

But while the notion of inventing helped separate humans from their bipedal cousins, inventions were not always created with the thought of practical purpose, or a means to an end. Indeed, many inventions—either on the drawing board or in actual usage—were often mental exercises, created from the curiosity of an imaginative thinker. Most of us know of Leonardo da Vinci (1452–1519) and his diagrams and drawings, detailing intricate designs of flying machines, and of bicycles and para-chutes. How practical he felt these devices were is moot. He was living in a time when technology was not capable of manufactur-ing what he saw in his mind's eye.

One of the most enlightened thinkers of the 13th century was Roger Bacon (*c.* 1214–94). In an age of superstition and ignorance, Bacon believed that through "the shaping and plan-ning of skill alone," rather than by way of magic, works of marvel could be made. "Instruments for navigation can be made without rowers, so that the largest ships, both on river and on sea, are steered by one man only in control at a greater speed than if they were filled with men," he wrote.

> Similarly, carts can be made to move without animals at an incal-culable velocity . . . [and] flying machines can be made so that a man sits inside the machine rotating some ingenious contraption by means of which the wings, artfully arranged, beat the air like a bird flying.

Bacon garnered most of his visions of the future from the ancient Greeks except, he admits, the flying machine, which was con-jured up in his own time by a fellow thinker. But regardless of his sources, Roger Bacon could imagine such "ingenuities" without carrying them to any logical conclusion about their use.

The Greeks created numerous inventions that force us to

wonder how modern we really are. But their inventions came about because they admired machinery, not because they saw any labor-saving value in what they invented. (Joseph II admired machinery, as we have seen, but he was also afraid of its consequences for employment. The ancients had no worries in that area.) The Greek priests of the 1st century A.D. actually used coin-operated machines to dispense sacrificial water in the temples—a trick clearly overlooked by the medieval Roman Catholic church. There were also machines that opened doors, made sounds, and moved objects.

Perhaps the greatest Greek inventor was Heron of Alexandria (c. 2nd century A.D.), who invented a steam engine. Yet he only used the device as a toy. The invention channeled steam from boiling water through a pipe into one side of a hollow ball. The other side of the ball was held in place by a similar solid tube to allow the ball to rotate. The ball had two bent pipes sticking out of opposite sides, and when the steam blew out of these it caused the ball to spin rapidly.

Had it occurred to him that a practical use might come of his steam engine, the locomotive could have been invented 1,500 years earlier. Although he was a great thinker, Heron of Alexandria would have had a tough time at the Harvard School of Business.

SOAP THAT FLOATS, SHOES THAT ROLL

Nowadays, unlike our ancient and medieval forebears, when entrepreneurs and daring corporate heads want to offer something new, they begin with a variety of tools: market research, lifestyle analysis, perceived needs, required benefits, and so forth. After all, it can cost millions of dollars to introduce a better mousetrap or a new widget, to say nothing of the basic startup costs for producing those brainstorms and the machinery required to manufacture them. While it is true that doing your homework can often lead to success, sometimes the most meticulous planning will get you nowhere. The videodisk, which came out at about the same time the videotape was storming the market, is an example of an interesting product with no future at the time: Few consumers wanted it, at least not in the quantities required to build an industry.

Quite often, however, products and industries grow up without the benefit of market research, let alone the daydreaming of a da Vinci or a Bacon: they just sort of happen. When Walter Hunt needed to pay off a $15 debt in 1849, he decided to invent something useful to fulfill the obligation. In just three hours, he came up with a device that allowed him to repay his loan: the safety pin. No market research there, but people quickly found uses for it.

Another example is the familiar story of the accidental discovery by Dr. Alexander Fleming (the son of a Scottish farmer) as he worked in a bacteriology lab in London. In 1928, he noticed a mold forming on several plates of nutrients exposed to the air—a growth that was dissolving a colony of staphylococcus aureaus bacteria he was cultivating. Fleming tried in vain to interest his colleagues in the bacteria-killing mold, which he named penicillin. It took World War II and thousands of infected soldiers to convince researchers that penicillin was useful.

A footnote to the story is even more curious: In 1896, some 32 years before Fleming's discovery, a French medical student named Duchesne discovered penicillin through careful investigation, and not by accident. Although he tested it on animals as a possible antibiotic, he never pursued its potential. Fleming did and ended up with a Nobel Prize.

Most children grow up marveling at how clever Procter & Gamble Company was to make its Ivory soap float. Wonder of wonders, when it was developed, Ivory sank like any other soap. But one day, a Procter & Gamble worker forgot to turn off a soap-making machine when he left the laboratory, and upon his return he was greeted by a foamy mixture. The company did not want to waste this concoction, so it made soap out of it and was rewarded with mail from elated purchasers who wanted more floating soap. The result: Procter & Gamble discovered that the unfinished soap had been mixed with air, creating a product that was lighter than its predecessor and less expensive to make because it used less mixture. It was a rare development in the history of retailing: Consumers were thrilled with *less* product for the same money.

Perhaps the oddest origin of an industry based on an accidental invention occurred in 1759, when a musical instrument-maker named Joseph Merlin was invited to a costume party in London. Merlin wanted to make a grand entrance and decided to roll into the party on wheels while playing his violin. Unfortunately, Merlin allotted just two wheels to each foot, believing this would give him the necessary stability. It did and it didn't. The violinist flew into the hall, fiddling away, only to watch himself zoom toward a huge mirror mounted at the opposite end of the room—he had not considered how to stop himself. The crash was spectacular, breaking mirror and violin. But people got the message that something fun had happened. By the 1860s, roller skates had four wheels and break pads, leading the way to an industry that today in the United States provides 30 million people with a good time.

We should continue to research and develop new products, and to learn as much as we can about their potential salability. But it cannot hurt to watch out for life's little accidents. They often lead to big payoffs.

CYLINDER SEALS AND FLOPPY DISKS

We have mentioned computers several times in our exploration, and it is evident that recent advances in computer technology have allowed individuals, as well as corporations, to partake in one of the necessities of modern-day life: recording and conveying information. The Information Age of the late 20th century is portrayed as a world drowning in a deluge of paper while simultaneously demanding to know more and produce more. Is this need for more and more information a recent phenomenon, or is it only the result of technology run amuck? Is it because we are capable of producing vast quantities of information that we do so—and with a vengeance?

When reviewing how our ancestors handled the problem of information, it is clear that improvement was always on their minds, too. Writing, and the recording of information for later use, probably obtained its initial trial run in ancient Sumer near the Persian Gulf, about 5,000 years ago. Writing took the form of pictures—not far removed from the art work etched on cave walls—and these were incised on thin clay tablets. The earliest written records were economic: inventories of sheep received for sacrifice or lists of wages paid to workers.

But it soon became apparent that tablets were not the way to go for brief messages, and small stone cylinders began to be engraved with symbols in relief. These cylinders could be easily carried abroad and rolled over a wet tablet to form the message. Cylinder seals have been discovered in ancient Egypt, leading to speculation that the two civilizations—Sumerian and Egyptian—had a cylindrical tête-à-tête going on. The Egyptians also used pictures, or hieroglyphs, and although they never developed a nonpictorial alphabet, as did the later Sumerians, the pictures began to represent the ideas and syllables that led to the development of our own alphabet. And like the Sumerians, the Egyptians saw the need to develop something better than clunky tablets for conveying information from place to place. They used the stems of the papyrus plant to create a paper used for writing.

The Chinese entered these ancient literary circles during the Shang dynasty (c. 1500 to 1000 B.C.). They perfected a writing system with characters representing individual words (rather than sounds) some of which are still used today. When the Chinese discovered paper in the 1st century A.D., they incorporated the ancient technique of using stone seals to make ink stampings on the paper. This led to a process of block printing in the 7th century. Although it never advanced very far, the Chinese saw block printing as most suitable for a language that was written by word characters and not by an alphabet. This probably led them to be the first inventors of movable type, sometime in the 11th century.

It took Johannes Gutenberg, and the passage of four centuries, before the inventions of paper and movable type were put to greater use. The production of Gutenberg's Bible (1454) set in motion a continuous quest for better ways to store, convey, and reproduce information.

The late 20th century and its technological wizardry could not have been imagined by those ancient writers—although as we have seen, the Greeks and many medieval thinkers were not very far off. Yet even Gutenberg would have had a hard time facing the fact that his entire Bible can be transmitted by satellite in one second.

The ancients nonetheless may have had one up on us: Many of their documents have survived over thousands of years. As we watch our books and papers turn to dust and our floppy disks lose their documents, we might ponder the wisdom of keeping our car titles and mortgage receipts on clay tablets—messy, but still there tomorrow.

STONEHENGE—THE FIRST COMPUTER

It is easy to take a myopic view of scientific thought or achievement. Indeed, the advancements of the last century alone seem to outdistance the accumulative knowledge of mankind over the last 5,000 years, or perhaps since the very dawn of the species. After all, despite similar needs and similar uses, it is nevertheless hard to envision a relationship between a large clay tablet recording a single sale of grain, and a square of silicon six millimeters per side which stores a million bits of memory. Why the confusion? It is because the modern world has confused machine with mind. There is an immense difference between generating a thought and evolving a technology capable of taking that thought to its uppermost physical limit: Heron of Alexandria would have loved working with the scientists at Rockwell International, but he couldn't. Few realize that Sir Isaac Newton (1642–1727) had the equations to go to the moon. He lacked only the technology to get there. If the mind and the machine were out of sync in terms of technological advancement for ancient societies, they did, however, work together to create the wonders of the ancient world. Can people today ever know how complex an ancient structure was, or understand its true purpose, or must they concoct theories that include architects flying in from other planets to build them?

Stonehenge is a prehistoric machine that captured the various religious, agrarian, and scientific aspects of Neolithic society. Whether a pagan temple, an elaborate calendar, or a predicator of the various manifestations of the heavens, it has come to represent the crowning achievement of our ancient ancestors. It is ironical, however, that even with all the accumulated knowledge from scientific discoveries, some of the mysteries of this ancient device are not yet understood today. And Stonehenge was built long before the advent of computers, adding machines, arithmetic books, or slide rules—let alone pencil and paper.

It is quite clear from recent research that Stonehenge is linked to the movements of the sun and the moon, significant movements which could prove useful to people capable of deducing their meaning. Despite conflicting theories as to its ultimate purpose, all agree that Stonehenge is both an astronomical laboratory and a computing device. To understand how it works—or may work, since no one is certain—requires a high degree of knowledge in astronomy, astrophysics, and what is now called astroarchaeology. Wouldn't the builders of Stonehenge be surprised that they were that "advanced"! Those unfamiliar with astronomy may find it difficult to distinguish between an azimuth and an Asimov, although both are by now in the encyclopedia. Yet even the basic assumptions of what this gigantic monument lying in Salisbury Plain in England was used for illustrate a clever multidimensional device, one that in fact does relate to present technology.

Although its history is long, suffice it to say that Stonehenge was built over a thousand-year period in various stages, beginning about 2800 B.C. Its builders have been identified variously as the Phoenicians, the antedeluvian kings from Atlantis, the Druids, the Romans, the Danes, and on a rather inspired day, the wizard Merlin who brought the megalithic stones from Ireland. The final work consisted of a circular ditch with a double circle of 82 bluestones from Wales; an inner circle of enormous upright *sarsen* stones (for Saracen, or "foreign"); a semi-elliptical arrangement of five huge post-and-lintel structures known as trilithons inside the sarsen circle; a series of holes around the ditch; and several standing stones, including the Heel Stone in the avenue outside the entire structure.

How this was all accomplished is not known—the sarsen stones alone are about 20 feet long and weigh between 35 and 50 tons—and it has taken modern imaginations to reconstruct what the thing is and how it worked: The ancients clearly knew what they were doing. Nor is any theory certain beyond the observation that the midsummer sun (June 21) can be seen rising over the Heel Stone when one is standing in the center of Stonehenge. But something awe-inspiring must have been happening here. In the 1960s, using 22 key stone and hole positions of Stonehenge in various alignments, 32 important sun and moon orientations were tracked, including all the equinoxes and solstices. Moreover, these alignments were predictable long before the structure was completed in its final form.

Such alignments would serve a useful purpose to an agrarian society. Knowing when spring arrived or when fall began would signal the planting and harvesting of crops, and perhaps even the celebration of certain religious/agricultural festivities. But were there other phenomena in the sky which an ancient people would want to predict? One answer—a most frightening event for a primitive society—is the eclipse. Whatever significance is placed on an eclipse of the sun or moon, from the anger of the gods to a beast swallowing the heavens, such an event literally overshadowed all other celestial activity as viewed from earth. Not long ago, it was discovered that Stonehenge seems to have a mechanism for predicting eclipses using the holes surrounding the structure. This theory led to some infighting among modern astronomers still at a loss for how the "primitives" figured it all out. But one thought most could agree upon was that the ancient builders, in fact, probably did predict eclipses. Using Stonehenge, we can't, despite our *sophisticated* methods and machinery.

But the question might be, for whom is this formula too sophisticated? Obviously, the functions of Stonehenge were comprehended by the people who built the machine—they knew how to work it. Perhaps the problem is one of the late 20th century, and its inability to accept the fact that mathematical competence of this magnitude—indeed any competence in politics, government, economics, religion, culture—could and did exist in a culture 5,000 years earlier. However, by becoming familiar with the past, we can call upon a thousand teachers to tell us about how human beings continue to act and think, and how they create machinery—in the mind, and on Salisbury Plain.

There is little doubt that Stonehenge was a multipurpose computer built to predict the astronomical phenomena associated with the sun and the moon. Research continues today—with the aid of *our* most sophisticated computers—to try and decipher the meaning of Stonehenge, its various uses, and its sophistication. What was derived from the machine in terms of social behavior may never be discerned. One can imagine the priest-king telling his people the moon will be swallowed whole this week—and that *he* will make it reappear! One can also see the power gained by the *users* of Stonehenge. The power to predict the actions of the heavens would enable an agrarian society dependent on the seasons to survive.

On perhaps a simpler level, the architects of Stonehenge wanted to bring to earth the mysteries of the universe in a way mankind has always endeavored: to discover the earth's powers through observation, contemplation, and a workable solution. The solution had to be visible to be truly believable, despite religious fervor. Geometry is fine on paper, but its tangible use makes it believable. Whether it is a theory for a nuclear chain reaction, or countless observations of lunar positions, human beings need to test what they believe to be true. So it was with Stonehenge. Scientists, archaeologists, and historians are just beginning to understand the technological aspects of this Neolithic computer. Today's investigators of Stonehenge may never have a full understanding of what the builders had in mind.

"BORROWING," THE GUPTAS, AND THE ORIGINS OF THINGS

Stonehenge was but one of hundreds of monolithic structures of the ancient world, many of which still boggle our minds as to what they were built for and how they worked.[1] There are two main theories as to why certain inventions or developments occur at about the same time throughout civilizations separated by vast distances. The first is simply that groups or societies reach certain stages where such developments "had to happen"—

---

[1] The rows of megaliths found at Carnac in France—several thousand of them—should keep our supercomputers whirling their disks for some time to come!

meaning, perhaps, that what humans do is predestined since we can't seem to help doing what we do. A second theory contends that humans borrow from each other—in today's world of patents and copyrights we might call it stealing ideas. In this scenario, and using ancient megalithic structures as an example, travelers visiting a stonehenge would be impressed, learn the process, and return to their home town to reproduce what they saw. Or else, a traveling group of builders might trek across whole continents, selling their services as master stonehenge-makers.

What we can safely say is that when a good thing happens, it happens everywhere, and in the 20th century within a very short space of time. The telephone, television, and videocassette recorder are inventions that spread rapidly throughout the globe. Moreover, the origins of such advancements often get lost once the invention becomes commonplace. For example, early classical Greek sculpture was, well, Greek to the Greek world. Yet if one studies the oldest examples, such sculpture appears Egyptian, probably because the Egyptians had been at it awhile and people noticed, including Greek sculptors who knew a good thing when they saw it. Yet a citizen of Athens admiring a statue might not know its origins.

The Western world has become accustomed to clothes made of cotton. While it was the Arabs who helped westernize this important fabric, they imported it from where it was made: India. It was originally called *quittan,* which in time became the word *cotton.* Indian culture during the Gupta dynasty (beginning about 320 A.D.) spawned many other advancements that found their way to other parts of the world, contributing to all facets of life, from business to art and leisure. Most people are unaware that these originated in India. This enlightened period ushered in the height of Sanskrit literature, the development of Hinduism, and the expansion of East-West trade. The most famous Indian story—that of Sinbad the sailor—found its way into the Arabian Nights fables. Other of their tales were borrowed over the centuries by some of the giants of Western literature, including Boccaccio, La Fontaine, Chaucer, the Grimm brothers, and Kipling.

In astronomy and mathematics, India was what we might call state-of-the-art. One scientist, Aryabhata, wrote about the value of pi (which we are still calculating out today on supercomputers), quadratic equations, solstices and equinoxes, and the spherical shape and rotation of the earth. Other Indian thinkers predicted eclipses, calculated the diameter of the moon, and pondered the effects of gravity. We now know that even the Arabic numerals and decimal system we presently use originated in India, including the value of zero. In manufacturing, some of the world's finest steel was forged in India. The country also produced soap and cement, both readily accepted and used in the West. India was perhaps best known for its fabrics, even in ancient times. Besides making cotton cloth, its people created other materials that became familiar items all over the world, including calico, cashmere, chintz, and bandanna.

As it is with all enlightened dynasties—and there have been but a few over the millennia—the Guptas succumbed to a combination of internal and external forces. But the contributions made for the enrichment of life were not lost to the rest of the world, even if their origins began to fade over time. One wonders what the United States of the 20th century will be remembered for when future nations contemplate the origins of certain material and aesthetic possessions. We hope it will be more than soap operas, fast food, and toy laser guns. On the other hand, if chop suey and pizza survive as admired delicacies, how many people will link them with their American origins?

There is another side to this: a country or culture keeping its eyes open for developments around the world to see how they might apply them to their own quality of life. It is certain that cultures borrow from other groups when the acquisition is desired and can enhance their lives. The Japanese are masters at keeping tabs on every research project and every technical paper being written around the world to see how it might provide their country with a new idea or an old one they can improve upon. They recognize, as did ancient people, that something borrowed could be something gained.

MICKEY MOUSE, CELTICS, AND KNOCKOFFS

Mickey Mouse may be an American-made character, but more and more he is being reinvented outside our magic kingdom. The same is true with Snoopy, Raggedy Ann, and other well-known names that have occupied retail shelves for decades. The imitation icons are "knockoffs"—unauthorized (and unlicensed) replicas of the real thing that can be quickly and cheaply produced abroad, especially in Japan and South Korea. Indeed, some knockoff experts believe that the Japanese can get hold of a product and reproduce it correctly in just 48 hours! Although imitation may be the highest form of flattery, the innovators at Disney, Gucci, Christian Dior, and elsewhere are hardly ecstatic. Instead, they are going to court to block the sale of knockoffs, since it is difficult to stop production thousands of miles from home. This is not the borrowing of old, where royalties and licenses and patents were yet to be discovered as a source of profit and a protection for inventions. This is blatant stealing of ideas for profit.

In other times, flattery may in fact have been the only thing a culture could reap when its products or ideas were purposefully copied by other people in other lands—and not simply passed on from culture to culture as with the Gupta dynasty. One group of people known for imitating the ideas of others were the ancient Celts. By the 3rd century B.C., the Celts were widely spread across Europe and into the British Isles. Yet despite the numerous artifacts from their culture, it has not been easy for modern archaeology to identify what the Celts produced as opposed to what they picked up from others. For example, in the realm of art the Celts do not seem to have created any new ideas. They did, however, pick up concepts and styles of art from the various peoples they traded with or made war upon, only to turn those ideas into simple, Celtic decorations. As one historian has written, "Once the Celt had borrowed an idea from his neighbors he was able to give it such a strong Celtic tinge that it soon became something so different from what it was originally as to be almost unrecognizable."

But the true Mickey Mouse ripoff artists of the ancient world were our now-familiar friends the Romans—and they did it literally. After conquering Greece, they brought back thousands of statues and other works of art to Rome. (The British did the same in the 19th century, but we credit them with an indigenous culture that often enjoyed mimicking the styles of the lands they conquered—a subtle difference in here somewhere.) Although the Romans did develop a "Roman style" of sculpture, they also used Greek sculptors to create works for their villas and public places.

When it came to painting, the Romans simply copied the Greek Hellenistic styles and motifs. In literature, they translated famous Greek works such as the *Iliad* and *Odyssey* into Latin, and more Roman dramas or epics were written in blatant imitation of the Greek form and style. For their very religion, the Romans lifted the Greek myths almost verbatim and Romanized them. So the king and queen of the Greek gods, Zeus and Hera, became Jupiter and Juno to the Romans, and each Greek god and demigod had his or her Roman counterpart, sometimes without latinization (Hercules instead of Herakles).

The Romans copied a nice thing when they saw it or read it. As it turned out, most of those things were Greek, and had there been trademark and copyright laws, the Greek lawyers would have been very busy—if allowed to bring suit in a Roman court of law.

Although companies today will continue to create new products and surround them with legal protection, the knockoff artists will continue to manufacture cheaper imitations with the hope of making a few bucks before anyone is the wiser. It is no longer a game of flattery or lack of creativity—it is a game of big business and big profits, and art for art's sake has become a motto with a price tag dangling from it. Such is life in the modern world.

PREDICTING COMPUTER ADVANCES IS PLAYING WITH FIRE

The computer, for human beings today, represents the enormous, rapid technological advances that have occurred in the last century—although no more rapid than other advances that brought about stark changes (the stirrup, the bow-and-arrow, the chisel). But computers also reflect an important need of late-20th-century man and woman: the need to make life more controllable, more efficient, more effective. Put another way, people use data and data use people—a relationship that began back when the cave was everyone's condominium. We have already seen our preoccupation with statistics (Chapter 7). The art of computing is very old, with the ancient examples of the abacus and the alignments of Stonehenge coming down to the modern world as reminders of our analytic nature.

It has only been in the second half of this century that computers have become far more than computing devices. They serve as surrogate people in the office and on the factory floor. They break sound and sight into myriad parts for manipulation and reconstruction. They provide the tools for management and often manage those tools. And they beg an interesting question: What's next? Given the incredible achievements of late in the area of artificial intelligence, we are just now trying to understand where this all is headed and what it means to the workplace and the home. Did we know in the 1930s, when television was invented, that it would be used on space craft, as a vehicle to play video games, and as a two-way communications tool far beyond the telegraph or the telephone? Can we know what the computer has in store for us?

Human beings have been confronted with such awesome potential before the advent of the computer. But it is precisely because we are in awe of our current creation that we forget a very basic discovery that had as much of a profound effect on the human condition—if not more—as the almighty computer: fire. Humans, of course, did not invent fire—they discovered it. Whether through lightning, friction, volcanic eruptions, or chemicals, the early users had the sense to realize there was a use for fire in the first place.

It is anyone's guess how fire was first put to work. Conquering darkness would have been an obvious benefit, as would providing warmth and warding off wild animals. The heat from a fire would also have allowed early men and women to live in less tropical, more frigid, climates. Cooking food was probably also an accident that went down well for the first daring gourmets. And the melting attributes of fire provided a means to forge metal implements, allowing for better efficiency when embarking on two favorite human activities: hunting and warring. The same has been true for the modern computer, which began as a task-saving machine and has moved into the realms of military machinery and strategic planning, as well as machines ranging from ovens and cars to airplanes and toys. But something else happened with fire that we may want to ponder a bit.

Fire became a god.

Fire was carefully preserved. It was used in religious ceremonies and it became the focus for all life: the word *focus* is Latin for *hearth*. The ancient Greeks felt it was the premier gift to mankind, stolen from the gods by Prometheus, who suffered greatly for sharing such power. Today we use fire much as in primitive times, and when it becomes a symbol for us, it usually represents enlightenment: We begin and end our Olympic Games with a torch. But most people take fire for what it is—a source of energy, not a magical gift from the gods.

It will be interesting to see what happens to civilization as the computer becomes more and more integrated into our daily lives, and our dependency grows. Could it become a god? Nothing is impossible. When the fire went out, the primitives moaned and feared the consequences of life without fire—they had become dependent to the point where fire was now the true meaning of life. This reaction is not dissimilar to what happens in an office when the computer "goes down." And like our primitive ancestors, we call in the priests—in this case computer technicians—to make things better. We are more dependent on a machine than we realize, and we will face the terrifying consequences our forebears did when the fire went out.

POWER AND OLD BEN

Before we leave inventions and the notion that our "new" things are not so new, we might spend a little time with a discovery that links past, present, and future. For while we marvel at what the latest personal computer or microwave can accomplish, we usually forget the reason that these new technological wonders even work: electricity. Ben Franklin would be shocked to learn of our neglect, almost as shocked as he probably was when his kite experiment during a lightning storm demonstrated the enormous power available to humans.

Speaking of Old Ben, probably the first electric cooking was done by this American statesman and scholar in 1749 in Philadelphia. From a letter he wrote in that year, it appears that the first meal cooked without a wooden or charcoal fire was a turkey: "A turkey is to be killed for our dinner by the electrical shock and roasted by the electrical jack, before a fire kindled by the electrical bottle." Other than a few experiments, however, it wasn't until the 19th century that electricity was thought of as a practical source of power. In 1831, Joseph Henry invented the electric bell, an extension of his work on electromagnets. His designs for magnetic coils increased the lifting power of the magnet from nine pounds to 3,500 pounds, power unthinkable beyond the enormous manpower needed to build pyramids or cathedrals. Since his time the basic design of insulating metal coils is still in use.

The shift from mechanical uses to communications occurred in 1827, when Harrision Gray Dyar set up a two-mile telegraph relay at New York's Long Island racetrack. Iron wires attached to insulators on posts allowed electric current to make red marks on litmus paper at the receiving end. The time difference between sparks determined which letter of the alphabet was sent. Although the telephone supplanted the telegraph as the major form of electrical communication, skeptics had problems with it in the beginning. On October 9, 1876, Alexander Graham Bell in Boston spoke with Thomas Augustus Watson in Cambridge, using a private two-mile-long telegraph wire attached to telephones. Because many people could not believe that the new invention was superior to the telegraph, or that it even worked, both Bell and Watson had to publish independent accounts of their conversation in a Boston newspaper so people could see that, in fact, they actually did speak to each other "over the wire."

Other time-saving inventions blossomed as the power of electricity became recognized as a universal force that had almost limitless application: the electric printing press (1839), the electric light bulb (1879), the electric street car (1885), and the electric toaster (1926). The first electronic computer arrived late in the story of electricity. Its name was ENIAC, for Electronic Numerical Integrator And Computer, and it was built at the Moore School of Electrical Engineering at the University of Pennsylvania in 1946.

Today we take for granted that our personal computers occupy only a desktop or a lap, and have enormous capacity and speed. ENIAC was kept in a room that was 30 by 50 feet. Its structure housed some 18,000 vacuum tubes and ran on 130 kilowatts per hour. So as we downsize, speed up, redesign, and modernize our electric machines, we might pay brief homage to that small spark that started it all—and keeps it all started. For in the forseeable future, it will be electricity that fires the inventions. Nuclear power in the home and in the office is still on the drawing boards.

INACCESSIBILITY AND ROMAN REMEDIES

The assumption should never be made that because inventions and technological advances become operational they are suddenly used by everyone. Even as prices come down and products reach wide distribution, not everyone can take advantage of what is out there. Where this becomes critical involves beneficial or even life-saving products or services that simply are not accessible to the masses, including those desperately in need of them.

One example is the health care crisis, especially in the United States, where costs increase as quickly as new developments in modern medicine, and where life-saving remedies are not affordable to many who might thereby save their lives. Further, the economics of keeping hospitals open are not simple and the rash of rural hospital closings is another crisis symptom. The American Hospital Association believes almost three out of every four rural hospitals, some 2,700 in all, are in financial trouble. Worse, these hospitals serve a large segment of the population, and about one quarter of them will probably shut down in the near future.

When people cannot receive adequate health care, either through lack of money or lack of facilities, they usually revert to homemade cures or simply avoid any treatment. This, in turn, can lead to a rise in the death rate, as people who otherwise might have been treated successfully are neglected. In the United States alone, consumers spend an estimated $25 billion a year on health quackery. Annual sales of vitamin and mineral supplements are growing and have already hit the $3 billion mark. And many "nutrition experts" sell products and services that are untested or simply unsound.

The ancient Romans, as we have seen, were one of the most advanced civilizations on the planet—the great builders of fortifications, roads, buildings, and a "modern" civil service. But when it came to health care, they were as in the dark as the barbarians they often conquered. Worse, they knew it. In his book on natural history, Pliny (23–79 A.D.) noted that "Medicine is the only one of the arts of Greece that serious Romans have not yet begun to practice." (They sure took everything else!) Because of this, he feared that "trust is at once put in any man who declares himself a doctor, whereas there is no form of deception that entails greater danger."

This has happened today as health care costs rise beyond a person's reach, and cheap, promising remedies become attractive. Or as Pliny put it, "so seductive is the hope [of a cure] which every patient entertains." Pliny listed some of the current "cures" going around Rome that people had complete faith in. For snake bites, applying "the spittle of a fasting person" seemed a reasonable remedy. Broken bones had a quick fix as well: "The ashes of the jawbone of a boar or swine; likewise boiled lard, tied around the broken bone, knits it with marvelous rapidity." A fever that wouldn't quit was cured "by wearing the right eye of a wolf, salted and attached." Other kinds of fevers required "the liver of a cat killed during the waning moon, preserved in salt, to be taken in wine just before the attacks." Depression was handled by drinking wine boiled "with calf's dung"—that would sure jolt most people out of a blue funk! And for lethargic people, arousal was simply a matter of "applying to the nostrils the calluses from an ass's legs steeped in vinegar, or the fumes of goat's horns or hair, or wild boar's liver. This is also given to drowsy persons."

This is not to say that lack of available health care facilities or the latest innovations will plunge the country into feverish searches for wolf eyes and calf's dung, although the statistics on dollars spent for similar cures is alarming. But as health care reaches fewer and fewer people in need, the only alternatives are store-bought and homemade remedies, or those offered by modern-day medicine men on the lookout for a quick buck. In an era where our knowledge of diseases and remedies is light years ahead of Pliny's day, it would be a travesty to keep that knowledge and the remedy it brings for only those who can afford it. Many of Pliny's people were ignorant of the maladies of the day; we are not. We must keep in mind that research, technology, and new creations in all fields—not just medicine—should have a purpose: to increase our knowledge or stimulate our thoughts, to the benefit of human beings. That is what the thinkers of the past always had in mind.

9
CHAPTER

ON CORRUPTION, DEATH, AND TAXES

We come to the three inevitable aspects of the human experience, aspects that surface from age to age since people began to organize in groups to share the burdens of existence. And we begin with one of the most basic attributes of human behavior: People do things considered unacceptable to the group, and usually at the expense of other humans. A recent example: When Hurricane Hugo came roaring into the Caribbean Islands in the fall of 1989, people prepared for the worst. But the worst did not simply mean damage from high winds and sea-swept shore lines. It meant looting by the very people who were pulling themselves together to battle the natural disaster *as a people*. And sure enough, after the storm had completed its damage, troops patrolled the streets to prevent looting and plundering . . . in vain, since most of the "human damage" had been done before their arrival. The same was true for Charleston, South Carolina: The storm decimated the town; then the troops came in to prevent the population from decimating itself. (In Panama, U.S. troops freed the Panamanians of a dictator; the Panamanians then freed the stores of their wares through looting.)

While this is hardly the place to delve into the reasons why humans do unto others what they don't want others to do unto them, greed is clearly a motive for any form of corruption that leads people into illegal or immoral activity. And there is no better place to start an examination than at the top—the government—to see how little "progress" we have made, and how we must expect corruption to be with us until such time as we create a way to prevent it or minimize it.

CASH AND KINGS: A TALE OF TWO RICHARDS

There are many modern examples of governments, and their leaders, plundering public funds or contributions for their own enrichment, or using power to their own end. The late Ferdinand Marcos and his fashion-addicted wife, Imelda, stand as exemplars of governmental leaders bilking the public of enormous quantities of money, much of it coming in as unaccountable foreign aid. Many others have done the same, and we might reexamine the most famous example in modern times: Watergate. It is a case where corruption entered the hallowed walls of the Oval Office in the White House, forcing the resignation of the President of the United States, Richard M. Nixon. And while the purpose here is not to go after a fallen elected official, it brings to mind an example from 800 years earlier with some interesting observations, both on the scandal and on the ambitions of leaders, past and present.

The office of the presidency provides not only power and prestige but a chance to become financially secure. Gerald Ford entered office in financial straits; he left office better off than most men on earth. A few men have no doubt viewed the office as a financial opportunity, and this may have been the case with Richard M. Nixon. In another era, he might have looked good snooping around to find ways of upgrading his lifestyle. An historical comparison between this president and another leader might provide insight into this subject of cash and kings, and corruption:

> Richard Milhous Nixon, President of the United States, 1968–1974. Known as "Tricky Dicky." Suffered political death as a villain.

> Richard Plantagenet (Richard I), King of England, 1189–1199. Known as "The Lion Heart." Gloried in physical death as a hero.

One Richard sounds, and perhaps was, a bit more valiant and awesome than the other. Yet besides both being Richards and rulers of large nations in their respective times, both used their immense powers to obtain money or the benefits of money. And at least on the surface, it appears that each was thinking only of himself, hoping to benefit only himself.

Richard I, however, made it look good.

When he succeeded to the throne of his father, Henry II, in 1189, the Third Crusade was taking shape. All of Christendom was charged with the task of freeing the Holy Land from the sultan, Saladin, and his horde of infidels. But Crusades—like other wars—required money. King Richard had not been in England a fortnight before he began devising ways to use his position to finance the Crusade. He started selling bishoprics and abbacies for cold cash: a practice, as we have seen, that was deemed illegal and sacrilegious by the Roman church. And the development of town charters received an historical boost as Richard began granting them for sums of money. He also dismissed sheriffs and allowed them to buy back their offices.

But these were just openers. More money was needed, and the possibility of Richard carving a kingdom out of Jerusalem for himself while freeing the Holy Land pushed him on to bolder schemes. By 1189, Scotland was under the feudal jurisdiction of England. King Richard now sold back the sovereignty of Scotland to its king, William the Bold, for 10,000 marks: a phenomenal sum in the 12th century. Richard also sold the archbishopric of York—second only to Canterbury in power within England—for 3,000 pounds. It did not matter that this was a blatant misuse of power, or that the purchaser was his half-brother, Geoffrey! As one historian has written: "The relation between romantic chivalry and common honesty is not always clear."

Yet Richard the Lion Heart became a legend in his own time, as well as in his own mind, spending less than six months in England during his 10-year reign. He died while laying seige to a castle he believed to be overflowing with ancient treasure. The legend began before the tomb was sealed.

Some 785 years after his death, another leader faced his demise: Richard Nixon. This ruler used his power not only to protect his growing paranoia over the opposition (the Democratic party), but to acquire personal wealth and aggrandizement. But he did it in secret, unlike the medieval warrior king.

Richard Nixon made his quest for wealth look bad.

So San Clemente and Key Biscayne—two lavish, costly estates on both coasts of the United States—became "retreats" for presidential business and relaxation, upgraded and kept at public expense. One of the first laws signed by this ruler included the doubling of his salary—perhaps overdue for the office, but clearly not a national priority during the height of the Vietnam war and the "war on poverty."

But his most infamous action, ironically causing his own downfall, was the secret taping of the conversations of individuals in the White House. After the 1972 Watergate break-in and trials, the scandal spread to within the confines of the White House. The tapes, many of which were made public after White House scrutiny, revealed that Nixon spent much of his second term in office trying to "contain" the Watergate revelations. They also show a president rationalizing in his own mind the legitimacy of the illegal or unethical activities planned or executed by his closest aides and their assistants. To hide this corruption, Nixon brought forth the mythical defense we have seen as the shield for many a king: executive privilege.[1]

But it didn't work, and once the existence of the tapes was revealed to the public, all Nixon had to do was destroy them, especially since so many of the conversations revealed corruptive minds around the president, if not corruption in action. But Richard Nixon did not destroy the tapes, and one theory is that the promise of wealth (and no doubt glory) from the sale of the tapes or their use in other salable media prevented the beleaguered president from this course of action. Richard M. Nixon fell from office disgraced, and he has spent the remainder of his life trying to rewrite a more pleasant place for himself in history.

---

[1] On September 10, 1983, White House attorneys filed a long brief in the U.S. Court of Appeals arguing that those who discussed Watergate with the president of the United States, including the key White House players in the sordid affair, were not bound by the laws of the land to come before a Grand Jury. The reasoning was rather medieval: "it is more important that the privacy of the Presidency be preserved than that every possible bit of evidence that might assist in criminal prosecutions be produced."

Thus there were two rulers, seeking fame, regal living, and a lofty place in the course of human events. But the king lived in a time when rulers were expected to be powerful, greedy, and resourceful. The president found his century suspicious of wealth and corruption in high places and appalled at cashing in on the highest office in the land and using it as a base for corruption. There is no lesson to be learned, just an observation: The later Richard could not play the king in an age which no longer understood the word; he could not even find a cause that resembled a Crusade.

DEFENSE PROBES AND FRIED FRENCHMEN

The burgeoning debt of the United States should have been a major focus of debate during the 1988 presidential campaigns, but it took a back seat to *ad hominem* remarks and name-calling. Democrats and Republicans alike now realize that the spending spree is over, and that fiscal responsibility is necessary to reverse the country's status as a debtor nation. Not a small part of the debt derives from spending for special interest groups, including the Pentagon and the vendors that have contributed to a multi-billion-dollar arsenal build-up. Recent allegations of payoffs and cheating for defense contract awards make better procedures to assure honest spending crucial as America enters the last decade of the 20th century.

More than 250 years ago, a leader took hold of the reins of a government deep in debt and financial corruption, hoping to clean up a mess not at all dissimilar to the current malaise in America, and no doubt other countries. His name was Philippe D'Orleans, and in 1715 he assumed the regency of France after the death of the old Sun King, Louis XIV. The heir to the throne of France was his five-year-old great-grandson, Louis XV, a minor who required a regent to rule in his place until he reached his majority.

Philippe, the son of the old king's brother, was a personage both likable and devious, who could spend millions of francs at a whim or contribute to the poor with the ease of a saint. His first task, however, was to deal with a national debt of 2.4 billion livres and additional floating debt that left the government bankrupt. Philippe took bold steps to shrink the debt: He drastically reduced the army to cut heavy military spending; taxes were reduced and many of the previous abuses in tax collection were condemned or abolished.

But his boldest stroke was to address public rage at the fraud perpetrated by those dealing with the government: merchants, financiers, and weapons manufacturers. (There seems to be a ring of relevancy here!) Philippe set up a Chambre of Justice, not unlike the occasional special prosecutor the United States calls into being from time to time, including the ones during Watergate. The Chambre began prosecuting those groups and people accused of defrauding the government. To encourage a widespread investigation, the Chambre offered incentives for whistleblowers: one fifth of all the funds recovered through their assistance. To protect informers, the death penalty was instituted for anyone interfering with their testimony.

Confiscation was one of the punishments bestowed upon a guilty party. Any person lying about how they obtained their finances could lose their property and be condemned to a ship's galley for life. Some were actually hanged or put in pillories; several committed suicide. Unfortunately, corruption continued, only this time it was in the Chambre itself. Court officials and influentials in government solicited bribes from guilty parties, who in return got their sentences or fines reduced. When one courtier offered to have a guilty party's fine of 1.2 million livres rescinded for a bribe of 300,000 livres, the amused criminal said, "My dear Count, you come too late. I have just concluded a similar arrangement with your wife for half that sum."

Early in 1717, the Chambre was dissolved, the government admitting that "corruption was so widely spread that almost all classes were infected with it, so that just punishments could not be laid upon so great a number of guilty persons without dangerously disturbing commerce, public order and the state." It was a cop-out, but nonetheless a recognition that corruption is a hard animal to flush out and catch, especially when the hunters are tempted to lay down their weapons and join the hunted.

INSIDE TRADERS' BUBBLE NOT FIRST
TO BURST

The world of business provides the best grist for the mills of corruption; it is a world of high finance, big money, and phenomenal riches to those willing to take the risks and ride out the hard times. (We briefly explored ethical behavior and business in Chapter 4.) The 1980s provided an environment for corruption in several areas. One of them was *inside trading*. This involved obtaining confidential, pre-announced information about a company that can affect its stock price, and acting upon it prior to public disclosure for the chance of reaping quick profits. It is quite simply illegal, and it quite simply became the sport of high financiers and arbitrageurs, many of whom were found in the confines of Goldman, Sachs & Company; Kidder, Peabody & Company; and other prestigious Wall Street investment houses.

Yet the fall of an elite inner circle bent on dreams and schemes for wealth is not new. One historic example with perhaps greater claim to tragedy by the team at the top is the South Sea Company debacle in the early 18th century, known to posterity as the South Sea Bubble. In 1711 in England, a unique trading company was formed to extinguish—of all things—the English national debt. The South Sea Company assumed the debt and in return was given exclusive British trading rights in South America and parts of the Pacific Ocean. Moreover, His Majesty's Government guaranteed interest payments for a specified period, to be offset by import duties. By 1720, the public came to believe that enormous profits could be had by buying into the South Sea Company, and despite warnings of illusory expectations, millions were invested.

In the first half of the year alone, the stock price rose from 138 pounds to 1,000 pounds. The bubble burst when it was learned that much of the money went into fraudulent companies, and the share value made a downhill run that ruined vast numbers of people. But the most visible casualties were found at the top: several key Cabinet members were implicated in the fraud, and many of the directors had their property taken to help recoup some of the monies lost by stockholders.

How much did those ministers and directors make off with?

Did they ride the wave of rising stock prices knowing full well that the tide was soon to turn? While such questions beg too much speculation of the scholarly kind, it is clear that an elite few knew what was taking place and had the most to benefit by not sharing that information. This situation has not changed a quarter of a millennium later. Opportunities for wealth are discovered by those who most likely can afford to go after them, legal or otherwise. It is a problem of coming up with the best watchdog, and placing him where he can detect a blip on what we might call the Greedometer. The problem is, we don't exactly know where to place our greedometers, and too many of them would smack of an invasion of privacy. It is a dilemma that will not go away as long as greed is here to stay . . . which it is.

THE HERMIT WOMAN AND THE SWINDLING PILGRIM

Most civilized societies that encourage private enterprise must put up with those less-than-civilized means by which monetary success is achieved: the swindle, the fraud, and the outright theft. True, many people almost beg the bad guys to take their money, whether by investing in Arizona swampland, putting 50 percent down on a house repair that will never take place, or buying into a little piece of "heaven on earth" from a *man of God.* (For that last charade, see Chapter 3.) The big business of bad business has always flourished despite numerous laws to protect the unknowing from the unrelenting. But laws alone cannot stop the swindler. If only there were a mechanism to get back at the guy who has taken your money. . . .

Well, there is a medieval story that relates the swindling of a swindler, and it gives one pause to wonder how this might be achieved today. It suggests that the best weapon against a thief is to play his own favorite hand—greed. The story was told by Petrus Alphonsus, a 12th-century collector of Arabian fables, especially those that taught a moral lesson. According to Petrus, a Spanish pilgrim traveled to Mecca via Egypt and, fearing to take all his money on the trip, entrusted most of it to an old man known for his honesty and integrity. Upon the pilgrim's return from Mecca to reclaim his money, however, he ran into some difficulty.

It seems that the trustworthy old man let the loot go to his head—or at least to a safe hiding place—and he now denied ever meeting the pilgrim, let alone taking his money. The neighbors refused to believe their old man was anything but honest, and although the pilgrim protested day in and day out, the greedy geezer only rebuked him. But then, an old hermit woman heard of the pilgrim's plight and decided to help him. "Bring me a man from your country whose words and actions you can trust," she said. When this was done, she ordered the man to bring her 10 boxes decorated in beautiful colors and fastened with silver-plated iron and good locks. Each box, however, was to be filled with rocks before being sealed.

The honest friend brought these to her and she now ordered him to find 10 men, each to bring one of the boxes to the old man who had swindled the pilgrim. The old woman accompanied the first man and his box; the pilgrim stayed out of sight. As the first box-bearer appeared, the old woman knocked on the old swindler's door. "A man from Spain has been a guest of mine and wishes to go to Mecca, and asks me for a trustworthy man to whom he can hand over his money that is in 10 boxes to be kept until his return," she said. The old man watched as the first man put down the colorful box, with nine more men coming down the path carrying similar boxes. Suddenly, the pilgrim he had swindled appeared, right on cue.

Uh oh—the old man had a dilemma. If the pilgrim started asking for his money again, the old woman would think the old man untrustworthy, and he would lose his chance at the 10 boxes of money. But that meant coughing up the money he had stolen from the pilgrim. As with all greedy people, it was no contest. "Friend, where have you been so long?" the old man said to the pilgrim he had deceived. "Come and get your money that you entrusted to my reliability long since, for I found it and I am tired of keeping it any longer."

The pilgrim received the money and thanked the old man upon departing. Then the old woman told the swindler: "You wait until we return, and take good care of what we have already brought." Needless to say, the swindler waited a very long time, and was not a very pleased pilferer when he opened the first box.

Rather than using tapped telephones and hidden video cameras to nab a swindler—which usually gives little benefit to the victims—it might be more effective to be a little creative and trap the crook at his own game. That way the victims get their losses back and the swindler might learn a lesson when he himself becomes a victim. Otherwise, he sees his capture as bad luck and merely a pause in his career. When it comes to corruption and swindling, maybe Hammurabi's "eye for an eye" isn't such a bad idea.

THE REHABILITATION OF THE ÎLE DE SEIN

We all go astray from time to time. The hope is that doing something wrong reflects a sudden slip off the path of what is right, and not a plunge into illicit activity on a regular basis. Yet time and again we learn of successful people getting nabbed for ill-doings. The Greylord investigation in Chicago during the 1980s convicted several judges; the Abscam investigation in Washington, D.C., convicted several elected officials.

Although some are cynical about prison systems that promise reform and rehabilitation—in light of the large number of repeat offenders—it is always refreshing when a group of nasties ends up becoming shining examples of what good people should be. An ancient island off the northwestern coast of France provides such illumination: The Île de Sein is a small, flat island once inhabited by the Druids. Today, the scant population consists mainly of fishermen and women tending barley fields. But several centuries ago, the people of Île de Sein had a more adventuresome occupation: wrecking ships.

Known locally as the "sea-devils," the citizens of Île de Sein lured boats onto the reef, where they were wrecked and plundered. It was undoubtedly the most lucrative source of business for the islanders, despite the severe laws against such activity. But in the 1600s after the Jesuits started spreading the Good News, the people of Île de Sein decided to mend their ways—

forever. And in what must be a major role reversal for any group of people, that in fact is what they did.

The islanders actually began *rescuing* crews of ships caught in harsh storms, and showed great courage in saving the crew of the British naval ship "Bellissima" in 1835. Sixty years later, the island was washed over from high winds, but the islanders, undeterred, rebuilt. The women were major contributors to the maintenance of the city of the island. During the 1860s and 1870s, the church of Île de Sein was built by stones carried on the heads of the women from the harbor to the church site!

At the onset of World War II, the men of Île de Sein joined the Free French by using their own boats, and helped 3,000 French soldiers escape the clutches of the advancing Germans. At the end of the war, General Charles de Gaulle personally visited the islanders and presented them with the Cross of Liberation.

It is not beyond reason that people who pursue a career of bad deeds can turn it all around within their lifetimes. Furthermore, positive role models can keep a group from lapsing into the old ways—there is nothing more powerful than positive peer pressure. In the case of Île de Sein, the pressure has lasted almost four centuries.

ODYSSEUS: TRAVELING THE LOW ROAD

When all is said and done, one person's morality is another person's sin. And each generation or society defines what its morality will be for the coming season. True, the Ten Commandments were carved in stone and not on a chalk board, but few people recall them during a clandestine meeting, the exchanging of classified information, or a good old-fashion bank heist.

One age that defined its morals in a way we might view as abhorrent today was the Heroic Age of the ancient Greeks, some 1,000 years before Christ, plus or minus a century or two. What's more, being deceitful was not only admired, it was regarded as a virtue. The Achaeans (Greeks) of the Trojan War era and after had a rather interesting outlook on life. Human life was cheap, war a way of life, and piracy a rather noble profession. Kings would even mount expeditions against cities, devastating them and enslaving the population. The 10-year Trojan War was probably no more than a series of raids by the Achaeans against a rival trading city, Troy—the abducted Helen may have been pretty, but hardly a good enough reason to launch a thousand ships so soldiers could face spears and swords for a decade of warfare.

The ultimate symbol of this amoral age—or premoral, as one historian has coined it—was the hero of *The Odyssey,* the cagey Odysseus, whom we have run into several times during our journey. This boastful king of Ithaca was proud to relate, for example, the story of how he and his men were running low on food. His response to the problem was to destroy the city of Ismarus and fill up his ship with their supplies. He also bragged about raiding villages along the Aegyptus river "to pillage the splendid fields, to carry off the women and little children, and to kill the men." He was a swell guy.

Odysseus was also a consummate liar, an attribute admired by his age. When he and a colleague captured a Trojan scout, Odysseus promised to spare the scout's life if he gave them certain information. The scout readily consented and was then killed anyway. One need only hear the words of the goddess Athena in Homer's great poem to realize that this would have been a man ripe for the wheelings and dealings of Wall Street:

> Cunning must he be and knavish who would go beyond [Odysseus] in all manner of guile, aye, though it were a god that met you. Bold man, crafty in counsel, insatiate in deceit, not even in your own land, it seems, were you to cease from guile and deceitful tales, which you love from the bottom of your heart.

As one historian observed, "Every weakling is fair play: The supreme virtue, in Odysseus' view, is a brave and ruthless intelligence." Odysseus is clearly with us today; he will be with us tomorrow. Watch the headlines.

DEATH: THE GREAT EQUALIZER

Besides the ever-present temptation for corruption, human beings also share a common experience that no one has yet to escape, if we can set aside religious beliefs and cryogenic preservation: death. At some point in our lives we will all face Nature's little way of telling us to slow down, and several decisions must be faced prior to that Final Moment. There are the finances to set in order, the legal requirements, the disposition of property. And there is that last bit of memory to be passed on to future generations once the house is gone, the money is spent, and the paper remains are scattered to the winds or the landfill: the tombstone and its inscription. For while wills are written, fulfilled, and filed, that message on the final resting place is a person's only shot at immortality. (The mighty, however, can build lasting monuments as described in Chapter 2.) And in most cases, those who missed Andy Warhol's promise of 15 minutes of fame while alive can grab years or centuries of it once they have moved on.

Our now familiar friends, the ancient Romans, spent a lot of time sorting out their financial affairs and preparing for death much as we do today. Death was an important business and lawyers took an appropriate role in setting up the right formulae for the disposition of goods, land, and money. But time was also taken to prepare a final statement for others to see. Fortunately, many of these still survive.

As with today, some were quite simple: "Laturnia Januaria, lime burner, lived 45 years." Others went into detail about the work they put into their final burial chambers:

> To the spirits of the departed. Gaius Calenius Hermes built this for himself and his family . . . and for Antistia Coetonis, his wife . . . he built a chamber on the right of the entrance; [placed] sarcophagi on the pavement outside; and opposite [the entrance] and to the left, in two walls, made niches with [funerary] urns and sarcophagi.

Although it was hoped that the soul of the departed would go to the underworld—which is what the Romans called Heaven—they were still concerned about what happened to their earthly remains. One citizen attempted to ward off vandals:

> To the spirits of the departed. Gaius Tullius Hesper built [this] tomb for himself, where his bones are to be placed. If anyone does violence to him or removes them hence, I wish for him that he may live a long time in bodily pain, and that when he dies the gods below may not receive him.

We have already seen the decline of the institution of marriage in ancient Rome, with the accompanying loose morals and behavior. Perhaps that explains why many couples wanted the world to know that their marriage was a good one, and set phrases were used in inscriptions relating to a blissful union while on earth. One example expresses this concern: "To the spirits of the departed. To Cerellia Fortunata, dearest wife, with whom he lived 40 years without the slightest cause for complaint, Marcus Antonius Encolpus built this."

Today, our private lives have become too private to share with the general public—that role is filled vicariously by television soap operas depicting sordid affairs most people only think about. Maybe the sudden prodigious costs involved in laying a person to rest, coupled with the thought of death itself, keeps our minds off the very last salute to mankind that we are allowed to make. Or maybe our approach is more realistic, like the inscription of one Roman who may have said it for all of us:

> To the spirits of the departed. Titus Flavius Martialis lies here. What I ate and drank is with me here; what I left behind is gone forever.

ABBOT IRMINON AND THE INTERNAL REVENUE SERVICE

We come now to the third leg of life's inevitable experiences, or perhaps more properly the third point on God's trident that we all get stuck with: taxes. Since the dawn of civilization—or perhaps pre-dawn since such systems set up so quickly—governments have required money from the people they ostensibly represent, and those people put up with some form of tax on what they make or do while walking the earth. In ancient Mesopotamia, the priests exacted payment in kind (mostly grain) in return for the blessings of the gods and the freedom to work the land. The Romans were adept at collecting taxes from their own citizens and conquered countries. And while the New Testament tells us that Jesus enjoined his followers to "Render unto Caesar what is Caesar's," paying taxes always was a sore point among the populace. It is no coincidence that the Gospel of Luke, describing the people who listened to Jesus, lumped the tax collectors with the sinners (Luke 15:1).

We have seen that, soon after William the Conqueror landed in England in 1066, an audit of the country was ordered to determine what each person owned. From this *Domesday Book* (1086), William could determine what taxes could be levied on the conquered Anglo-Saxons. Payments to the state came indirectly, through a local lord or landowner. Much of Europe operated the same way, and one interesting example of tax payments comes from the reign of Charlemagne, ruler of the Franks in the 9th century and, as we have seen, a model orator (Chapter 7). The source is the estate book of the Abbey of St. Germain des Pres near Paris, kept by Abbot Irminon. The Abbot, like William the Conqueror two centuries later, kept track of every tenant on his lands, what they had, and what they owed him. He passed some of the last on to Charlemagne in the form of an army tax. When we consider typical farmers on the abbey lands, we see that they had to make numerous payments, in kind if not in money. Besides payment of an ox and a certain number of sheep, a farmer had other obligations for privileges granted him on his land. He might have to carry a load of wood to the abbey house in return for being allowed to gather firewood in the forests. He might pay some hogsheads (casks) of wine for the right to pasture pigs. And every third year he had to give up a sheep for the right to let his animals graze upon the abbey's fields.

As if this were not sufficient, the 9th-century farmer owed the abbey three chickens and 15 eggs every year, along with a number of planks to keep the abbey house in repair. Often he had to give up some pigs, and sometimes he was asked for corn, honey, wax, soap, or oil. If the farmer also possessed a skill, he might have to build furniture or barrels.

So while it is true that taxes are taxes no matter what form they take, we might be glad that it ends with our checkbooks. It is difficult to believe that a dentist would take kindly to cleaning an internal revenue service agent's teeth for free. And just imagine a lawyer cheerfully defending an IRS agent in court as a professional courtesy!

INCOME TAX: BLAME NAPOLEON

Americans are proud of their ability to rise to the occasion with their own money when it comes to helpless whales or earthquake victims. But when the income tax monster comes to the door, it is time to hide under the covers, wallet in hand. Of course, rational minds realize that it costs money for a government to do all the things it thinks its subjects want it to do, and you can only tax goods and services so far before they can no longer be purchased or made. But personal income tax has always thrown rational thinking to the winds. What many Americans may not realize is that this annoying invention was borrowed from abroad.

The 16th Amendment to the U.S. Constitution made the federal income tax legal in 1913, although attempts to impose an income tax before that time—for example, in 1861 during the Civil War—proved to be ineffective. It was the British who led the way to legitimatize income tax during a time when people could accept such a demand on their personal worth—they could buy into the objective (discussed in Chapter 1). Eventually, it reached their former colonies.

By 1800, Napoleon Bonaparte had become master of much of Western Europe, with no end in sight to his scheme of French world domination. Despite Admiral Nelson's impressive naval victory over the French in 1798 near the entrance to the Nile in Aboukir Bay, England was smarting from the enormous costs of the war and the inability to keep the trade lanes open to the Continent. England's prime minister, William Pitt the Younger, had been running the government of George III since 1783, and he was well aware of England's depleted capital at the hands of France's self-appointed emperor. When Napoleon stopped trade from the Rhine, he also put a halt to 75 percent of all grain imports from the Baltic. England was in a dangerous economic situation.

Yet Pitt was the first to admit that his fellow countrymen were already immersed in a sea of taxes. Everything from windows and houses to servants and carriages carried a tax, and it was doubtful he could squeeze more currency out of existing burdens. So in 1798, Pitt created a graduated tax on earnings for all those making 60 pounds a year or more. At the high end, for those making more than 200 pounds annually, the rate was 10 percent, a very low rate by today's standards but a screaming injustice to Georgian England.

Politics and unpopularity finally did in Pitt, who was forced to resign in 1801. His successor, Henry Addington, abolished the income tax and made peace with Napoleon. But it merely bought time for the "little corporal." For while England relaxed and disarmed, Napoleon planned his next move, and in May 1803 declared war on an unprepared England. Addington was a lost man, but before his fall he reimposed the income tax—at half the rate—with the hopes of rearming the English war effort. Pitt came back into office as prime minister in 1804, Nelson triumphed at Trafalgar a year later, and the rest is history.

Americans and citizens of other countries will continue to fear a rise in income taxes as the debate goes on about how much the government should spend on its people. At least the debate often concerns wars on poverty, drugs, and crime . . . and how to pay for them. Wars in faraway lands are hard to pay for with much enthusiasm, unless the world, or the homeland, is at stake. Nevertheless, let us hope that U.S. senators and congressmen, who should read history books as a daily diet of *new* information, gloss over the fine print when it comes to taxes: There are numerous ideas sitting there waiting to be activated. War with Napoleon was just one of them.

CONCLUSION

The past is present. Yet our neglect of what has happened before our time robs us of perhaps the most important guidepost for the present, and the future. We began by noting Santayana's observation that those who cannot recall the past are condemned to repeat it. Clearly, that condemnation will be widespread in the 1990s: Surveys continue to show that college graduates are at a loss when it comes to the past. At the end of 1989, one survey of American college seniors discovered that 25 percent of them had heard of Christopher Columbus but didn't know when he arrived in America. Almost half were unaware that the American Civil War took place between 1850 and 1900. More than half didn't know that the Mayans lived in Mexico; that Thomas Jefferson wrote the Declaration of Independence; that the Magna Carta was the cornerstone of British parliamentary government (more than one third thought it was "the charter signed by the pilgrims on the Mayflower"). And in a year when communism was crumbling in Eastern Europe, almost one quarter of the seniors believed the phrase "from each according to his ability, to each according to his need" was found in the U.S. Constitution; it is, in fact, the fundamental concept of communism, written by Karl Marx.

A recent report by the National Endowment of the Humanities noted that almost 80 percent of colleges and universities in the United States do not require a course in the history of Western civilization, and more than 80 percent of college students need not take an American history course.

From Stonehenge to Star Wars, through 5,000 years of history, there is a wealth of knowledge available to help us cope with the present and plan for the future. History is not simply the surviving records of the winners who trumpeted their victories and the losers who rationalized their defeats. It is an enormous body of information waiting to be pieced together to give us a clearer picture of what happened, and why. All we need to do is recognize the importance of the past and commit to understanding it. The present can then become a less complex, more comprehensible, peaceful place to live. And that means the future, with the help of the past, will take care of itself.

NAME INDEX

SUBJECT INDEX